SORTITION

SORTITION

THEORY AND PRACTICE

Edited by Gil Delannoi and Oliver Dowlen

imprint-academic.com

Published in the UK by Imprint Academic
PO Box 200, Exeter EX5 5YX, UK

Published in the USA by Imprint Academic
Philosophy Documentation Center
PO Box 7147, Charlottesville, VA 22906-7147, USA

ISBN 9 781845 401993

A CIP catalogue record for this book is available from the
British Library and US Library of Congress

Contents

    Note. These papers on the lotteries and their political use were presented at the conference held at SciencesPo (Institute for Political Sciences), Paris, November 27–28, 2008.

Contributors

Hubertus Buchstein, Professor of Political Theory at Greifswald University. Research areas: Modern Democratic Theory, the history of Political Science and the history of Political Thought.

Gil Delannoi, Research Director at Sciences-Po Paris (Centre de recherches politiques) is a philosopher and an historian. At the present time his main activity as a professor is the history and theory of democracy. His research fields are democracy, evolution of political forms and regimes, and the history and conceptualisation of relativity.

Oliver Dowlen is an independent scholar who works primarily in the area of random selection and its capacity to produce democratic regeneration and political consolidation. During the 1980s and 1990s he was extensively involved in practical political work and was a founder member of the Society for Democracy including Random Selection (SDRS). During this time he also studied Marx's concept of alienation for a part-time MPhil. In 2002–6 he took a full time doctorate in politics at New College, Oxford for which he explored the political potential of sortition.

Gerhard Göhler is a Professor Emeritus and taught political theory and the history of political ideas at the Free University, Berlin, until 2006. He is currently co-ordinating 'Governance in Areas of Limited Statehood', a research project on power and soft control at the Berlin Research Centre. His research interests include the theory of political institutions, theories of power and control, the history of political ideas in modernity and the history and theory of political science. He is co-editor of the collected works of Ernst Fraenkel, one of the founding fathers of German political science after 1945 (6 volumes, 1999–2008). He has written on the early Hegel, Marx's dialectic, liberalism and conservatism in the nineteenth century and institutional theory ('Institution Power Representation: What Institutions Stand For and How They Work', 1997). Email: goehler@zedat.fu-berlin.de.

Barbara Goodwin is Professor of Politics at the University of East Anglia, Norwich. Her research interests include ideologies, social justice, utopianism and moral responsibility. Recent publications include *The Politics of Utopia* (with Keith Taylor, 2nd edition, 2009), *Using Political Ideas* (5th edition,

2007). She is General Editor of the Imprint Academic series 'Sortition and Public Policy'.

Michael Hein, research assistant at the Chair for Political Theory at Greifswald University. Research areas: politics in South Eastern Europe, European Integration, Constitutional Politics, and Systems Theory.

Yves Sintomer is Professor of Political Sociology at Paris 8 University, and Invited Researcher at Neuchâtel and Lausanne Universities. He is a Doctor of Political and Social Sciences (European University Institute, Florence) and has a Habilitation to direct research (Paris 5 University). He has also studied at Paris 8, Paris 10, Frankfurt/Main, and Harvard Universities. He has been Deputy-Director of the Marc Bloch Center (Berlin) and he has written various books and articles on participatory and deliberative democracy, most recently, *Les budgets participatifs en Europe*, La Découverte (Paris, 2008, English translation forthcoming).

Peter Stone is an Assistant Professor of Political Science at Stanford University. His articles have appeared in such journals as the *Journal of Political Philosophy*, the *Journal of Theoretical Politics*, *Political Theory*, *Rationality and Society*, and *Social Theory and Practice*. His book on lotteries, *The Luck of the Draw*, forthcoming with Oxford University Press. He has a website at www.stanford.edu/~pstone

Antoine Vergne is a PhD candidate at the Freie Universität (Berlin, Germany) and the Institut d'Études Politiques (Paris, France). He works on the theory and application of sortition in politics. He has specialised in the development and practice of the Planungszelle—the Citizens' Jury model—in international contexts and has observed and assessed participatory democracy in projects in France and Germany. He has published several papers on this topic.

Introduction

Oliver Dowlen

The Modern Revival of an Old Idea

The group of international scholars of sortition who met in Paris in November 2008 share one thing in common. This is the intuition that our subject, the use of random selection or sortition in the public or political arena to choose people or allocate goods, is something special. But just what is so special about sortition that so engages those who study it?

To begin with it promises to bring something new to today's political landscape, something of potentially world-changing significance. For those in the west who are aware of the deficiencies of the current liberal, representative, paradigm of government it offers to make up for what is perceived to be a democratic deficit. The modern use of sortition opens the prospect of creating practical equality between citizens in respect to public office and the possibility of bridging the gap between the citizens and what is too often seen as a detached political elite. It could also help to create more impartial institutions in a political arena too often dominated by partisan intrigues and pressures. For those in developing democracies it promises to inhibit the canker of corruption and to help to bring rival factions into a stable, unified political process. As a possible new addition to modern politics its introduction would fit comfortably onto the agenda of those advocating a more participatory model of democracy. Likewise it could appeal to those promoting greater citizen responsibility, those of an egalitarian persuasion or those demanding greater political transparency and accountability in public affairs. Above all it could serve to strengthen the hand of those seeking social progress through greater political engagement.

In this respect, therefore, the primary task of the modern explorer of sortition would consist of demonstrating in advance, in theory, what practical benefits sortition could bring to the modern polity. The fact that members of the political community are now openly advocating citizen's jury schemes makes this need for clarity and understanding that much more urgent. As schemes get up and running, moreover, they would also need to be critically evaluated so as to inform further initiatives. The role of theory would therefore be to ease the passage of sortition into practice.

One of the complications of this vision, and another special quality of sortition, is that it is not just a new idea. It may be new to today's politics but was systematically used in Ancient Athens and in late medieval Italy — two formative periods in the development of what we know as politics or the political process — and in many other places besides. This tells us, in the first instance, that sortition is not an untried mechanism: there is a considerable body of practice to inform modern theory.

But while this body of practice is a valuable resource for the modern advocate, it does not come without difficulties. Although sortition survives in the important institution of the randomly-selected jury, the last republic in which it was extensively used in the central organs of government — the Second Florentine Republic — fell in 1530. In the face of this discontinuity, all evaluation has to come through the prism of history. In order to make the historical precedent relevant to any possible modern application, therefore, the modern researcher has to be acutely aware of the differences and similarities between the lot-based polities of the past and our own political landscape. Moreover this situation is further complicated by the fact that remarkably little theoretical writing on sortition exists from these periods. It is as if the successful use of sortition in practice meant that commitment to theory was thought of as unnecessary — the use of lotteries was just a matter of common sense.

In these circumstances the symbiotic relationship between theory and practice takes on another twist. It is inevitable that those looking to past practice will do so from the viewpoint of the present — and I see no problem with this if it is done intelligently. There is thus a sense that we need some sort of view of what constitutes political progress and a thorough understanding of what a lottery process actually does before we can interpret what was actually happening in those somewhat distant republics. The more consciously articulated these views become, I would suggest, the more they can tell us about why sortition was valuable then, and why it could be valuable now. There is a sense, therefore, that as well as looking towards the future, today's scholars of sortition, are, in fact, writing the theory that will help us to unravel the past practice of sortition.

This is not to suggest that looking back to past practice is the only way forward, but I would claim that this 'discontinuous' nature is a very special feature of the practice of sortition which helps makes it a particularly all-sided and rich arena of study. Unlike completely new devices, sortition has played a part in our political inheritance. While new sortive measures might well be unfamiliar territory for the modern politician, we also have to realise how whole areas of our modern political world — ideas of equality, impartiality and the purity of the political processes for example—emerged from political contexts where sortition was widely used. Thus a study of sortition can also act as a means of re-examining our received views of the political process.

At the same time it is equally true that modern political science and political theory can bring new insights to the study of sortition. The most obvious change in the way we understand lotteries has come from the advent of statistical probability theory. But there is also much to be gained by approaching sortition from the premises of rational choice theory, game theory or in terms of the modern disciplines of conflict resolution or constitutional design. It can form part of the philosophical exploration of the role of the rational in politics as well as contributing to the ever-present debate on the distribution of social goods. If sortition has the ability to belong equally well to a variety of political platforms, it can also potentially straddle a number of different academic approaches to politics.

One reason for this, and the reason, I would suggest, that it is so fascinating for those who study it, lies in the complex nature of the lottery itself. It is a process that deliberately excludes both reason and desire—yet it is used for rational ends and to produce desired outcomes. It has been used as a link with the divine, and also for the most frivolous of games. It offers equality of opportunity to its participants, but because there is one winner in a lottery, that equality differs from the process of distribution by equal shares. A lottery is a mechanical process and the outcome is determined without the aid of any human faculty: be it love, hate, reason, passion, profound wisdom or wilful prejudice. One application can therefore be useful for any number of reasons at the same time. It is this chameleon-like nature of lot that teases and exercises the minds of all who engage seriously with the subject and seek to elucidate its potential benefits. Faced with these complications the type of scholarly exchange that would enable us to view the same object from many viewpoints becomes an indispensable step on the path to greater understanding.

When the authors of this collection of papers met in Paris there was a real sense that a decisive stage in establishing a broad, pluralist international discourse on sortition had taken place. Such is the compelling nature of the subject, its natural complexity, its potential benefits to the modern world and the richness of its tradition in practice that I am fully confident of its continued growth and development.

Gil Delannoi

Exploring the Boundaries of Theory and Practice

When the authors of this book met in Paris in November 2008, it was certainly the right moment to convene such a conference. It had obviously become urgent to bring scholars together for a first meeting on the subject as the use of lots in politics is expanding throughout the world nowadays. It has been successfully experimented on from Canada to China,[1] from Germany to Australia, and has even gained ground in the oldest European representative democracies of Britain and France.

The authors of the present book have spent a considerable amount of time studying and debating this topic. Our Paris conference laid the foundations for a theoretical framework. This could not have been done without paying great attention to bygone procedures, recent experiments and new perspectives.

Even without especially delighting in theory we are aware that some necessary connections are missing if we wish to improve our knowledge and practice of sortition. Does such a statement as 'It works in practice' imply the following reply: 'Yes but does it work in theory?' Albert Einstein famously said: 'Theory is when we know everything and nothing works, practice is when everything works and nobody knows why.' We should therefore concentrate on keeping both approaches in mind: the theoretical and the practical. All the more so because when it comes to this division between theory and practice, what we find is a ceaseless interaction, blurred by a significant plurality of theories and practices.

---

1   A group of 107 citizens selected by lottery represented the people of Xiamen at public hearings held over two days in 2007. These hearings concerned the construction of a chemical plant. The hearings were also attended by eighty lawmakers and political advisors. Most of the representatives voiced their opposition to the project and a relocation was subsequently envisaged.

Theory and practice are not two worlds apart but two sides of the same reality. Theory has to explain the practice. Practice has to show the theory at work.

Let us begin with an important point of vocabulary concerning what I will call, for the moment, random selection. In some languages, such as French for example, there is only one expression for this (*tirage au sort*). In English we find a large number, including: random selection, use of lots, selection by lottery, sortition. Should we choose one word only from among these words? In a sense, it might be argued that we need such an exclusive tool.

I am nevertheless afraid that a sole catchword often obscures rather than clarifies. But it is possible and useful to define a special meaning and then to explore a field in which each available word can operate. To begin with, we can acknowledge that *random selection* is one way among others for sorting out, sampling, picking, electing or selecting persons or items. *Sortition* might then be defined as a general term refering to this method. Finally, *drawing lots* is the gesture by which such an event often takes place.

Is there still a life after vocabulary? Knowing many philosophers and theorists, I have some reasons to doubt this, but I am convinced that we must go ahead by defining the main terms more accurately. Any effort in this direction will develop our comprehension of the procedures involved and their value. Subsequently, by bringing together our work and thoughts, we might even try to improve the mechanisms of democracy.

We can never underline too often how flexible sortition can be. It opens up an immense field for theoretical and practical exploration. It should be noted that, despite appearances, random selection is a more flexible and more varied procedure than the elective vote. There is also considerable room for reshaping the rules which govern the electoral practices. Thus, sortition can be used to appoint a candidate (or few candidates) from among a larger pool of candidates. It might also be relevant to choose someone from among a whole population. In addition, the following question should be considered: should individuals who have been randomly chosen have the right to refuse their election, or be forced to accept it? These two choices of procedural definition alone provide considerable flexibility.

Since random selection depends on field, scale, code, and the set of laws extending or limiting the procedure, sortition is a procedure which is still underrated and too often discarded. There is only one exception to this flexibility: the procedure is rather rigid as an antidote to corruption. But who would complain about that?

In the academic field, advocating sortition should mean explaining its potential, devising experiments and implementing the best ones. All the contributors here are obviously more favorable than hostile to sortition, but this interest should be treated with caution. My standpoint is that sortition must be an addition, not as a substitution for existing arrangements, and certainly not used as a universal panacea. I don't want and I don't need (and would possibly fear) the idea that a radical choice has to be made between the different and varied forms of democracy, for example between the direct or the indirect, or between the meritocratic and the popular. Each form has a necessary purpose in a complete democracy and I would advocate sortition in much the same spirit. In the current climate where we have a great deal (and a great deal to complain about) in terms of administrative bureaucracy, political representation and superficial leadership, we have much less direct democracy and almost no sortition at all. The question we are posing is: why not revive, observe, evaluate and refine the latter?

At first I would recommend its flexibility. In other words: sortition with or without entrance qualification; mandatory or voluntary; consultative or sovereign. That said, I would not back any sort of proposal based on sortition just because it is radical, provocative or amusing. One of the most ill-advised operations, in my opinion, would be the replacement of a representative assembly by a new body whose members would be selected by lot on a basis similar to universal suffrage. This would just be like tying two opposite types of logics together with an Utopian knot. I would be prepared to bet that the outcome would contain the worst of what each approach has to offer. Adding bodies and procedures would work better than replacing or mixing them up. The will to correct representation by representative sortition puts me in mind of someone regretting that cars have replaced horses and then proposing to remedy that situation by putting a horse behind the steering wheel of a car.

Once the different types of logics are distinct (partisan representation is aristocratic at best and oligarchic at worst, sortition is democratic at best and populist at worst), I would back any attempt to create political bodies chosen by sortition, either qualified or not. The choice of one option rather than the other would depend upon the needs of each individual case. These bodies could be juxtaposed to the existing representative and legislative institutions and the experiments could be implemented at any scale (from local to international) and in any field (from politics to other activities).

Every process of trial and error leads to experiments. And, big or small, everything that can be done in our field is worth doing. Given the stark realities of politics and public opinion, I would support ways of instilling sortition in existing procedures as a first step. Together with local experiments this is the best way to understand the actual changes that this would promote.

The academic profession could be an interesting playground for such experiments. I taste them with delight in advance. In any case, a reform that succeeds is usually better than a revolution that fails or that never takes place. The utopian perspective nevertheless remains a fertile ground for the human imagination.

Following our conference we are appealing to all with a twofold request: let us continue what we have commenced with very specific and useful tasks of academic standardization, in vocabulary, in bibliography, in the collection of data. Thereupon, let us keep every kind of approach open. Let us be as pluralistic as possible. Far from being opposed to each other, these approaches are coherent and should derive mutual benefit from one another.

Note on citations

The bibliography at the back of this volume consists of selected works that deal specifically with the subject of sortition or works that the editors regarded as essential reading for the study of the subject. Works listed in the bibliography are cited by reference to the author's surname followed by the date of publication in brackets; works not in the bibliography are cited in full in the footnotes of each individual chapter.

Part I

Connecting the Past and Future of Sortition

1 Gil Delannoi

Reflections on Two Typologies for
Random Selection

This paper presents two typologies for random selection. The first typology is based on the <u>uses</u> of random selection: surveys, organized job rotation, neutralization of a procedure, allocating resources, a way to save time and means. The second typology sets out the <u>use values</u> of random selection: consultation, deliberation, impartiality, participation, response to rarity.[1]

1 A few preliminary points

1.1 Random selection and universal suffrage

1.2 Random selection and direct democracy

1.3 Random selection and election by vote

2 Typologies

2.1 On uses of random selection

2.2 On use values of random selection

3 Concerning these typologies

3.1 Surveys

3.2 Organized turnover

3.3 Neutralization of a procedure

3.4 Resource allocation

3.5 A way to save time and means

4 Provisional conclusions

4.1 Prevention of corruption

4.2 A broader typology

4.3 Forms of competence

4.4 Forms of equality

4.5 Mixing procedures

1   A first draft of this chapter was presented in 2005, reshaped and extended for the November 2008 conference. It is part of a theory of democracy in progress. The works cited in the original papers have been included in the Bibliography of this book.

The *theory* and *practice* of *politics* has its etymological origins in Greek antiquity. Although the Greeks invented the basic words of the political vocabulary, two important notions from ancient democracy have not survived: *psephos* (vote in ancient Greek) and *kleros* (sortition).

Both of these were essential procedures within Athenian democracy. Voting can be substantial and legislative (applied to texts or decisions) or elective and nominal (applied to individuals or parties). Sortition is indeed 'elective' despite the modern meaning of the word 'election', which is usually perceived to be at odds with selection by lottery.

Each procedure boasts a certain number of advantages. A closer examination of the Athenian system leaves little doubt about the way in which the first democrats saw the alternatives. Voting was used for a few senior political posts where considerable individual competence was required. Aristotle explained this by the fact that voting *in itself* is an elitist exercise: it may not reveal the best candidates nor elect the best from among them, but at the very least it designates those whom the community deems the best. Furthermore, when tasks call for exceptional abilities, the rarity of those abilities justifies unlimited re-election. There is no earthly reason to deprive a community of the services of those best equipped to deliver them. Similarly, selection by lottery is consistent with one of the founding principles of democracy: equality. Better still, whereas a universal suffrage brings equality by voting and potential equality in the eligibility (anyone has the right to be a candidate for election), selection by lottery brings more equality in eligibility and more equality in terms of the result. Any individual is eligible without having to be a candidate, and anyone in the pool can serve when the election procedure is by random selection.

In Athenian eyes, it would have been just as absurd to select leaders randomly as to elect jurors by vote. Sortition has a number of advantages but the first is the assurance of equality, since equality is, by nature inherent in this procedure more than in any other. In democracy's egalitarian triptych equality in the right to free speech and in the right to vote make up the first two elements. The equality of political involvement (or mandatory participation) brought about by random selection is the third.

Democratic equality is not, however, the sole benefit of sortition. One of its practical advantages is that it can function as a procedural restraint on corruption. The term 'corruption' conjures up the idea of something illicit which should be avoided in the name of fairness. It may be fraud or bribery or it might merely be a breach of rules, foul play or a conflict of interests in a broader sense. As an antidote to corruption, random selection can be defined positively as promoting probity or integrity. The use of lottery is less susceptible to corruption than any other procedure (there will never be an absolutely ideal procedure in any case). It can play an essential role in establishing procedural political rules and maintaining a high standard of political conduct. Thus, among the many reasons for using random selection that a typological approach reveals is its capacity to enhance integrity. The principle of integrity and its experimental effects was constantly seen in the practical history of sortition as well as in the theoretical arguments about its use. Random selection prevents intrigues, curbs passions and discourages factions.

1 A few preliminary points

1.1 Random selection and universal suffrage

Random selection of political officers has never been combined with *universal* suffrage nor has it been practiced on such a broad basis. Random selection from the entire citizenry does take place in some judicial systems, however. This is the case for trial courts in France, for instance, where popular juries are required to hear criminal cases. It is also used on this scale in experiments in consultative politics (public hearings, citizens' conferences in the field of deliberative and participative democracy) and in opinion surveys.

These domains touch on politics but are not directly political in comparison to the election of officials by universal suffrage. The use of sortition on the same scale as so-called universal suffrage is, at best, a marginal proposition in today's political climate.

1.2 Random selection and direct democracy

If we were to ask whether random selection is an agent of *direct democracy*, the answer would have to be: yes and no. Yes, in the sense that it entails more active participation of the people than is the case with representative or mandating procedures. No, because it produces office holders and elites that represent a whole population and who deliberate among themselves, apart from the citizenry. In this way, it is closer to representative democracy than to direct democracy. A typical procedure of direct democracy is the referendum, which is a vote for or against a law that has already been written by another political body. A similar, but even more direct procedure is the *votation* (to use the contemporary Swiss term). Here the citizenry choose between several legislative options that are either proposed by the government or put forward by popular initiative.

Sortition might best be described as an intermediary between direct and indirect democracy. This can be explained by its relation to both equality and sovereignty. In indirect democracy, the people, who are sovereign, elect representatives who pass the laws. The exercise of the people's sovereignty is therefore quite limited. Rousseau described it as occasional and sporadic. In the same way, equality among citizens is restricted and ephemeral. On the contrary, in direct democracy all citizens are equals, all act at the same time when they form the body politic for a referendum or 'votation'. In this sense, the equality, the scope, and the universality of the procedures of direct democracy is superior to those of most random selection schemes. In contrast, the specific equality of random selection stems from the practical involvement of all citizens in schemes where everyone has a realistic chance of being chosen at some time. This happens when the size of the pool and the frequency of rotation means that most citizens will occupy the post in question at one point or another. The current meaning of the word lottery obviously does not suggest this quasi-certainty. Although both are based on random selection, a rotational scheme is the opposite of a raffle, which relies on the idea that each participant has only a minimal chance of winning.

1.3 Random selection and election by vote

The mode of random selection used in antiquity has come down to us as a symbolic vestige rather than as a practical political proposition. It actually had little place in the history of republican ascendance. It has sometimes been mistaken for the notion of direct democracy, which is an anachronism when applied to ancient practices. In the Italian republics of the Renaissance limited forms of sortition were used to counterbalance procedures that combined elements of elective voting, co-optation, and appointment—a hybrid of genres.

Full political use of sortition based on the principle of the equal (or approximately equal) competence of citizens in matters of general (and certainly not technical) concern dealing with politics and morality is only really found in antiquity. The grounds for trusting its competence were presented by Protagoras both as reasoned argument and as founding myth in the famous Platonic dialogue of that name. His reasoning is challenged by Plato's Socrates. Aristotle takes an intermediate, conciliatory approach. For the most part he favours popular judgment so long as democratic prerogatives are accompanied by other procedures. Yet I would say Aristotle is closer to Protagoras than to Plato.

It is clear of course that equal ability is not the same thing as equal performance. This point must be stressed. Likewise, citizens of a given country or area all speak the same language, but they do not speak it the same way or with the same level of command. Even if popular sovereignty is no better than other types of sovereignty, it should not be discredited or considered useless for this reason. Tocqueville observed that a people as a whole can make as many errors as an individual does, but the former is quicker at self-correction. This can apply to the rectification

of errors, the instigation of urgent reforms, or, in extreme cases, the resolution of crises such as those caused by incompetent leadership, massa-
cres or civil war. The people of a country are more likely to change
leaders than to wait for unsatisfactory leaders in power to change the
way they think and behave.

Because sortition has been little used since antiquity, debate has been
minimal and was usually concerned with the qualifications of those chosen by it for a given job. From the Renaissance onwards, random selection
was no more than a device that had its uses. It was largely used by oligarchic regimes and therefore had no particular status as a democratic principle. There has been no attempt to inquire into the real reasons that would
justify intense or widespread use of it. The importance of its procedural
benefits, however, is obvious from its use in antiquity. The positive effects
of sortition are many and, in practice, include a curb on machinations,
intrigues, and partisan cleavages. In institutions that are more oligarchic,
more corporative, and more municipal than those of antiquity, random
selection is one guarantee against corruptions of the republican ideal.

We have inherited numerous potential uses for random selection from
ancient, medieval and modern history. The fullest usage was based on the
idea of equal ability for a given task with mandatory participation by all
in functions that are considered to be at the same time an honor and a
chore, a pleasure and a burden. Such is the case, for example, when a citizen is selected to be a member of a jury. A more negative and more restric-
tive use was defined and implemented to satisfy the imperatives of
republican civic virtue in medieval and modern city-states. Here sortition
was greatly diluted because it became only one of a series of procedures
and was often integrated with other mechanisms in complicated ways.
Moreover the point of application of these schemes could vary greatly
according to a spatial scale, from offices of major executive significance to
those that operated at a local grassroots level. Finally, the procedure can
vary in respect to the functional dimension of the post in question: from
sovereign decision-making to simple optional consultations.

It should be noted that, despite appearances, sortition is a more varied
and more flexible procedure than the elective vote. There is considerable
room for manoeuvre, not only in usage and in outcome, but also in the
rules that govern the practice itself. Thus, one might ask whether this
mechanism should only involve candidates with specialist skills or
whether it might be a relevant method for choosing from a whole population. One might also wonder whether individuals who are randomly chosen should have the right to refuse their election. These two choices of
procedural definition alone provide considerable flexibility in the way
random selection might be used.

Because sortition has never been combined with universal suffrage a number of theoretical doors have been left open. For Tocqueville, this limitation in past practice was reason enough to conclude that the democracies of antiquity were aristocratic. I will propose a typology that goes beyond the political and judicial domains, starting first with one that addresses *uses*. I will then move on to a second typology, which is based on *use values* or more general theoretical objectives. Finally I will attempt to correlate the two.

2 Typologies

Note that the two listings are not symmetric. The reading order could be reversed, starting with the second typology. However, this method might have been a little repetitive. It is nonetheless worth noting that this reversed way of reading also makes sense.

2.1 On uses of random selection

These categories describe the key areas or tasks where random selection can find its practical application. They are a response to the question 'what would I use random selection for?'

- Surveys
- Organized turnover
- Neutralization of a procedure
- Resource allocation
- A way to save time and means

2.2 On use values of random selection[2]

These categories refer to the general political benefits that could accrue when random selection is used. They are a response to the question 'what

---

2   Comment on typology 2.2: Gerhard Göhler rightly signalled the omission of an 'integration effect' in the working paper of this chapter. I had envisaged mentioning such an effect as well as a seventh one: a *lucidity effect*. However, I finally chose not to mention them, not because they were irrelevant, but because I did not have much to say about them, apart from indicating their existence. Though an integration effect is certainly relevant as an argument for sortition, it is still more relevant for direct democracy, which embodies an integration of the whole body politic, whereas selection by lot *conveys* the idea of integration more than it embodies it. From this standpoint, integration is a side effect. It has an impact in the mental environment in which it is used, but is not embodied by any procedure. Another possible effect is a sort of *lucidity* effect. By lucidity effect, I mean that the chance factor, either as a fluke or a risk, an opportunity or a threat, is generally underestimated in our rationalising societies which are driven by bureaucracies, managers and scientists (or pseudo-scientists). In such a context, using lots as an elective tool is an eye-opener that reminds us that chance counts for the best or the worst in human life. Intoxicated by routine forecasting, winning streaks and a lack of imagination, people today are so often 'fooled by randomness', as the broker turned thinker, Nicholas Taleb would say, that such a reminder of this inevitable frailty must contribute to any thoughtful and careful action.

are the political values that the use of random selection has capacity to generate?'

- Consultative effect **(C)**
- Deliberative effect **(D)**
- Impartiality effect **(I)**
- Participative effect **(P)**
- In response to **R**arity **(R)**

3 Concerning these typologies

This commentary follows the order of the first typology on formal usage and adds in remarks on use value as it proceeds.

3.1 *Surveys*

In a *survey* random selection serves as the framework for constituting population samples. It is based on statistical principle. Interestingly enough, not much more than a few thousand individuals are needed for a totally random survey (in other words, with no quotas or preliminary criteria) to be representative of a given population. In a country like France, the margin of error for a random survey is 1.4% for a sampling of 5,000 people.[3] Thus 5,000 randomly selected individuals constitute a highly reliable sample for voting surveys or to obtain simple answers to simple questions. A sample numbering no more than an ancient demos (20,000 for example) not only provides a decision-making tool roughly on a par with that of the entire population of a modern state, it also (though to a lesser extent) reduces distortions in the representation of different groupings such as, the sexes, different professions, social classes, etc. These latter are often misrepresented or indeed absent from traditional political representation. Obviously, this random sampling provides an equal distribution of the sexes and would reflect other factors such as age for instance, even if a bit less exactly.

This technique can be used to set up advisory and focus groups, or for in-depth surveys. It is frequently employed in marketing and opinion polls, albeit using the smallest samples possible. The same method of random sorting can serve to constitute groups to whom institutional political functions could be entrusted.

In the Athenian system, all citizens gathered in a popular assembly which convened around twenty times a year and voted on laws. Sortition was used for roles required for the execution of judicial and executive tasks. In contrast, nowadays, a sample aims to be as representative as pos-

---

3 According to D. Boy and J. Chiche, *Analyse des données* (Paris: Centre de Recherches Politiques de Sciences-Po).

sible. The idea that elective voting is not the only tool that can be used by representative democracy and that random selection can be employed to democratic ends may seem surprising. Nevertheless, it is used to select members of every popular jury, and less frequently, in experiments with consultative, deliberative, or participative democracy, which, in most instances, take place at local level. The technique can also be used on a wider scale, at State level for example, especially where assemblies of citizens are regularly organized to deal with specific subjects.

The potential use of representation by random selection varies greatly depending on the size of the population pool. With universal suffrage the pool is tantamount to the whole, but it can be made smaller by division into constituencies. With a randomly selected sample the use of tighter selection criteria or mandatory candidacies similarly affects its ability to be genuinely representative. Representativeness can also be adjusted after sortition has taken place. If clearly unsuitable individuals are chosen, they can then be disqualified, and a further lottery selection held. This would, however, detract slightly from the universality of the procedure.

What counts above all is that the sample be chosen on an egalitarian basis and that it be sufficiently representative of the population so that regular results can be inferred from it. Testing this regularity is not difficult and requires only two separate samples selected in the same way. It then becomes easy to compare how representative they are. It is even possible to make them work in parallel and to check whether the results produced by them are similar or not.

The objectives of such sampling are varied: from a simple count of ballots (one answer to one question) to the institution of a deliberative group which produces its conclusions either by vote or by written record.

This form of representative random sampling is particularly suitable for the use of Consultation (C), moderately suitable for Deliberation (D) and might possibly contribute to Participation processes (P). It also satisfies certain demands of Impartiality (I). Yet, other forms of survey sample, those selected according to quotas for example, cannot be called representative in the same way and are nonetheless no less reliable. Finally, since the procedure is in some way linked to response to Rarity (R), the fact that it is inexpensive (in means, time and strategies) is obviously not due to a shortage of population from which to select candidates. Rather, it is inexpensive as a result of economies of procedure and scale. A sampling takes less effort and costs less. Whatever the advantages, it is seldom proposed that the deliberations of representatives chosen by the body politic as a whole be replaced by the deliberations of a sample of citizens randomly selected from the same population. In the same vein, even though it would be perfectly possible to replace a vote by the population as a whole with a large-scale sampling (say 50,000 or 100,000 instead of a whole population of 50,000,000) this could be considered unreasonable and anti-democratic. It is not so much that the result would be altered: it would be practically identical in both cases. The symbolic value of equal participation and the collective experience of this equal participation embodied in the mass vote would be lost.

3.2 *Organized turnover*

Random selection can be used to determine a temporal order and thus fix the rotation of those appointed to a specific task. Such were the dynamics of the Athenian system. In this type of rotating procedure each individual knew there was a good chance (or mischance) of being selected. Most Athenian citizens were likely, sooner or later, to serve as jurors. There was a strong ethos of civic responsibility and there was a strong chance that they would serve, at least a few months during their lifetime in a small body of magistrates in the executive branch of the political system. Sortition designated who and when.

This way of organizing turnover has survived, but in contexts that render it barely significant: in competitive exams and electoral campaigns, for example, the order of passage is randomly selected: on French radio and TV networks, political campaigners are allotted equal time to deliver their speech and the exact moment when they deliver it is randomly selected. But the main significance of the rotation principle lies elsewhere. It was designed to foster mandatory democratic participation. It is therefore suitable for assignments considered to be both a right and a duty, both an honour and a chore. The equality of result brought by frequent turnover enacts this rotation principle in a way that is fundamentally different from the lottery principle. Common lotteries attribute prizes, resources, subsidies or tasks to one person (or to very few) singled out from a great number. I define *common lottery* as a lottery based on a chance competition in which people win money if they have previously chosen the numbers selected by the final drawing of lots. Such a lottery is egalitarian in terms of rights (provided everyone gets only one ticket), but not in terms of results. A *democratic lottery* is one which organizes a mandatory turnover among citizens. As the odds of being selected in such a lottery are very strong, a political lottery is the opposite of a common lottery. If the odds are not so strong, then the lottery is somewhere in between the common lottery and the political one. This intermediary type should perhaps be called a *political* or *social lottery*.

Random selection based on job rotation is not only egalitarian but participative. It embodies the Platonic concept of politics as an unavoidable chore for a free individual. It produces magistrates who are not preoccupied with advancing their careers. In this sense it reduces corruption. However, while drawing lots prevents corruption *ex ante*, it is no guarantee *ex post*. The impossibility of *ex ante* corruption as a result of the drawing of lots does not mean that once in office the magistrate will not corrupt or be corrupted just like in the fable of 'The Dog who Carried his Master's Dinner around his Neck'.[4] For this reason in Athenian democracy the public disclosure of accounts held while in office was a crucial moment for a randomly selected magistrate. The fact that magistrates ruled collegially also argued against corruption as the incompetence or dishonesty of one magistrate could be prevented by the collective manner in which decisions are taken.

Such random selection, when akin to rotation, suits participation (P) and impartiality (I) particularly well but it is not very relevant for C and D (consultation and deliberation) since the sampling is of short duration and on occasion similar to survey techniques. It has no connection with rarity (R) since it is designed to distribute to everyone in turn.

3.3 Neutralization of a procedure

This neutralization which random selection can bring about is often intended to suppress competition or to avoid conflicts of interest. Since random selection is instantaneous, it eliminates (or drastically reduces) the manœuvering that usually precedes other forms of choosing: intrigue, string-pulling, advertising, attempts at influencing and other tactics whether hidden or not. The notion itself of transparency (or opacity) has no meaning when one has recourse to random sampling. Rigging is still a possibility, but one far more difficult to put into practice and thus less frequent than in elective voting or other forms of selection. Recourse to drawing by lot does away with extra-ordinary ambition and suggests that political responsibility should be part of ordinary life.

To these effects (or rather non-effects) which precede the process itself, one should add the effects (or once again non-effects) which follow designation. 'Random selection offends no one,' wrote Montesquieu. It does not flatter the winner's vanity nor render the loser resentful. It moderates both arrogance and bitterness. With the exception of cases of fraud, it likewise does away with suspicions of partiality on the part of the organizers. This pacifying effect is individual, collective and systemic, that is to say all-pervading.

From the point of view of integrity, the neutralization obtained is procedural, tactical, and psychological. Is the remedy too radical? No, if the level of ability among the population concerned is roughly equal. This roughly equal level of ability is taken for granted (in the case of trial juries

4   See this fable by La Fontaine in the Appendix to this chapter.

for instance) or is obtained by a preliminary sorting out. Finally, it can be verified at the close of the procedure by an examination of the ability of those designated.

This procedural neutralization satisfies, above all, the demand for impartiality (I), and bypasses or suppresses the deliberative aspects (D) in at least two respects: determining who is to be chosen and who is to make the selection.

3.4 Resource allocation

When random selection is used to allocate *resources*, the term 'lottery' is appropriate. The lottery effect (a limited number of jackpots for a small number of winners) can nonetheless be rectified by using rotation or by increasing the number of lots drawn.

Unlike job (or prize) rotation, in which identical jobs (or prizes) are allocated over time, the lottery is far more pertinent for the equal allocation of rare (or finite) resources.

However, the combination of average availability and the equality principle entails a move away from pure lottery (defined as a massive participation and few prizes). Resource allocation can be thought of as a means to satisfy the need to award unequal benefits to a population made up of equals. Random selection is not often chosen to do this today, though it was used in Athens recently to distribute apartments in the former Olympic Village among interested citizens. It can also be used to distribute concert tickets, travel visas or fishing permits, for example, when demand is greater than supply. Even though these examples are minor, the principle on which they rely is important in terms of theory for it is radically different from other procedures, namely distribution by the market (supply and demand or auction) or on the basis of an interventionist policy (meritocratic, functional or traditional).

Barbara Goodwin takes distribution by random selection even further and suggests it could become a utopian alternative to be applied to society as a whole. This fundamentally egalitarian alternative then acts as a substitute for both the market economy and for bureaucratic administration.[5]

The Goodwinian utopia revives the egalitarian dream which was dealt a death-blow with the failure of communist egalitarian (or pseudo-egalitarian) dictatorships. For Goodwin, the only areas not suitable for random selection are the family and education. It could be adopted in every other area of life to equalize opportunities. It should be underlined here that only the chances are equal whereas the benefits remain unequal. By 'equality' here, I mean absolute equality of opportunity which must

5   See Goodwin (2005).

rotate in order to be fair in a system where resources are unequally distributed. As I have frequently and emphatically noted, corruption and conflict of interest are impossible in such a system.

Each job (each social or 'professional' function) would then be assigned by drawing lots on the understanding that there would be a preliminary training period as soon as the person was designated. Thus, each citizen would, in turn, serve in several capacities and the constant renewal would (in part) counterbalance variations in results. This is nothing less than a generalized form of lottery linked to a medium-term commitment on the part of each citizen. Goodwin brushed aside the notion of an associated risk of incompetence with an ironic quip: for the most part, in competitive societies, it's the fact of being an office-holder that provides a semblance of competence rather than real competence earning a place for the meritorious.

This utopia is more equalizing than it is egalitarian since it assumes, as principle and as fact, that even a completely egalitarian education produces non-egalitarian results. Basically, as proposed, this radical antidote no longer seeks to put an end to all inequalities: on the contrary, it bows to fatality but then sets out to make up for inequalities by mechanical correctives.

But is this not a new form of tyranny? Goodwin replies that randomness is not really tyrannical since it lacks the motivation that characterizes the true tyrant. Chance is indeed innocent, but arbitrariness is also a form of tyranny, and tyranny without a tyrant is just as disturbing and oppressive.

In practice, this type of job rotation is more limited today than it was in Athens, for there is no longer any question of one person fulfilling all social functions in the course of a lifetime. However, the arguments justifying such a rotating lottery are similar to those used in the past: in principle, the certainty that one will change job several times discourages individuals from abusing their power as it could be turned against them when they came to occupy a subordinate rank. Goodwin characterizes her system as 'socialist, individualistic, and anarchistic'. Regardless of whether it elicits horror or sympathetic interest, one must concede that the system sheds light (for the benefit of theory) on the mechanisms by which random selection allocates resources. Moreover, it raises the possibility, utopias aside, of a similar, albeit more limited use elsewhere.

One way to apply the principle of equality fully would be to organize a lottery where the participants themselves were rotated. The use value would be participative (P) in terms of rotation and of the involvement of all, and above all impartial (I) to the point of innocence created by the arbitrariness of the procedure. Here, random selection is cast in the role of the eternal child-king moving counters in a game, just as in Heraclitus' allegory of time. Goodwin does not disavow the tragic dimension; she even alludes to the fatal Babylonian lottery imagined by Borges in one of his apologues.

3.5 *A way to save time and means*

The final type (*a way of saving time and means*) covers pretty well everything left over — as is true for the last category in most typologies. It essentially concerns the need to gain time, money or simplify procedures for one reason or another. It is usually used by necessity but can also be by choice. Lack of time, lack of means, impossibility of proceeding otherwise: these are the factors that define such use. For example: in a given situation there are only a few seconds left to choose someone for an urgent job. If either no one or everyone wants it, the only way to choose is by drawing lots because of the shortage of time.

Equality here is only a by-product of random selection. It is not the point of departure and is even less the result. The reasoning runs as follows: it is better to choose one person than nobody at all. Inequality is better than universal equality in a state of penury. Random selection is adopted in certain tragic cases, characterized by extreme rarity and extreme urgency (the transplanting of human organs for instance) where timing becomes a question of life or death.

Random selection is also used in cases where no urgency exists, but where the resource in question is unique or extremely rare. If there is only one item to be had and massive demand for it, it would be a nihilist conception of equality to attribute it to no one. One answer would be to organize a lottery, an egalitarian procedure with non-egalitarian effects. This would prevent the market from coming into play and the rare object would not be granted to the highest bidder. Random selection is justified by the fact that all other procedures have even greater drawbacks (as in the medical case).

The value of this last usage is almost exclusively as compensation for rarity (R), with some impartial effect (I). Participation (P) is, to say the least, passive and indeed fatalistic.

4 Provisional conclusions

4.1 *Prevention of corruption*

In comparison with the vote and the opportunities it provides (and often encourages) for propaganda, clientism, and indefinite re-election, sortition has, at whatever epoch and whatever its theoretical grounds, advantages in terms of honesty, neutrality and the prevention of corruption. This is one of the use values that argues in favor of certain random selection procedures. It is no doubt easier (and more convincing) to argue in favor of random selection on these grounds than on the grounds that all citizens are equally competenct.

At this point it should be remembered that whereas the anti-corruption effects of random selection are strong before designation or election by lottery (*ex ante*), the *ex post* effects are less certain. Corruption is as tempting for a person chosen by random selection as it is for a person elected by name. The fact that in ancient times there existed numerous procedures for preventing — or at least limiting — the corruption of magistrates chosen by lot proves that this temptation did indeed exist. The following case illustrates this point. Imagine that a representative assembly (the French National Assembly for example) is chosen by random selection. Once the assembly is convened, the influence of the surrounding society begins to be felt. Some of the representatives will be prey to lobbies, pressure groups, trade unions etc. There is no proof that randomly chosen representatives will be less corruptible than career politicians. Some may indeed be less corruptible given that they will not have schemed in pursuit of an objective, they have no career to pursue and no other ambition than to serve the common good. Others, on the contrary, might well take advantage of their short-lived position of power knowing that no sanction will be forthcoming as they will not be seeking a second term.

It is vital both to think through the theory and become familiar with the practice of sortition. But neither must we forget that laws provide, at most, half of the story. The other half is determined by custom, habit, and behaviour. The content of the procedures is only part of the problem and part of the possible solution. What Thoreau said of the elective vote applies just as well to random selection: 'The fate of the country' does not only depend on 'how you vote at the polls' — 'the worst man is as strong as the best at that game'; but on 'what kind of man' is acting on the political stage and in everyday life.[6] It matters how you vote but what matters even more is how you behave.

4.2 A broader typology

The classification methods and the theoretical considerations set out here fit into a broader framework than the typologies given above. In this broader framework one should distinguish between three possibilities: random selection as used to select persons (a juror or an official for example), to select objects (the attribution of an apartment for example), or to make decisions (a decision in a strong substantive sense: whether to go to war or not, for example). In each of the three cases, a different procedure is

6   'Slavery in Massachussets', *The Liberator*, 21 July 1854.

involved: in the case of *persons* it is an *election* (by vote, random selection or other means), in the case of *objects*, a *lottery*, and in the case of *decisions, the toss of a coin*, a deliberate manipulation of chance, understood here as fatality and not play.

4.3 Forms of competence

Finally, research should deal not only with questions of principle (equality) or result (neutrality). The question of competence should be framed in the broadest possible terms. Sortition assumes as a general rule that the level of competence required is approximately the same, either from the very start, or as a retroactive effect of experience since actual practice forces one to become competent.

If *competence* is taken to be *equal or roughly equal*, then random selection is based on the principles and practice of equality, justice, and the rotation of jobs and offices.

If competence is *unequal*, then the brutality of random selection will, at best, substitute one form of inequality for another, one form of arbitrariness for another.

If competence is *not an issue*, the criterion that defines it becomes redundant, as is the case with lotteries and (sometimes) resource allocation. What is being distributed here in no way raises the problem of competence.

Finally, there are *cases in which* competence is not uniquely associated with any one procedure since the required *competence varies* in respect of the content and not the form of the process chosen. In surveys, for instance, competence is not linked to the survey as a procedure but to the content itself, since competence varies according to the nature of the questions and the way in which they are formulated.

4.4 Forms of equality

To study the equality of a procedure, three *forms of equality* must be determined: equality *at the source of the procedure*, equality *in its mechanism*, and equality *in its effect*. In terms of equality at source, an election by vote in which there are no named candidates and all are eligible for office is as egalitarian as a lottery. However, this equality diminishes with the mechanism of choice as voters do not consider that every eligible candidate deserves to be chosen or has the same chances of being elected as any other. Selection by vote necessarily entails that possible choices be ranked. Finally, equality decreases because of the aristocratic effect which results from every vote and lasts until the next election (for all the psychological reasons already mentioned). This effect becomes palpable even in the unlikely extreme case where everyone votes according to chance.

This is because the winners would nonetheless believe that they had been elected by merit and not by random selection.

4.5 Mixing procedures

The mixing of different procedures opens up a wide field for experiment. It should be remembered that the basic decision to use lots is not taken by drawing lots. To decide whether to use a lottery or not by drawing lots would be mere fatalism and such a cult of randomness is very different from any theory of participation or representation. Moreover, such a question reverberates in an infinite regression. How might we choose to use lots or not in the decision to use lots or not? Selection by lottery is thus always connected to other procedures and other forms of decision-making.

Appendix

Nous n'avons pas les yeux à l'épreuve des belles,
Ni les mains à celle de l'or:
Peu de gens gardent un trésor
Avec des soins assez fidèles.
Certain Chien qui portait la pitance au logis
S'était fait un collier du dîné de son maître.
Il était tempérant plus qu'il n'eût voulu l'être,
Quand il voyait un mets exquis:
Mais enfin il l'était et tous tant que nous sommes
Nous nous laissons tenter à l'approche des biens.
Chose étrange! On apprend la tempérance aux chiens,
Et l'on ne peut l'apprendre aux hommes.
Ce Chien-ci étant de la sorte atourné,
Un Mâtin passe, et veut lui prendre le dîné.
Il n'en eût pas toute la joie
Qu'il espérait d'abord: le Chien mit bas la proie,
Pour la défendre mieux n'en étant plus chargé.
Grand combat. D'autres Chiens arrivent;
Ils étaient de ceux-là qui vivent
Sur le public et craignent peu les coups.
Notre Chien, se voyant trop faible contre eux tous,
Et que la chair courait un danger manifeste,
Voulut avoir sa part. Et lui sage, il leur dit:
Point de courroux, messieurs, mon lopin me suffit:
Faites votre profit du reste.
A ces mots, le premier il vous happe un morceau.
Et chacun de tirer, le Mâtin, la canaille,

A qui mieux mieux ; ils firent tous ripaille;
Chacun d'eux eut part au gâteau.
Je crois voir en ceci l'image d'une ville,
Où l'on met les deniers à la merci des gens.
Echevins, prévôt des marchands,
Tout fait sa main: le plus habile
Donne aux autres l'exemple. Et c'est un passe-temps
De leur voir nettoyer un monceau de pistoles.
Si quelque scrupuleux par des raisons frivoles
Veut défendre l'argent, et dit le moindre mot,
On lui fait voir qu'il est un sot.
Il n'a pas de peine à se rendre:
C'est bientôt le premier à prendre.

                                        La Fontaine (*Fables*, VIII, 7)

Our eyes are not made proof against the fair,
Nor hands against the touch of gold.
Fidelity is sadly rare,
And has been from the days of old.
Well taught his appetite to check,
And do full many a handy trick,
A Dog was trotting, light and quick,
His master's dinner on his neck.
A temperate, self-denying dog was he,
More than, with a load, he liked to be.
But still he was, while many such as we
Would not have scrupled to make free.
Strange that dogs a virtue you may teach,
Which, do your best, to men you vainly preach!
This dog of ours, thus richly fitted out,
A mastiff met, who wish'd the meat, no doubt.
To get it was less easy than he thought:
The porter laid it down and fought.
Meantime some other dogs arrive:
Such dogs are always thick enough,
And, fearing neither kick nor cuff,
Upon the public thrive.
Our hero, thus o'ermatch'd and press'd
The meat in danger manifest
Is fain to share it with the rest;

And looking very calm and wise,
'No anger, gentlemen,' he cries:
'My morcel will myself suffice;
The rest shall be your welcome prize':
With this, the first his charge to violate,
He snaps a mouthful from his freight.
Then follow mastiff, cur, and pup,
Till all is cleanly eaten up.
Not sparingly the party feasted,
And not a dog of all but tested.
In some such manner men abuse
Of towns and states the revenues.
The sheriffs, aldermen, and mayor,
Come in for each a liberal share.
The strongest gives the rest example:
'Tis sport to see with what a zest
They sweep and lick the public chest
Of all its funds, however ample.
If any commonveal's defender
Should dare to say a single word,
He's shown his scruples are absurd,
And finds it easy to surrender
Perhaps, to be the first offender.

(Translated from French by E. Wright, Boston, 1841)

2 Yves Sintomer

Random Selection and Deliberative Democracy

Note for an Historical Comparison

Sortition has been widely used in politics in the Florentine Republic. It has made a comeback in the last decades in contemporary democracies. To what extend can one talk of this as the rebirth of Ancient ideals? This chapter underlines the peculiar context of Early Renaissance Florence, and the specific use of sortition at that time. Combined with other procedures, such as co-option, it allowed development of a Republican self-government where all (or a lot of) citizens could be governed and governing in turn. This polity is contrasted with modern experiments, where sortition rests on the notion of the representative sample – which was unknown at the time of Leonardo Bruni – and implies deliberative democracy rather than self-government. This comparison enables us to understand better some of the challenges deliberative democracy has to face, most notably in relation to participation and decision making.

In 1439, the humanist Leonardo Bruni (1370–1444), the Florentine Republic's Chancellor, published a short treaty in Greek: *On the Florentine Constitution.*[1] At that time Bruni was probably the most famous European intellectual, and Florence was at the height of its splendour and power. Florence during this period had seen the invention of perspective in art, but, more broadly, the early Florentine Renaissance had also witnessed the development of new techniques in textile manufacturing and banking. For our purposes the most significant innovation of this period was

1   Previous versions of this paper have been presented at conferences at the Collège de France (Paris), at Amalfi (European Amalfi Prize for Sociology and Social Sciences/University La Sapienza, Roma), Berlin (Hertie School of Governance/Centre Marc Bloch), Bellagio (Rockefeller Foundation/CNRS/ Mac Arthur Foundation), and at the IEP Paris. I would like to thank all participants for their useful comments.

the rise of civic humanism, which has been identified as a fundamental source of the modern republican tradition. In this essay, which refers more to the regime that had been de facto abolished by the Medici when they took power in 1434, Bruni positively valued Florence as a mixed constitution.[2] The social composition of its citizenry, he claims, results from two exclusion principles: noble families (the magnates) are excluded from the most important offices (this is the anti-aristocratic principle), and manual workers are excluded from the political life (this is the anti-democratic principle). Three other main elements sustain the democratic dimension: the ideal of liberty (*vivere libero, vivere civile, vivere politico* is at the core of its institutions and political system; offices are held for short-term periods, usually two to four months, including the most important of them, the *Signoria*; those who hold the offices are chosen through random selection (*tratta*). The executive, the legislative councils and part of the judiciary are chosen in this manner.[3]

On 11 December 2004, after nearly twelve months of deliberation, a Citizen Assembly, selected by lot from the citizens of British Columbia in Canada, presented its *Final Report on Electoral Change* to the B.C. Legislature. It proposed to change the electoral system by introducing more proportionality (replacing the existing electoral system, the so-called First-Past-the-Post, with a new Single-Transferable-Vote system). This recommendation was then put to the electorate-at-large in a referendum held concurrently with the 2005 provincial election. Gordon Gibson, the creator of British Columbia's Citizen Assembly and councilor to the Prime Minister, justified the initiative in the following manner:

> We are [...] adding new elements to both representative and direct democracy. These new elements differ in detail but all share one thing in common. They add to the mix a new set of representatives, different from those we elect. As things stand now, both streams of decision-making are highly influenced — almost captured — by experts and special interests. The idea of deliberative democracy is essentially to import the public interest, as represented by random panels, as a muscular third force. The traditional representatives we elect are chosen by majoritarian consensus, for an extended period, as professionals, with unlimited jurisdiction to act in our name. The new kinds we

2   The readership of this essay has been limited in comparison with Bruni's other writings. However, it was probably the most incisive definition of the Florentine political regime during the first three decades of the fifteenth century that has been made by a contemporary scholar. Bruni's essay is to be understood in the line of an Aristotelian tradition (one year before, in 1438, Bruni wrote the first modern Latin translation of *Politics*, making it understandable for a wide public; at that time Greek was far less practiced than Latin and medieval translations were hardly readable).

3   Leonardo Bruni, 'Costituzione politica di Firenze', in *Opere*, ed. P. Viti (Utet: Torino, 1996).

are talking about are chosen at random, for a short period, as ordinary
citizens for specified and limited purposes.[4]

The decision seems only to have been the prelude to a larger wave of
similar experiments. Ontario, the most populous Canadian State, followed British Columbia's example in 2005. Two further examples can be
mentioned. On 4 June 2006, in the evening, 131 citizens selected by lot
voted for the socialist candidate in the town hall elections in Marousi, a
middle-sized town near Athens. Throughout the day, they had listened to
those who wanted to become candidates and, using facilitators in order to
have the best possible deliberation, they had discussed the suitability of
the candidates in a general assembly and in small groups. At the end of
the day the person who received the most votes was actually the one who
was least known to the citizens in the morning. The local socialist party
(the PASOK) organized this process following a proposal made by Geor-
ges Papandreou (who was the PASOK national leader and Socialist International's President at that time).[5] In the autumn of 2006, the French
presidential campaign was troubled for some weeks by a proposal made
by Ségolène Royal, the socialist candidate. Ms Royal wanted to set up citizen juries to evaluate politicians' actions. Ms Royal, had promised that, if
elected, she would reform the French Constitution through a process in
which the Legislative Assembly and a Citizen Assembly selected by lot
would work together to prepare a revised text that would then be put to a
referendum. It is surprising to see how many different participatory and
deliberative devices where random selection plays a role have been created in the last two decades, in very different contexts.[6]

It would, however, be ridiculous to compare early renaissance Florence
and British Columbia so strictly. Their contexts, institutions and political
cultures are completely different. Nevertheless two important questions
arise from this comparison. Firstly, can we claim that the recent interest in
random selection marks a resurgence of the democratic tradition that
accompanies the use of this mechanism — a tradition that was invented in
Athens during the classical period and reinvented in the Italian
city-states? Secondly what does this parallel teach us about deliberation,
participation and representation? In what follows, I will proceed in two
steps. First I will briefly describe the self-government based on random
selection that characterized the Florentine Republic and explore the

4   Gordon Gibson, 'Deliberative Democracy and the B.C. Citizens' Assembly',
     http://www.ccfd.ca/index.php?option=com_content&task=view&id=409&Itemid=284
     February 23, 2007..

5   Mauro Buonocore, 'Un weekend deliberativo all'ombra del Partenone', *Reset* 96 (July–August
     2006), pp. 6–8.

6   See Carson & Martin (1999) and Sintomer (2007).

ambiguous role that deliberation played in it. I will then contrast this polity with current experiments in deliberative democracy based on random selection and will discuss what this reveals about the processes of deliberation, participation and decision-making.

Self-government, random selection and deliberation in early renaissance Florence

As we know from the seminal works of Hans Baron, John Pocock and Quentin Skinner, the Florentine notion of *libertas* has been decisive in the formation of the modern political thought.[7] What is less known is that the ideal of the *vivere libero* included not only independence from foreign powers, the rule of law, political equality among citizens (or at least among those who were full citizens) and the right to take an active part in public affairs, but also the right to participate directly in the government of the Republic. Most of the magistrates were randomly selected and held their offices for only a few months.[8]

The role of random selection in the Florentine Republic

From 1282 onwards, the *Signoria*, which was similar to what we would now call an executive, was the most important power in the city. Its members represented the various corporations (*arti*) through a complex system of quotas. It was in charge of foreign policy, controlled the administrative bodies and had the right to initiate the laws of the Republic. Up to 1494, when a Major Council was created following the Venetian model, the *Signoria* decided when the two legislative councils had to meet. Even though this institutional system was continually evolving, its basic features remained the same until the end of the fifteenth century. During this period some of the most important political debates in the city concerned the repartition of political and administrative positions among the various corporations and the role of sortition in that process. From 1328 onwards the majority of official positions were attributed by lot (called *la tratta*). The candidates names were put in pouches (*borse*) and sortition provided the way of selecting those who would be in charge for a certain period. The members of the *Signoria* were selected by lot, and, during the

7   See Hans Baron, *The Crisis of the Early Italian Renaissance* (Princeton: Princeton University Press, 1966); *In Search of Florentine Civic Humanism* (Princeton: Princeton University Press, 1988). * J.G.A. Pocock, *The Machiavellian Moment: Florentine Political Thought and the Republican Tradition* (Princeton: Princeton University Press, 1975). * Quentin Skinner, *The Foundations of Modern Political Thought*, 2 vols (Cambridge: Cambridge University Press, 1978).

8   See Nicolai Rubinstein, 'Florentine Constitutionalism and Medici Ascendancy in the Fifteenth Century', in Rubinstein ed., *Florentine Studies, Politics and Society in Renaissance Florence* (Evanston: Northwestern University Press, 1968); * *The Government of Florence under the Medici (1434 to 1494)* (Oxford & New York: Clarendon Press/Oxford University Press, 1997).

republican period, most of the political and administrative offices were attributed according to a similar process.

The selection process actually took four steps.[9]

(a) In the first one, selection committees in each neighborhood had to choose those citizens who were considered apt enough to hold the office, according to strict personal and political criteria.

(b) During the second phase the list of those who had succeeded (the so-called *nominati*) was scrutinized by a city commission composed of pre-eminent citizens, the *arroti*. The names of those who achieved a qualified majority (two thirds of the ballots, in a process called *squittino*) were put in leather pouches (*imborsati*). For those offices that were attributed through quotas, there were different pouches for the major and the minor guilds.

(c) Sortition itself only took place in the third step when the names were withdrawn from the pouches. Ad hoc officials, the *accopiatori*, were in charge at this crucial moment. The names of those who had not been selected were left in the pouches for the next sortition. After an unusual or important political event (such as a revolution or a drastic change within the regime) had taken place a new *squittino* would be organized before the old pouches were empty.

(d) The last step consisted in eliminating the names of those who had been selected but who did not fit the necessary criteria for office (the so-called procedure of the *divieti*). If any of those chosen still owed taxes, had served in a similar capacity in the recent past, had been sentenced in respect to certain crimes, had a parent in a similar position or already held another important office, they would not be allowed to take up their posts.

Sortition, deliberation and self-government

What was the relation between sortition, election and deliberation in the Florentine Republic? It was very peculiar and very different both from how it operated in Athens and how it is used in our modern democracies. In the Attic city-state, offices were allocated either by random selection or, for the ten per cent most important, by election.[10] In the Florentine system election and sortition were combined. In addition, we have to be aware of the different political values denoted by the term 'election' in different historical periods and political cultures. Modern readers see elections as a process by which the grassroots select those who will then speak and act for them. Ancient Athenians would have had a similar understanding of

9   See Najemy (1982), p.169 ff.
10 See Moses I. Finley, *Politics in the Ancient World* (Cambridge & New York: Cambridge University Press, 1983). * Also see Hansen (1991).

the term. In Florence, elections were a top-down process, a kind of co-option of worthy citizens by the political elite or 'inner circle' where the political power of the state was concentrated. This only changed with the formation of the Major Council in 1494.

The meaning of the word 'deliberation' also varies in respect to the language and context in which it is used. In English, it usually implies a careful discussion of all sides of a question. It is with reference to this meaning that the concept of 'deliberative democracy' was created, and it is only in specific contexts that deliberation necessarily leads to a decision—most notably with a trial jury. In Early Renaissance Italy, the word had quite a different meaning. It implied the decision of a collective body, but not necessarily a collective discussion.[11] Francesco Guicciardini, a famous intellectual and politician who was Machiavelli's contemporary and one of the first theoreticians of representative government, wrote for example in 1512:

> I easily accept that laws could be decided in the [Great] council (*che la deliberazione ne sia in consiglio*), because they are something quite universal and concern every city member; but I like the fact that it is impossible to discuss them publicly, or only following the orders of the *Signoria* and in favor of what it proposes, because if anybody were allowed the freedom to persuade or dissuade others, this would lead to great confusion.[12]

Discussions on public matters were very lively and quite important for the decision-making process in the Florentine Commune. Where did they take place?

(a) There were political discussions in non-public places, for example in the big *palazzi* belonging to the most important families in the city. Such discussions also took place in spaces intermediately between the private and the public arenas: public meetings of a kind were regularly organized on the *bancs* which existed at the bottom of the *palazzi*, and in the open shops and the *loggie* in front of them. In this respect the Florentine inner city was in some way similar to the Athenian agora or the Roman forum.

(b) The general assembly of the people, called the *parlamento*, never had the role it had played in Athens. It had no regular meetings and was only organized from time to time. It was not an institution in which one could deliberate, and usually had a plebiscitary function.

11   This meaning remains the same in contemporary Italian and Portuguese. French and Spanish are somewhere in between. In German, conversely, deliberation excludes decision and a '*deliberative Stimme*' (a deliberative voice) is only consultative. These semantic differences partly explain the difficult diffusion of the concept of 'deliberative democracy' in West European languages other than English.

12   See Guicciardini (1932).

(c) A lot of discussions took place in the guilds, the *arti*, which were a basic feature of the medieval republican system. The *arti* could take decisions for themselves, had specific institutions and could partly designate candidates for offices. Their meetings were only open to members. With the Early Renaissance their importance strongly decreased and they gave way to a more unified political body.

(d) Discussions leading to decisions also took place in the numerous electoral commissions that selected those whose names were to be put in the pouches. These were not open public affairs, as we previously noted, except during the short period at the end of the fifteenth century and the beginning of the sixteenth when the Major Council (*consiglio maggiore*) was in place. Elections were not usually conducted from below and there were no public campaigns; moreover, at that time, parties and factions (*intelligenze*) were prohibited, even though they existed informally.

(e) Most of the offices — including the most important, the *Signoria* — were collegial. This meant that although discussion took place, again, it was not in public. Executive decisions were taken in these offices.

(f) The two legislative councils, selected by lot within much larger lists than the one which was used for the *Signoria*, had the power to pass or refuse the bills proposed by the executive; but they could not propose any bill by themselves and it was forbidden to criticize the proposals.[13] The only speeches allowed were in favour of the measure in hand and it is this arrangement that Guicciardini advocated in the above quotation. In addition, the sessions of the legislative councils were not public, i.e., they were not open to all citizens.

(g) A much deeper discussion took place in advisory bodies called *pratiche*, which the *Signoria* could call at will and which were selected by the most important political leaders. The quality of discussion was high in these bodies, they served to enlighten the public mind and forge a majority consensus, but they took no decisions and were not open to the public.[14] Their role was a crucial factor in the progressive loss of republican substance from the Florentine institutions at the time of early Renaissance for they heralded the emergence of a political class that was dedicated to politics on a full-time basis, that was

13 Along with the exclusion from citizenship of the working class, one the most important aristocratic features that Leonardo Bruni (op.cit., 1996) mentioned was precisely this point: that the legislative councils could not really discuss nor modify the bills proposed by the *Signoria*, but could only approve or reject them. According to him, the other non-democratic elements were that the councils could not decide their own schedule, and that there was no more conscription but a professional mercenary army.

14 See G.A. Brucker, *The Civic World of Early Renaissance Florence* (Princeton: Princeton University Press, 1977).

hegemonic in the electoral commissions and whose members could regularly pass from one public office to another.[15]

In this complex system, deliberation, in the sense of public discussion that is used in most theories of deliberative democracy, was an essential dimension. Even though none were democracies, it is for this reason that we can claim that the Florentine Republic along with the other Italian communes that developed similar systems 'reinvented politics'. As Moses I. Finley, Cornelius Castoriadis and Christian Meier suggest,[16] politics is something very peculiar and has not existed in all societies and at all times; it implies not just the struggle for state power, which takes place in every state society, but also the existence of a public sphere.[17] The articulation of deliberation and decision making in Florence was nevertheless very peculiar, and very different from what we find in modern democracies.[18] The decision-making bodies were not open to the public. The randomly selected legislature could take decisions but could not discuss the bills in question; the general assembly of the people could decide but not deliberate; and the body in which discussion was most lively, the *pratiche*, was co-opted by the inner-circle and was neither open to the wider public nor entitled to take decisions …

Sortition in this context had therefore an ambiguous relation to deliberation. Its main function was to ensure an impartial resolution of conflicts between the different factions that deeply divided the Republic.[19] However, this was not its only value for it also played a crucial role in establishing citizen self-government. Due to random selection and the rapid rotation of the offices (usually from two to six months), nearly all those who had the full citizenship were able, in theory, to have regular access to public office. Citizenship was essentially defined through the membership of one of the twenty-one officially recognized guilds. At the beginning of the fourteenth century this included between 7,000 and 8,000 persons from a population of about 90,000 people. In 1343, three-quarters

15   In his chronicles, Giovanni Cavalcanti estimated the inner circle at about seventy people and concluded: 'I had the feeling that the Republic would decay in tyranny and would be no more a free commonwealth (*e non vivere politico*), that its government was conducted outside the Town Hall […] The Commune was more governed in dinners and in privates offices that in the Town Hall; a lot of people were holding the offices, but only a few governed' (*molti erano agli ufficii e pochi al governo*) (quoted in Brucker, op. cit., 1977, p. 251).

16   See Finley, op. cit., 1983. * Cornelius Castoriadis, *Domaines de l'homme* (Paris: Seuil, 1986). * Christian Meier, *The Greek Discovery of Politics* (Harvard: Harvard University Press, 1990).

17   Jürgen Habermas, *The Structural Transformation of the Public Sphere: An Inquiry into a Category of Bourgeois Society* (Mass.: MIT Press, 1991).

18   This explains the mixed feelings of familiarity and strangeness that we get when reading Machiavelli's *Istorie Fiorentine* (*Florentine Histories*, Princeton: Princeton University Press, 1988).

19   See Sintomer (2007), Dowlen (2008), Buchstein (2009).

of the citizenry were nominated to take part in the *squittino* for the *Signoria*; around 800 passed the test and were *imborsati*—and were thus destined to hold one of the major offices in the years following the vote. In 1411, at the time of the birth of civic humanism, more than 5,000 citizens were *nominati* and more than 1000 *imborsati*. The Major Council created in 1494 had around 3,000 members.

Apart from the highest executive positions there were plenty of other offices that used sortition as a means of selection during this period. If one includes those held by Florentines in the occupied territories, there were between 1,000 and 2,000 political offices and between 2,000 and 4,000 administrative offices in the various institutions and in the guilds subject to random selection. The rule was clear: the more important the office, the harder the competition.[20]

Florentine citizenship was clearly restricted to a minority of the population. The ratio of full citizens to population was larger than that of Venice during the same period,[21] smaller than that of classical Athens,[22] and comparable with the proportion of full citizens to the population of Great Britain at the end of the eighteenth century.[23] Florence was not a democracy in the meaning we presently give to the term. It was not self-government by all and, as we have seen previously, a large part of the power tended to be de facto in the hands of the inner circle during much of this period. Despite this, it was more self-government than representative government and, compared to other regimes of its time, it embodied to some extent the ideal of self-government by the many—*governo largo*. The discrepancy between the constitutional ideal and the political practice in this matter, moreover, was probably no greater than in a modern democracy. The ideal of the *vivere libero* was at least partly embedded in the real life of the Republic of Florence and included the equal participation of the full citizen in public life and an equal—and real—opportunity to hold a pub-

---

20 See G. Guidi, *Il governo della città-repubblica di Firenze del primo quattrocento* (Firenze: Leo S. Olschki, 1981), vol. 2, pp. 43-4. * See G.A. Brucker, op.cit., 1977, p. 253. * See G.A. Brucker, *Florence. The Golden Age, 1138-1737* (Berkeley: University of California Press, 1990). * See Najemy (1982), pp. 177 and 275.

21 Venetian citizenship was basically restricted to the Great Council members: around 1,100 persons for a population of 90,000 at the beginning of the fourteenth Century, and 2,600 for a population of 250,000 before the 1575 plague. See Lane, *Storia di Venezia* (Torino: Einaudi, 1978), pp. 120, 295-7 and 372.

22 Between 30,000 and 50,000 citizens, for a population of 250,000 to 300,000 people. In both cities, women were excluded from citizenship, but in addition, in Florence, manual workers (the *popolo minuto*) had only access to citizenship during the revolt of the Ciompi in 1378, when for a few months 13,000 new persons gained access to citizenship through the creation of three new guilds; peasants from the neighbourhood (the *contado*) remained totally excluded, together with the people living in territories under Florentine domination (the *dominio*).

23 338,000 persons within 8.5 million people.

lic office. This ideal was realised through random selection and the rapid rotation of offices — techniques that were used in order to avoid or limit any division between state power and the citizenry. This polity was thus very different from the absolutist regimes that were emerging in the European countries at the same time, but also very different from the representative democracies that appeared two or three centuries later. It was not a democracy but it was mixed regime, as Leonardo Bruni rightly concluded. The debate between the 'democratic' and the 'aristocratic' dimensions was explicit, and we find it both in the archives and in a large number of contemporary analytical works from this period. At the end of the fifteenth century the old Aristotelian opposition between elections, considered as basically aristocratic, and sortition, that was seen as a democratic tool, seemed to revive in Florentine politics,[24] and was well synthesized in a dialogue by Francesco Guicciardini.[25] The main Tuscan city was a Republic, in the sense that it had a largely self-governed citizenry, and the republican ideal that was elaborated in this city-state helped to establish a radical tradition of self-government that can be found throughout the history of modern democracy.

A renaissance of deliberative democracy?

During the early renaissance, Florence was frequently compared with Athens. Although it has been less influential at the political level than the Greek city, it has played an important role in the development of the modern republican tradition.[26] Our analysis of its political system provides a valuable viewpoint from which to understand the specific features of modern deliberative democracy and the challenges it might have to face.

According to most supporters of participatory instruments based on random selection, the return of this technique in politics, after centuries of eclipse, implies that some of the ideals of ancient democracies are coming back. A good example of this can be found in the writings of Lyn Carson and Brian Martin, two of the most coherent advocates of random selection. They write:

> The assumption behind random selection in politics is that just about anyone who wishes to be involved in decision making is capable of making a useful contribution, and that the fairest way to ensure that everyone has such an opportunity is to give them an equal chance to

24   G. Cadoni, 'Genesi e implicazioni dello scontro tra i fautori della "tratta" e i fautori delle "più fave" 1495–1499', in *Lotte politiche e riforme istituzionali a Firenze tra il 1494 e il 1502*, Istituto storico italiano per il medio evo, Fonti per la storia dell'Italia medevale, Subsidia 7, 1999, pp. 19–100.

25   See Guicciardini (1932), pp.175–95.

26   See Baron, op.cit., 1966 and 1988. * Also see Pocock, op.cit., 1975 and Skinner, op.cit., 1978.

be involved. Random selection worked in ancient Athens. It works today to select juries and has proved, through many practical experiments, that it can work well to deal with policy issues [...] For democracy [...] to be strong, it must contain the essential element of citizen participation, not just by a self-selected few but by ordinary people who rightly can determine their own futures. Given the difficulty of involving everyone in such a deliberative process, we argue that random selection is an ideal means by which a cross section of the population can be involved. [27]

For sure, there are evident and huge differences in the social, political, economical and institutional contexts of modern democracies on the one hand, and of Athenian or Florentine Republics on the other. Nevertheless, can we speak of a partial resurgence of the ideal of self-government taking place in the contemporary experiments in deliberative democracy?[28] These experiments might well be signs of a new democratic trend in the early twenty-first century — but this is by no means certain. This trend could develop further or random selection in politics could remain what it now is: a minority concern or niche. The experiments themselves embody a larger critique of those paternalist traditions — be they liberal, republican or socialist — that tend to reduce democracy to representative government. Their supporters consider that civic participation in politics is crucial for the good health of our political system. They claim the political equality of all citizens in public discussion and, in some cases, in decision-making. They think that democratic legitimacy is closely linked to the expansion of deliberation in the sense of public debate: the more a decision comes from a lively and well-organized public debate, the more it will be legitimate, both normatively and empirically.[29] This line of thought is clearly a response to the growing distrust of the political system by the citizenry, which is a current and significant trend, at least in Europe. In the deliberative democracy corpus, sortition has a visible space.[30]

It is important, nevertheless, to stress the obvious differences between Florence and experiments like the British Columbia Citizen Assembly. In

---

27 The 'fair cross section of the community' is the notion that the U.S. Supreme Court referred to when it imposed the reform of the trial juries at the end of the 1960s in order to select them by lot among the all citizenship and not only among a particular group of it ('The Jury Selection and Service Act', 28 U.S.C., secs 1861-69, quoted in Abramson (2000). * See Carson & Martin (1999), pp.13–14.

28 This has been a central question in Röcke (2005), Sintomer (1987) and Buchstein (2009).

29 Bernard Manin, 'On Legitimacy and Political Deliberation', *Political Theory* 15 (1987), pp. 338–68. * Also see Jürgen Habermas, *Between Facts and Norms: Contributions to a Discourse Theory of Law and Democracy* (Mass.: MIT Press), 1998; and Habermas, op.cit., 1988. * See J.S. Dryzek, *Discursive Democracy. Politics, Policy and Political Science* (Cambridge: Cambridge University Press, 1990).

30 See Dienel (2002), Fishkin (1995), Warren *et al.* (2008) among many others.

Canada, as in other Western countries, nearly all adults are full citizens. The technique of random selection is not a routine, nor part of normal constitutional activity; it is only used at particular moments, when a public authority freely decides to organize a citizen assembly, a citizen jury, a consensus conference or another kind of deliberative device. Up to 2009, no law has made sortition mandatory beyond the judicial domain. The political experiments based upon sortition usually operate on the margins of politics, and the British Columbia experiment is the exception rather than the norm.

The notion of representative sample

A further — less evident but crucial — difference concerns the meaning of random selection. In Florence, as in Athens, sortition and a rapid rotation of the offices enabled citizens to be governing and governed in turn. This is why one can speak of self-government, and this is why, in the classical political thought from Aristotle to Guicciardini, random selection had been associated with democracy and elections with aristocracy. The contemporary use of random selection is quite different. The real chance to be selected in the British Columbia Citizen Assembly or in any other scheme of this type is very low. The idea, clearly expressed by Lyn Carson and Brian Martin, is to use sortition in order to select a microcosm of the citizenry, a group that has the same features and the same diversity as the citizenry, but at a smaller scale. This would form a 'minipopulus', as Robert A. Dahl first said,[31] or a 'mini-public', the word that is now most common. This possibility is statistically plausible when one takes a representative sample of the citizenry. A fair cross-section of the population is, at a small scale, similar to the population at large. The notion of representative sample is familiar to the twenty-first-century reader due to decades of its intensive use in statistics and opinion polls. It was unknown in Athens or Florence, however, and the idea that random selection statistically leads to a cross section of the population was not scientifically available. The 'microcosmic' reasoning that implied that political representatives had to be the social or cultural mirror of the people became important during the age of the French and North-American revolutions. But because it was impossible to rely on the notion of a representative sample, its promoters ignored sortition and put forward other technical solutions.[32] The Anti-federalists proposed small constituencies in order to favour the lower middle-class — a proposal that was not particularly con-

31   Robert A. Dahl, *Democracy and its Critics* (New Haven: Yale University Press, 1989), p. 340.
32   See Sintomer (2007).

vincing and that was successfully criticized by the Federalists.[33] Another solution suggested the separate representation of different social groups through corporatist methods—a proposal that was possibly too closely identified with the Old Regime to convince radical democrats.[34] In the nineteenth century, the higher classes' de facto hegemony among representatives regularly lead to the idea of the specific representation of subordinate groups, and particularly of the working class.[35] The representative sample is an invention of the end of the nineteenth century. It was first introduced in politics with the opinion polls in the middle of the twentieth century[36] and it only became the instrument for selecting trial juries and various political juries and committees at the end of the 1960s and in the 1970s.[37]

In the large communities typical of modern democracy, the deliberation of a cross section of the people is not the same as the self-government of the people. It gives everybody the same chance to be selected; but because this chance is very small, it does not allow all citizens to hold public office in turn. It leads instead to a counterfactual opinion of a mini-public that is only representative of what the larger public opinion *could* be. This is quite clear when we read James Fishkin, who invented the deliberative poll, another technique of deliberative democracy that uses random selection:

> Take a national random sample of the electorate and transport those people from all over the country to a single place. Immerse the sample in the issues, with carefully balanced briefing materials, with intensive discussions in small groups, and with the chance to question competing experts and politicians. At the end of several days of working through the issues face to face, poll the participants in detail. The resulting survey offers a representation of the considered judgments of the public.[38]

When traditional polls consist only in a 'statistical aggregation of vague impressions formed mostly in ignorance of sharply competing argu-

---

33 See Manin (1997).

34 See among others Comte de Mirabeau, 'Discours devant les états de Provence', 30 January 1789, in *Œuvres de Mirabeau* (Paris, 1825), t. VII, p. 7, quoted in Rosanvallon, *Le Peuple introuvable. Histoire de la représentation démocratique en France* (Paris: Gallimard, 1998).

35 See among others the 'Manifeste des Soixante', *L'Opinion nationale*, 17 February 1764, quoted in Rosanvallon, op.cit., 1998.

36 See Blondiaux, Loïc, *La Fabrique de l'opinion* (Paris: Le Seuil, 1998).

37 The 'fair cross section of the community' is an approximation of the representative sample when the group is too small to be truly representative.

38 See Fishkin (1995), p. 162.

ments', deliberative polls allow us to know 'what the public *would* think, had it a better opportunity to consider the questions at issue'.[39]

Challenges of deliberation

Another difference between the Florentine Republic and contemporary randomly selected bodies is the relation between deliberation and decision making. The modern schemes based on random selection tend to reveal a larger dynamic of deliberative democracy, which seems appealing but has also to answer some important challenges. In this paper I will not discuss deliberative bodies such as supreme courts or administrative committees such as the Food and Drug Administration. I will focus instead on those that are open to ordinary citizens. Schemes of this type seem to offer a number of promises. They offer the possibility of establishing a countervailing power to the existing media-dominated democracy;[40] they promise to limit the distance between the political class and citizenry and to promote better communication between them. In this role they could constitute an alternative to the old mass parties that have dominated the European political arena during the last century. At the same time, however, they are confronted with three sets of challenges.

The first one is that *the counterfactual opinion can differ from the real opinion* of the people. When the proposal of the British Columbia Citizen Assembly was put to the electorate-at-large in a referendum in 2005, it failed to pass the test: because it was considered as a constitutional matter, the referendum required approval by sixty per cent of votes and simple majorities in sixty per cent of the districts in order to pass. Final results indicate that the referendum failed with only 57.7% of votes in favor, although it did have majority support in seventy-seven of the seventy-nine electoral districts. When the proposal was put again in a referendum in May 2009, the gap was even larger: only 38.7% of valid votes and seven of eight-five electoral districts were in favour of the proposal. In Ontario, the Citizen Assembly proposal convinced only a minority of voters and there will be no second chance. In Europe, the PASOK candidate selected by a cross section of Marousi citizens was not the one who won the elections some months later.

The tension between the counterfactual deliberation and the real public debate seems to be inherent to deliberative democracy, as far as it takes an institutional form. This tension appears in several dimensions.

---

39   Fishkin (1995), pp. 89, 162.
40   A. Fung and E.O. Wright eds, *Deepening Democracy, Institutional Innovations in Empowered Participatory Governance* (London & New York: Verso, 2001).

(1) *Learning process.* The more the members of a representative sample learn in a Citizen Assembly, the more their knowledge and opinion will differ from the public opinion at large. The most interesting schemes, which lead to a real empowerment of the participants, tend to differ more from the average public opinion than the bad ones.

(2) *Numbers.* When the number of participants grows, the deliberative quality of the discussions tends to decrease.

(3) *Publicity.* Jon Elster and others have shown that the publicity of the debates does not necessarily lead to a better discussion.[41] In some context at least, a discussion behind closed doors will be of a better quality. In Canadian Citizen Assemblies the public sessions open to all alternated with closed discussions in small groups. Most citizen juries discuss without any audience. In this context, it is more difficult to involve the wider public and to increase its understanding of the case in question. Thus the meetings tend to be schools of democracy for the few, not for the many.

(4) *Learning through discussion or through action.* The deliberative devices are conceived in order to foster and improve political education. However, they usually allow participants to meet only 'for a short period, as ordinary citizens for specified and limited purposes', as Gordon Gibson puts it.[42] In social movements or in NGOs, the deliberative quality is probably lower but the intensity and the emotional commitment of the participants is much higher. In some cases personal ambition, rather than the desire for democratic progress, could even become the main motivating factor.

Deliberative democracy has also to face another set of challenges. Because it focuses on the (deliberative) rule of the game, *it often tends to forget or at least to underestimate power relations and the relationship between deliberative schemes and the broader democratic transformation of society at large.* Those participatory devices that select individual by lot, without any tie between them, constitute an instrument that is not embedded in actual social relations. It therefore makes it difficult for these mechanisms to change existing power structures. This induces serious difficulties.

(1) *Power in the deliberation itself.* One of the most discussed problems is the influence of power on the deliberative process itself. A formally equal procedure can leads to unequal outputs if it remains blind to the differences in social, economic or cultural capital that strongly influence the input side of the process.

---

41   Jon Elster, 'Arguing and Bargaining in the Federal Convention and the Assemblée Constituante', Working Paper, 4, The University of Chicago, Center for the Study of Constitutionalism in Eastern Europe, 1991.

42   Gibson, op.cit., 2007, see note 4.

(2) *Top-down and bottom-up.* In addition, deliberative processes are nearly always top-down. It is therefore not very probable that radical changes will take place in which the power of those who have set up these instruments would be truly challenged.

(3) *Individual vs organized citizens.* A lot of deliberative designs, especially those that employ random selection, valorize individual citizens. They consider organized interests, including NGOs and organized citizens with some diffidence because they are supposed to defend particular interests. These deliberative instruments can even be used against the organized civil society, without which any progressive civic change is hardly conceivable.

(4) *Consensus and dissent.* In consensus conferences, citizen juries and some other devices, deliberative democracy is supposed to lead to a consensus.[43] But do real changes usually come through consensual arguments? Historically, the progress of justice and democracy has been imposed through huge social struggles, not through reasonable consensual discussions. The deliberative devices often tend to be inhospitable to politicization.

(5) *Argumentation and passions.* As suggested by Jürgen Habermas, a good deliberation is usually considered to favor the force of the better argument. However, in order to make real transformations in a world in which the structural resistances are huge, passions seem necessary; such transformations are hardly the product of mere rational argumentation. Rhetoric and emotions are crucial. In order to be strong enough to regulate the world markets, politics has to make people dream of another world. In this process arguing can only be one dimension among others.

(6) *Deliberative democracy and social justice.* Last but not least, the relation between deliberative democracy and social justice remains unclear. Machiavelli said during the late Renaissance that some equilibrium between the wealthiest and the poor has to exist in order to have a stable republic, and that social inequalities have to be limited.[44] It does not seem that the majority of the instruments that deliberative theory has analysed are linked with movements of emancipation of the subordinate classes or of outsiders groups. Nor do they fit particularly well with the critique of the new forms of inequality that are produced by contemporary capitalism. In order to find a real articulation of this relationship, one has to consider participatory instruments such as the participatory budgeting in Porto Alegre.[45]

43   This is not the case for deliberative polls.
44   Machiavelli, *The Discourses* (Harmondsworth: Penguin, 1998).
45   Rebecca Abers, *Inventing Local Democracy: Grassroots Politics in Brazil* (London: Lynne Rienner Publishers, 2000); Leonardo Avritzer, *Democracy and the Public Space in Latin America* (Princeton: Princeton University Press, 2002); Yves Sintomer, *The Porto Alegre Experiment:*

(7) *Enlightened decision making vs. counter-power.* To summarize these points, deliberative democracy often tends to be a way of producing a more enlightened decision making and a more enlightened consent. This is important but hardly enough.

Random selection and legitimacy

There is an apparent trade-off between deliberation in the English meaning (good discussion) and deliberation in the Latin languages meaning (decision of a collective body). The deliberative bodies open to ordinary citizens are not usually entitled to make decisions. Among the collective bodies that theorists tend to present as good examples of deliberative democracy, those that are entitled to take decisions, or whose advice is directly integrated with decision-making bodies, are mostly expert commissions such as supreme courts, ethics committees or neo-corporatist bodies. Among those open to 'ordinary' citizens, most are only consultative or advisory boards: they are only 'weak publics'.[46] Why is this? Is it only a contingent phenomenon? Can we expect the situation to change in a next future?

The classical Athenian or Florentine Republics relied on a clear principle of self-government (combined with the rule of law). Representative democracy relies on another relatively clear principle, the consent of the people expressed through elections (articulated with the notion of the sovereignty of the people, the rule of law and the human rights). In both cases, they rely strongly on the legitimacy of number, and especially on the majority principle. However, an important feature of our political regimes is that growing numbers of decisions are taken through expert committees. In some cases these committees apply the majority principle; in others they function by consensus. Their legitimacy cannot be based entirely on number, but has a strong epistemic dimension: it relies on expert knowledge and on well-designed procedures that favour good deliberation.

Participatory schemes made up of ordinary citizens selected at random cannot rely on the legitimacy of number or on the legitimacy of expert knowledge. This is why they are not usually entitled to take decisions. Nevertheless, they have their own kind of legitimacy. First of all, contemporary participatory devices are most often employed in order to enable an enlightened discussion to take place. One of their basic assumptions is

Learning Lessons for a Better Democracy (New York: Zed Books, 2004); Gianpaolo Baiocchi, *Militants and Citizens. The Politics of Participatory Democracy in Porto Alegre* (Stanford: Stanford University Press, 2005).

46 N. Fraser, 'Rethinking the Public Sphere', in *Justice Interruptu, Critical Reflection on the 'Postsocialist' Condition* (London & New York: Routledge, 1997).

that a careful deliberation will lead to reasonable results. This is why *the counterfactual opinion tends to be more reasonable than the wider public debate*. In fact, the epistemic quality of deliberative devices based on random selection is important. These instruments usually differ from the modes of participation that were more common in the early seventies, such as the General Assembly in which the discussion is badly organized and in which, very late in the night, those who are still there decide in the absence of the vast majority.

In addition, deliberative participatory devices may have some epistemic advantages compared to representative government or expert committees. Most deliberative democrats rely on a negative argument, well expressed by John Dewey: 'A class of experts is inevitably so removed from common interests as to become a class with private interests and private knowledge, which in social matters is not knowledge at all.'[47] This statement can be extended to the political class. Deliberative democrats also propose more positive arguments. One of the most common is that *good deliberation needs to include various points of view, so that the range of arguments can be enlarged, and the reasons better balanced*. In this line of thought, participatory devices based on a random selection tend to be better than participatory devices based on voluntary involvement or on the organized civil society because they rest on a cross section of the people and maximize the epistemic diversity of their deliberation. This is why they can bring something valuable to what is, in fact, a context of increasing complexity.

A third argument for participatory devices is political. Their promise comes from the fact that discontent is growing against the actual functioning of representative democracies. There is a perceived need to counter the tendency to reduce politics to rhetorical shows, to limit the autonomy of the political class and to make it more accountable to the citizenry. *Participatory devices are instruments that promote better communication between the political class and the citizenry*. Those based on a representative sample of the population enable political communication to take place among ordinary people and not merely between 'professional citizens'.

The fourth argument is also political, but is more radical than the third one. Democratic theoreticians of representative government (as opposed to its elitist advocates) often concede that the best democratic system would be real self-government, but add that, because self-government is impossible in the large communities typical of modern democracy, the second-best solution is representative government. One could however

---

47   John Dewey, *The Public and Its Problems* [1st ed. 1927] (Athens, Ohio: Swallow Press/Ohio University Press Books, 1954), p. 207.

argue that: *since the best democratic system is real self-government; and because self-government is impossible in the large communities typical of modern democracy, the second-best solution is actually to let the counterfactual citizenry selected by lot decide.* In this way at least it offers citizens an equal chance to participate in decision making.

The fifth argument for participatory devices based on a representative sample of the population is *impartiality*. Elected representatives, experts, and organized interests tend to be moved by particular interests rather than by the notion of the common good. In contrast, random selection ensures that the large majority (or even nearly everybody, due to the possibility of recusal as in a trial jury) will judge according to what they consider the best for all without taking a partisan stance in any controversy. This impartiality advantage may be strengthened when the advice or the decision has to be taken by a qualified majority or reached through consensus.

Taking into account these five types of legitimacy that participatory devices based on random selection can claim, what can be said about the potential of these contemporary experiments?

When the imperative of impartiality is high in respect to a particular topic, random selection offers a worthwhile method by which to select those who will deliberate. An important distinction has to be made, however. It is interesting to note how Hegel defends the institution of trial jury composed of lay-persons. Their participation is justified, he writes, insofar, and only insofar, as what is at stake is not the universal, the right or the law, but a concrete and subjective judgment about a particular case.[48] One can be less strict, but one has to recognize that it is not the same thing to decide on concrete particular cases and to enact a law. In particular cases, participatory instruments based on random selection have enough legitimacy to discuss, but also, at least in some contexts, to decide. This is true in trial juries,[49] and this has been the case in the Berlin citizen juries that, in seventeen neighborhoods, decided the attribution of half a million euros each to sustain local projects in the frame of the urban renewal policy.[50] This could be developed much further.

On the other hand in cases where impartiality is crucial but where a law is at stake, as in British Columbia, it would seems promising to couple a

48 Hegel, *Elements of the Philosophy of Right*, § 227-8 (Cambridge: Cambridge University Press, 1991).
49 See Abramson (2000).
50 Röcke, Anja & Sintomer, Yves, "Les jurys de citoyens berlinois et le tirage au sort : un nouveau modèle de démocratie participative?", in Bacqué & Rey & Sintomer eds., *Gestion de proximité et démocratie participative: les nouveaux paradigmes de l'action publique*, La Découverte, Paris, 2005, p. 139-160.

proposal made by a Citizen Assembly with a referendum, as was done in the Canadian Provinces.

It is undeniable that expert committees have an important role to play in cases that rest on highly technical questions. To ensure impartiality, however, it would be necessary to include lay-persons in the decision making, either at particular moments in the proceedings, such as in the consensus conference on scientific issues invented in Denmark.

In cases where general political issues are at stake, participatory devices based on random selection do not have enough legitimacy to make the decision: the counterfactual opinion is not the same as an actual self-government. Two options could be considered. The first one is to give these devices a mere consultative function and then let elected representatives decide. The idea is to produce a more enlightened consent and a more enlightened government. This is the mainstream option, and we will probably see many processes of this kind proposed and adopted in the next decades. An alternative would be to combine the counterfactual deliberation with larger participatory mechanisms. This would be a movement in the direction of a participatory democracy that would combine representative government and deliberative democracy with forms of direct democracy. It could be worth making some steps forwards in this direction.

Conclusion

The idea of deliberative democracy is an important contribution to the renewal of politics and could improve the efficiency and legitimacy of public policies. It is precisely because we live in a complex world that the need for public deliberation increases. Deliberative democracy is a good counter-tendency to populist tendencies, and to the domination of charismatic leaders.

Because of its inherent tensions, deliberative democracy cannot stand alone and has to be combined with participatory democracy, which is different and which has something to do with the principle of self-government that was so important in early renaissance Florence. Participatory democracy implies the actual participation of a large proportion of the citizenry in politics, and in particular the involvement of previously dominated groups. It not only relies on institutional devices, but also on social movements. The good deliberation of the mini-public has to be linked with a better debate in the larger public sphere. The British Columbia scheme, which couples a Citizen Assembly with a referendum, indicates a path we could follow if we were to go in this direction.

Deliberative democracy and participatory democracy, even taken together, cannot stand alone. They are part of a broader evolution that modifies the meaning of political representation, and they are dimensions — until now, secondary dimensions — in the development of multi-level governance. The classical division of power between the executive, the legislative and the judiciary has always been an open process, rather than a stable equilibrium. By addressing the limits of representative government, some schemes of deliberative and participatory democracy propose to modify this supposed equilibrium by introducing a fourth power into the equation. While this makes the situation more complex, and a good equilibrium is not easy to find, this is a promising path.

Random selection for public offices has a role to play in this process. Coupled with the rapid rotation of the offices, it was crucial in the early renaissance Florence where it enabled a limited but real self-government to emerge. Contemporary schemes based on random selection rely on the notion of representative sample, which was unavailable before the end of the nineteenth century. They established the notion of the counterfactual opinion — what the larger public could be if it could truly deliberate. They are therefore closely linked to the ideal of deliberative democracy, which is something very different from the Florentine *vivere libero*. They offer sources of legitimacy that have to be combined with, rather than opposed to, the legitimacy of either representative or direct democracy.

3 Oliver Dowlen

Sortition and Liberal Democracy
Finding a Way Forward

The author's approach to the relationship between liberal democracy and sortition is to start from the qualities of the lottery process itself and what it has the capacity to bring to the political process. By combining this perspective with a critique based on policy types it is possible to see sortition as broadly commensurate with liberal democracy's concerns with protecting the integrity and fairness of the political process and guarding it against the rise of political absolutism. The electoral process and selection by lot can therefore be seen as complementary mechanisms. Where the introduction of sortition might challenge the institutions and ideals of liberal democracy is in respect to the dominance of political parties, the impartiality of the state, and the greater involvement of the citizenry in the body politic.[1]

As a polity type liberal democracy is broadly recognisable by a series of characteristics. These include the selection of political officers by the citizenry in periodic elections, the structural separation of powers between different branches of government, the rule of law, open government and the active presence of a plurality of political voices — usually channelled through the medium of legitimate political parties. While the manner in which these major characteristics are manifested might vary between regimes bearing that name, the absence or neglect of any of the above would usually cause us to doubt the democratic credentials of the state in question.

---

1 I would describe this paper as an agenda-finding exercise. It stands at the end of my earlier explorations of the potential of sortition and at the beginnings of what I hope will be future work on the implications of its modern application. Thus, roughly speaking, the first half, the discussion of approaches, is a summary of the findings of *The Political Potential of Sortition*, (see Dowlen (2008)) while the second part is a brief attempt to see how these might relate to liberal democracy. The first part is 'post-research' and the second, to a large extent, 'pre-research.'

If the structural and institutional characteristics of liberal democratic states can be agreed upon for the most part, the political values that they embody or aspire to are open to greater debate.[2] The term 'liberal' suggests that liberal democratic states are linked to a distinct school of ideas: the primacy of the political and economic freedom of the individual (especially against the centralised power of the state); a downplaying of the classical notion of the citizen as active political agent; religious and political tolerance; and a faith in the inherent reasonableness of human nature in the search for political solutions.[3] 'Democracy', on the other hand, indicates rule by the people — a notion that sits somewhat awkwardly with liberal emphasis on the private life of the individual and the promotion of a limited, professional, political caste.[4] At the same time, however, we must recognise how these two strands of thought and practice both involve a commitment to open, accountable government and to a shared political process. Moreover they both recognise that the greatest danger to such public goods is posed by the exercise of arbitrary power.

Sortition, in contrast, is a mere mechanism of selection involving the use of lots or other random selection procedures. If we abstract it from any particular context in which it is applied it is an ideologically neutral problem-solving device and does not necessarily speak to any set of political values. In practice, however, it was used by democrats in Athens and by republicans (both popular and elitist) in northern Italy during the late medieval and renaissance periods. For this reason it is often associated

2   This relationship between an institution-based understanding of liberal democracy and the reading of this governmental form based on the values and ideals it espouses is not always easy to assess. This is possibly because they have traditionally occupied different areas within the academic political arena. The question of the modern application of sortition, however, demands that some accommodation be made between them. Perhaps the best starting point comes from works such as David Held (*Models of Democracy*, Cambridge: Polity 2006) and Samuel Finer (*History of Government from the Earliest Times*, vol. 2, Oxford University Press, 1999) where constitutional design and political meaning are explored together.

3   The debate on the changing nature of liberal values is well covered by J.G. Merquior in *Liberalism: Old and New* (Boston: Twayne Publishers, 1991) and summarised in Ernest Gellner and Cesar Cansino, *Liberalism in Modern Times* (Budapest & London: Central European University Press, 1996), pp. 7–37. * Also see A. Arblaster, *The Rise and Decline of Western Liberalism* (Oxford: Blackwell, 1984).

4   There is a sense that the term 'liberal democracy' is used pejoratively to express the idea that it falls short of full democracy or, merely serves the interests of those of a liberal philosophical or economic disposition. Democrats regard it as regrettably liberal, and liberals as regrettably democratic (see Arblaster, op. cit., 1984, pp. 75–9). Here I tend to take the governmental form of liberal democracy as a given. It is (with its variations) simply one of the current paradigms of government and as such necessarily embodies a mixture of inherited ideas and practices. I am less concerned about why it is called what it is.

with polities that show a commitment to public governance and to citizen participation, rather than with regimes of an overtly despotic nature.[5]

The relationship between liberal democracy and sortition is thus a complex one. It is especially complicated by the fact that, with the notable exception of the randomly-selected jury, sortition plays little part in the modern liberal democratic polity. Compared to those who practised it regularly, publicly and as part of their central governmental apparatus, we are, on the whole, much less familiar with its modus operandi and its benefits. At the same time, owing to its consistent use in Ancient Athens and medieval/renaissance Italy it is very much part of the tradition that spawned our current political practices and values. It has made, as it were, a hidden contribution.[6] The complexity of this relationship is also brought into sharp focus by the prospect of a reintroduction of sortition. Without a more thorough first-hand knowledge of sortition it is difficult to know just how we should evaluate the impact of this ancient but little-known mechanism on modern political practice in general and on liberal democracy in particular.

One way forward is to assess sortition simply as a response to perceived problems in current liberal democratic practice. This requires that we first form an opinion as to which features might require replacement or improvement and why. We then have to decide whether these problems can actually be solved by the application of this type of mechanism, and which are better served by other means. We must therefore bring to the equation some form of assessment as to what a lottery does well and what distinguishes it from other forms of choice or decision making. To this we must add the condition of good design. The use of sortition itself cannot guarantee favourable results and benefits to the political system if it is part of a badly designed scheme or if too little attention is paid to the relationship between sortitive elements and other elements in the scheme itself or in the constitution as a whole.

To this essentially 'problem-based' approach we can add the more general political question of how we are to assess the impact that a *consistent*

---

5   Sortition can be, and has been, used by those wishing to bypass the conscious leadership of their opponents — be they democrats or oligarchs. It was used by the thirty Tyrants in Athens in 404 BCE and by the ruling group in Florence to diminish the influence of the leadership of the guilds. See Najemy (1982).

6   Perhaps we should think of it as hidden because it was ignored, and ignored because it was not fully understood. Certainly the connection of lotteries with chance and superstition prevented many of those from an enlightenment or utilitarian tradition from exploring its possible benefits. See Godwin (1971) pp. 241–3 and Condorcet in K.M. Baker, *Condorcet: from Natural Philosophy to Social Mathematics* (Chicago: University of Chicago Press, 1975), p. 449 n. 156. It would also be true to say that predominantly aristocratic arguments about the capability of those selected obscured the more general political reasons why sortition was employed. See Dowlen (2008), pp. 233–4.

and *widespread* use of sortition might make on our political values. It is here that comparison between the political priorities of those polities that made use of sortition and those of today's liberal democracies becomes relevant and we can use our critique of polity types to identify which aspects of the older dispensations are relevant to the modern discourse and which are not. We should not expect to recreate the conditions of either Ancient Athens or medieval Florence in the modern world. However, an intelligent reading of how lot was used in those contexts and how those older polities differ from our own forms of government can tell us much about what to expect from a reintroduction of sortition.

In this paper I will argue that both approaches are necessary if we are to form a genuinely all-round theoretical approach — one that can successfully guide us in our understanding of sortition in practice. But I will insist that to find the best and most reliable way forward we must start with the lottery mechanism itself and try to define what it does best and what it has the capacity to bring to the political process. With this approach at the centre of my critique I then turn my attention to liberal democracy. I sketch out some of the areas that I believe could form a future agenda for exploring the impact and implications of a modern reintroduction of sortition.

The limits of the Aristotelian approach

My first port of call, however, is to take a quick look at two critical perspectives on the political use of lot. The first, Guicciardini's *Del modo di eleggere gli uffici nel Consiglio Grande*, comes from the early sixteenth century.[7] Nonetheless it pre-empts some of its features and problems of liberal democracy. The second, Manin's *The Principles of Representative Government*[8] comes from the late twentieth century, a period during which many of the claims of liberal democracy were coming under increasing critical scrutiny.[9]

Sometime around 1530 Guicciardini wrote a pair of fictitious speeches, one defending the use of sortition, the other opposing it and advocating the wider use of preference elections. The speeches are loosely based on the events of 1494–9 when, during the Second Republic, Florence first adopted an elective scheme on the Venetian model, and then reverted to the use of sortition for the election of its major officers.

---

7   See Guicciardini (1932).
8   See Manin (1997).
9   See Barber (1984); and C. Pateman, *Participation and Democratic Theory* (Cambridge: Cambridge University Press, 1970).

The first of Guicciardini's speeches follows a predictable pattern. Government is concerned with the management of the city; this requires that those with most ability be selected. This is to be achieved by conscious selection rather than the action of chance. The use of lot, moreover, constitutes a dereliction of our moral duty to make judgements about the qualities and abilities of our fellow citizens. The second speaker, however, portrays the proposed voting system as a loss to the citizenry at large who will then be divided between those who govern and those who merely vote. This he regards as a state of 'servitude' because, despite assurances that voting is a means of reflecting the public will, government will inevitably devolve to the rich and educated stratum of society. For our purposes this second speaker is important because he portrays preference voting as a means by which an aristocratic elite can retain power by giving with one hand and taking with the other.[10]

Guicciardini is regarded by some as the first 'liberal'. I would certainly agree in the sense that he visualises and advocates a new form of popular republicanism in which periodic preference elections replace the older form of sortition as a means by which citizens gain access to public offices. He certainly stands on the cusp of political change since he was a major player in the fall of the Second Florentine Republic and the demise of the particular popular, inclusive form of republic that it aspired to and occasionally achieved.[11]

This contrast between the older lot-polity and the new form of elective republic is taken up by Bernard Manin in his important *Principles of Representative Government*. Manin recognises that representative government is designed to protect government from the perceived chaos of democracy rather than to grant influence to the masses via the elective process. With hindsight not afforded to Guicciardini, he presents representative government as a contradictory mix of forms and ideals. It is democratic in name, but the voting system relies on the principle of distinction that will inevitably divide the citizens between office holders of one class and voters of another.[12] Representative government does, however, bring the idea of popular consent into political practice in a manner impossible in a predominantly lot-based polity. Manin's descriptive narrative of sortition *outmoded* by new forms and ideas contrasts with the normative arguments

---

10 For a fuller account of these speeches see Dowlen (2008), pp. 123–32.

11 Cecil Roth in *The Last Florentine Republic* (New York: Russell and Russell, 1968), p. 91, describes Guicciardini as a 'creature of the Medici'. His role in the papal overthrow of the Second Florentine Republic somewhat belies his overt support for the idea of the mixed polity. Thus he attacked popular republicanism from the middle ground in theory while supporting absolutism in practice.

12 See Manin (1997) pp. 236–58, plus Chapters 3 and 4 respectively for the principle of distinction and the elective aristocracy.

of Guicciardini's second speaker who presents sortition as *usurped* by the conscious introduction of a new voting system. There is in Manin, however, a sense that modern representative democracy still has room for improvement.[13]

These two contributions ask us to make some sort of valuation of the respective benefits of the lot polity and the representative, liberal democratic, model that followed it. It is important, however, that we also attempt to understand the overall theoretical approach that these writers adopt when dealing with the vexed question of sortition. The first thing to notice about these contributions is that they present sortition in opposition to preference election. This is a particularly Aristotelian formulation of the question based on the distinction between polity types found in *The Politics*.[14] Election by lot is the democratic way of doing things, preference election that of the aristocracy. While there is some value in this approach it also presents us with difficulties. To begin with it does not adequately reflect the complexity of the political use of lot: lot was used instead of preference election in some contexts, but it was also used *in combination* with elections, both in its medieval and its ancient context.[15] It was used by democratic regimes, but also in mixed and predominantly aristocratic regimes, such as the Venetian republic.[16] More importantly the central question of this approach—the question *'who governs?'*—does not, of itself, constitute an inquiry into the specific advantages that lot can bring to the political process as a whole. It merely tells us how the use of lot might favour one group of people (citizens at large) compared to another (a select group of citizens) in any constitutional arrangement. This, arguably, has more to do with the size of the pool and the overall constitutional design (both pre-lot rational decisions) than the action of the lottery itself. Aristotle is, in fact, remarkably silent about what sortition actually does and how it does it; a lacuna that is also present in Guicciardini's

13   See Manin (1997), particularly in the conclusion p. 237 where he talks of how the voters' will is rarely translated into action by an incoming government, but in its dismissal of a government the voters wish becomes an unqualified demand.

14   In Aristotle's *Politics* on this issue see particularly book IV, 1299a–1301. This view is also reflected in Montesquieu's *Spirit of the Laws*.

15   In Athens the generals and a number of other specialist posts were subject to election by the Assembly. In late medieval Italy the two main sortition schemes both involved preference election. The *brevia* was a form of indirect election in which the electors were first selected by lot. The later *scrutiny* involved random selection from a previously elected pool. See Dowlen (2008) pp. 67–97; Wolfson (1899) on the *brevia* and Najemy (1982) on the *scrutiny*.

16   The Venetians used a complex system of sortition to select nominating bodies. Those nominated would then be put forward for election by the Grand Council. See D.E. Queller, *The Venetian Patriciate* (Urbana & Chicago: University of Illinois Press, 1986).

piece.[17] While Manin makes some astute observations on why sortition was used, or might have been used, in particular contexts, he does not start with the lottery process itself.[18] In both contributions, therefore, the second approach (the exploration of sortition in respect to polity type) takes precedence over the first (the exploration of the problem-solving potential of sortition).

My response is to assert that if we start from the lottery itself, this can lead us to some important conclusions about what sortition can bring to the political process and to the political community. This in turn lays out the ground for how we can successfully explore the relationship between sortition and liberal democracy. In short: the problem-solving approach supplies the key to understanding the relationship between sortition and any type or genre of government.

The 'blind break' — at the centre of lottery theory

I start from the premise that the lottery is a human invention. It is used as a means of making decisions when there is competition between options. At the centre of every lottery is a feature or characteristic that sets it apart from all other decision-making processes. This is the deliberate exclusion of all human judgement and rational evaluation from the point where the option is chosen. I call this feature the 'blind break' and it can be illustrated as follows:[19]

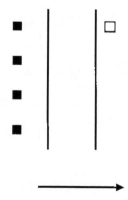

---

17 While Aristotle refers to the use of lot in Heraea to prevent electoral intrigue, he does not apply this reasoning to its use in Athens. See Aristotle, *Politics*, book V, 1303a.

18 See for example Manin (1997) p. 41 for a summary of the use of lot in Athens which does not include reference to its anti-factional potential; see p. 31 for its use as an adjunct to rotation, and see p.52 for its use in medieval Italy as an anti factional device valued for its impartiality.

19 This approach is developed in Dowlen (2008), pp. 11–30.

On the left is the pool of options. I show these after the options have been stripped of their particular values and converted into symbols of equal appearance or with equal physical characteristics. At the centre the parallel lines depict the blind break. It is a break because the chain of rational, purposeful activity that has governed the decision to use a lottery, the size and nature of the pool of options and the general nature of the outcome is broken by the intervention of a decision-making method of a different order. It is blind in the sense that the decision cannot be predicted and cannot be manipulated or deliberately influenced by any party.[20]

Since a lottery is a mechanical process of decision making *all* human qualities are excluded. Reason cannot influence a lottery decision; but neither can emotion, prejudice, irrationality or flawed reason. It is best, therefore, to describe a lottery, not as an irrational, but as an *arational* process.

From this position it becomes possible to distinguish between those applications of sortition that make a positive use of the blind break, and those that, for whatever reason, do not. Those applications that make optimum use of this form of decision-making in respect to their desired aims I call strong applications of lot. If a lottery is used when there is no real need for an arational process, or where the use of such a mechanism contradicts the general intentions of those designing and operating the scheme, I call this a weak use or application. In these cases it would probably be more efficient to use a conventional decision-making process that relies on human reason. In most successful cases of lottery use the disadvantages of arationality are outweighed by the advantages it can bring to the particular context of application. In a strong application there is a clear reason for using an arational mechanism. In a weak use there is no clear link between the stated aim of the procedure as a whole and the arational characteristic of the lottery process.

This formulation supplies us with a theoretical perspective with which to approach and discuss any application or possible application of

---

20 A point of contention arises here in respect to the modern use of lot in sampling theory to produce a representative sample of, for example, the electorate. This would imply that a lottery (in accordance with probability theory and the law of large numbers) will inevitably produce a proportionate outcome sufficient for the job in hand—a kind of population in miniature. This would indicate that the blind break is, in this respect, somewhat less than blind and the outcome could be subject to a level of meaningful calculation. Probability law, however, is based on the simple lottery itself. It cannot tell us anything more about the outcome than we already know from the size of the pool expressed as a ratio to the number of outcomes. Sampling theory, moreover, uses the lottery primarily to ensure that the choosing of the sample is not subject to subjective variation, not to create demographic proportionality — this task is usually achieved by stratifying the sample. See F. Conway, *Sampling, an Introduction for Social Scientists* (London: Allen and Unwin, 1967). See also Jackson & Brashers (1986); Dowlen (2008), pp. 20–8.

sortition. It is an approach firmly anchored in the practical qualities of the mechanism itself and is based on establishing whether a lottery is 'fit for purpose' in respect to any projected use. It also helps us to address the more general question of what benefits sortition has the capacity to bring to the political process.[21]

Lotteries in political practice

If we now apply this perspective to the cut and thrust of real political contexts where groups of people are actively attempting to establish rule-governed procedures for governmental decision making, a distinct conclusion emerges.[22]

This is that it is possible to identify what I call a 'primary political potential' of sortition. This is *one* function that lot performs that is more politically significant than all others. It is a function that derives from lot acting at its greatest capacity (using the blind break positively) and one from which all subsequent benefits derive. This primary potential can be expressed as *the capacity of sortition to protect the process of selection of public officers from wilful manipulation by those who wish to control it for their own ends*. In this way sortition breaks up concentrations of power within the body politic by preventing those with wealth, influence or the physical means of oppression from engineering public appointments. It is this aspect of sortition that enabled it to be used against the arbitrary power of tyrants and against the operations of competitive partisan factions seeking absolute power.[23] By these means sortition has the capacity to defend the shared political community and strengthen its ability to operate according to publicly agreed rules and procedures.

This function, capacity or potential has the effect of generating further secondary political benefits. These are all dependent on the primary potential of sortition in one way or another. If a large pool is used, the threshold to participation in the political process is lowered to enable greater numbers of citizens to play an active role in the body politic without possessing pre-existing advantages. In contrast to preference elections a candidate does not have to 'seek power' by trying to drum up

21 This approach is not contradictory, but complementary to the approach that seeks to define different types of lottery. Sooner or later every designer or operator has to ask whether a lottery is the right mechanism for the job in hand and has to have some criteria with which to make that decision.

22 What follows is a summary of the conclusions to the historical analysis found in Dowlen (2008) pp. 215–32 .The method of inquiry was to combine an analysis of lottery form and function with an historical investigation of the political use of sortition.

23 The best example of this is the advocacy of sortition by a grouping of republicans opposed to the de facto Medici dictatorship in Florence in 1465-6. See N. Rubinstein, *The Government of Florence under the Medici.1434–1494* (Oxford: Clarendon Press, 1966), p. 157.

support. These citizens, moreover, have a direct relationship with the polity unmediated by the influence of any other grouping. In such circumstances the polity itself can be understood by all as impartial—literally non-partisan — and the citizens entering office are independent — literally non-dependent — on the power of any other for their passage into government. Because sortition is an arational mechanism, it also excludes all irrational elements from the lottery choice. Not only can the use of sortition curb excesses of competitive partisanship and power-broking within the body politic, it can also inhibit the effects of the organised hatred, blind adoration or revenge.

Of the greatest critical importance, however, is the conclusion that, if we place the blind break at the core of our approach to sortition, we at once place the exploration of sortition within a general discourse on political power. Sortition is a means by which wilful power over the process of appointment can be inhibited. But while it is a 'taking away' of power in one respect, it can constitute a restoration of power in another, in so far as it helps to establish agreed, shared political procedures.[24]

Sortition and liberal democracy

If we now return to the relationship between sortition and liberal democracy, the identification of the primary political potential of sortition and the placing of sortition within the context of a discourse on power gives us new insights. To begin with it focuses our attention on how liberal democracy claims to deal with the phenomenon of concentrated power and the dangers posed by the arbitrary exercise of that power. This in turn helps us to assess which institutions address this task, the extent to which they are successful, and the extent to which other institutions might compromise or contradict that success. At the same time we need to ask where within liberal democratic structures a greater preponderance of shared political power might be valuable.

This is, I must admit, a long-term project of some complexity. It is fraught with difficult questions about how we define liberal democracy, about how we distinguish between different variations on the basic model, about how we understand the discrepancy between its ideals and its achievements and about how we understand its pattern of development. We also need to understand how liberal democracy and the earlier lot-based polity differ from each other and how, at the same time, they are

24 It has to be realised, however, that the effects of sortition could be undermined by other elements within any political or constitutional context, especially those linked to concentrations of power. There could be no interference in the selection procedure if a proper lottery (i.e., one not fixed or manipulated) were held to select a jury in a totalitarian state, but the jurors selected in this way could be subject to other pressures to secure their compliance.

part of the same tradition. In this paper I can only give a first indication of some of the arguments and areas of study that are suggested by this agenda.

Liberal democracy and partisan power

It is clear that, of all modern forms of government, liberal democracy holds the protection of the political process from arbitrary subversion as a cherished aim and has developed a panoply of measures, traditions and devices to further that end. Some of these derive from the earlier republican model; others do not. The separation of powers is one active principle that fulfils this role in the design of new liberal-democratic constitutions; rotation in office (although never to the extent of Athens or Florence) is another. The subservience of all public officers to the rule of law is a further important principle in the battle against both low-level corruption and high-level subversion. For our purposes the ideal that those enforcing the rule of law should be impartial is of particular importance. From a later age comes the idea that absolute dictatorial power can be inhibited by competition between governmental and loyal opposition parties: the notion of political pluralism. We should, however, recognise that this is, in fact, a relatively modern presentation of the much more fundamental republican premise that the political process should be public and political expression should be free and open.

If, however, we look at the other side of the equation — the concentration of power — this very relationship between political openness and the political party becomes a point of divergence between modern liberal democracy and the lot-based polities that preceded it. Political parties were illegal in both ancient Athens and late medieval Florence, and in both these cities a major task of those seeking to establish the rule of law and due political procedure was to keep the locus of power within public institutions. Parties were synonymous with covert intrigue, subversion and the culture of political dependency. They were seen as a major threat to the political process, encouraging either tyranny or factional fragmentation.

Political parties also exemplify the greatest difference between the respective political values of the lot-based republic and those of liberal democracy. In the lot-based republic the ideals of the general interest and the notion of entering office to serve the interest of all prevailed. Partisanship meant supporting one sector of the population against another and was considered a danger to the inclusive political process. In the modern liberal democracy, however, it is considered desirable, even essential, for parties to pursue their particular interests to the utmost (within the limits of the constitution) and make few compromises with their rivals.[25]

Concentrations of power in the internal structures and procedures of political parties can also be problematic. Michels, back in the early twentieth century noted how the concentration of power within mass political parties posed a threat to democracy.[26] Michel's attention was on the tendency of parties to act beyond their established constitutional confines; but even where the role of parties is carefully prescribed, the tendency for parties to concentrate power still remains. In liberal democracy, moreover, it is not easy to divide the sectional, partisan and potentially hegemonic objectives and the essentially private modus operandi of the political party from its legitimate political role. Parties are vulnerable to extra-constitutional factional control and their internal structures demand partisan loyalty and political dependency—political 'vices' that sortition was originally introduced to counteract.

What becomes clear, therefore, is that arguments for the modern application of sortition have to address the issue of how lot-based systems will relate to political parties and their culture. My current thinking is, yes, political parties *can* act as conduits for the exercise of unconstitutional power (power operating outside the aegis of the open political process); yes, excessive partisanship *can* discredit the political process; but it is also possible for parties to play a responsible political role. There is considerable investment in the political party system and as an institution they harbour both problems and potential benefits. My intuition is that the presence of more non-partisan sortive elements within the body politic in general, rather than in the place of party structures, could be used to counteract or counterbalance these dangers.

Sortition, government and state

In this respect it is important to look at the distinction between government and state in liberal democracy and the opportunities that this can afford for the use of sortition.[27] One of the main reasons for the political success of the randomly-selected jury is that it is an organ of the state judiciary the selection of which is out of the control of any partisan or poten-

---

25   See Schumpeter, *Capitalism, Socialism and Democracy* (London: Allen and Unwin, 1976). There is a sense that Schumpeter's platform is both prescriptive and descriptive of liberal democracy. His advocacy of a democracy of competing elites, however, relies on safeguards against the possible hegemonic ambitions of any party and the idea that the state bureaucracy should be impartial.

26   See Roberto Michels, *Political Parties* (Glencoe: Free Press, 1949).

27   While a strong case has been made for the use of sortition to select citizen-based bodies in the legislative and executive branches of government, the potential of sortition for generating impartial state institutions can easily be overlooked.

tially partisan force. In this respect at least, it is understood as an impartial bastion against the exploitation of the weak by the powerful and of the individual citizen by the state.[28] At the same time, of course, the jury is itself an organ of the state. It is the first step in the modern era by which the citizen body was asked to take an active responsible role in the state and the first stage at which it is possible to talk of the modern state as belonging to its citizens.

Even if we recognise the need for governments to embrace some level of partisanship, the danger that party rule could slide into permanent partisan hegemony would be thwarted by the presence of more demonstrably impartial institutions within the state apparatus. These could include greater use of jury-like groupings within the judiciary, citizen bodies within the state bureaucracy and some elements of citizen oversight within the security services and armed forces.[29] As a basic principle the more that sortition-generated organs operate within significant sectors of the state apparatus, the more the state can be understood as genuinely impartial.

Sortition and the transition to democracy

From this it is also evident that sortition can help states in transition to democracy or open government. While liberal democracy is seen as a desirable end product for many states undertaking a transition from more absolute forms of political rule, how this is to be undertaken is invariably far from straightforward. New democracies are often modelled around the more developed nation states of Europe and America without any consideration being taken of the long period that it took to achieve political stability in the more mature democracies. It is in these circumstances that the vulnerability of the liberal democratic form to concentrations of power becomes most apparent.[30] The political party is particularly open to corruption, and is often seen as a mere conduit for those

---

28 The randomly-selected jury first emerged in South Carolina in the late seventeenth century. The lottery element came from English republicanism and its interest in the Venetian constitution. Its extension to England and Scotland in 1730, however, was not inspired by any higher political motivation than the prevention of bribery by the under sheriffs in charge of choosing jury members. See Dowlen (2008), pp. 172–83.

29 An example of this is the 1994 proposal by Keith Nilsen of the *Labour Committee for the Democratic Accountability of Secret Services* that monitors for the secret services should be randomly selected. For more details see www.sortition.org.uk. (accessed January 2007).

30 This becomes more than obvious from the difficulties experienced in the transition of the ex-communist Eastern European states to a quite eccentric range of democratic and semi-democratic regimes. In most of these cases concentrations of partisan power within self-selected elites (from left and right) considerably impeded the transition to stable open government. See Jan Zielonka, *Democratic Consolidation in Eastern Europe*, vol.1, Oxford Studies in Democratization, 2001.

with personal political ambition. Democratic consolidation, moreover, is often attempted following periods of deep social division, if not open conflict. These divisions and the hegemonic ambitions of their leaderships are likely to spill over into the new political settlement making political stability and trust in the new institutions particularly difficult to achieve. In these conditions there is a strong case for the introduction of non-partisan political organs and the use of sortition could be an important means of guaranteeing impartiality.

As a caveat to this argument it is clear that communist states have traditionally distrusted liberal democracy on the grounds that it cedes too much power to capitalist elites and private economic interest groups.[31] The ability of sortition to break up or diffuse concentrations of power within the body politic could go some way towards assuaging these fears: effecting a transition towards open government without endangering the gains made by the working class.

Sortition and political participation

I end this paper with a brief mention of what is, for most, the strongest grounds for the introduction of sortive schemes in liberal democracy: the division between those who vote and those who govern — the political division of labour. Here we are back with the arguments of Guicciardini's second speaker and Manin's critique that representative government is a form of mixed polity. My point, and the point of this paper is that it is the lottery's ability to create non-power relationships that is its primary contribution to the political process. It is this that enables citizens to participate in government without having first to seek and gain personal political power. It is the same role of sortition in inhibiting the politics of power that helps create a 'level playing field' of rule governed procedures and promotes the idea that the body politic belongs to all — in the sense that it cannot be dominated by partisan groupings. The lottery is not just an instrument for engendering political participation, *it creates participation of a particular type and can help create a polity of a particular type.* The basic unit of this polity type is the politically aware independent (non-dependent) citizen;[32] its governing principle is procedural fairness

---

31 This has long been the communist objection to liberal democracy, epitomised by Lenin on democracy ('The Proletarian Revolution and the Renegade Kautsky' in Lenin, *Collected Works*, vol. 28, London: Lawrence and Wishart, 1938). Lenin's venom is mainly directed against Kautsky's presentation of democracy as pure, or non-partisan. The Marxist world view (on which Lenin's attack is based) has difficulty with the idea of impartiality, but it is also clear that sortive democracy could go a long way to assuage Lenin's concerns.

32 The independent actively involved citizen of the lot polity is to be distinguished from the largely private citizen of liberal democracy. In a broadly based sortive scheme there would be

and its chief enemy the accumulation and exercise of those forms of partisan power that pose a threat to open, inclusive government.

In this respect it is not the system of voting and the citizen's periodic consent to government that is problematic in liberal democracies. This can be seen as belonging to the same tradition of open, shared political process that produced sortition. The difficulties in fact lie in the domination of the elective process by partisan groupings. This is exacerbated by the growing gap between the essentially private citizenry and a professional political caste (often linked to extra-political lobby or interest groups) that can leave citizens disenchanted with the political process and relatively powerless to change it. By giving citizens an active, responsible role in the body politic in a systematic, direct and impartial manner sortition can complement and enrich existing electoral arrangements and moderate the potentially harmful effects of this division.

Conclusion

In this short paper I hope to have presented a way of approaching the possible re-introduction of sortition and what that could mean for polity of the future. It is an assessment built on political practice and on the recognition that the lot-polities of the past and today's liberal democracies are part of the same tradition in their promotion of open, accountable, government and a strong, shared political process. What becomes clear, however, is that wider use of sortition in the context of modern liberal democratic states could have the effect of strengthening certain aspects of liberal democracy while challenging others.

By identifying sortition as a mechanism capable of breaking up concentrations of potentially despotic partisan power we can see it as able to rectify the possible tendency for the liberal democratic states to become oligarchic through their party structures or extra-political through their links with lobby or interest groups. While seeking to improve liberal democracy, this usage would also be very much in keeping with the overall orientation of liberal democratic governance and its concerns over the misuse of power.

On the other hand, the politically active citizen is, for the most part, absent from the institutions and ideals of liberal democracy. If sortition were more widely used to select citizens to the state apparatus this could begin to create a new relationship between citizen and state that would diverge significantly from the liberal democratic model. Citizens would no longer be disengaged, essentially private, individuals needing protec-

no contradiction between the notion of the independent, impartial citizen and the ideal of collective (i.e., citizen-wide) political endeavour.

tion *from* the state. Instead they would begin to see themselves as part of the state itself. It would be a state, moreover that could be seen as belonging to all in the sense that no party or interest group could be understood as organising the appointments in question. It is in this area that I see sortition mounting its greatest challenge to the current liberal democratic paradigm and it is here that it has the potential to generate the greatest change to our understanding of the political process.

4 Antoine Vergne

A Brief Survey of the Literature of Sortition

Is the Age of Sortition upon us?

This chapter offers a brief survey of the main texts on sortition. In addition it gives an account of the extent and diversity of the literature that deals with random selection in politics. In particular it considers texts in which authors present the potential of sortition in current political contexts (exploratory texts) and those in which proposals for the introduction of a scheme of sortition are made (advocacy texts).

Introduction

Clearly, the age of random selection is upon us.

Sid Leiman[1]

According to some scholars there is a growing interest in the subject of sortition or random selection, especially among those concerned with political practice or political philosophy. This affirmation — which would underpin the opinion formulated by Leiman — is founded not only on the fact that there appears to be an expanding literature on the subject but also on the observation that sortition schemes seem to be spreading in political practice.[2] This paper is a brief attempt to look at how this body of 'lot-specific' literature is developing and an attempt to differentiate between the different threads of ideas, motivation and orientation that run through it. Through these means I also have the opportunity to address a number of questions concerning the nature and range of this literature,

---

1   Leiman (1978), p. 8.
2   The latter point has been already tackled by recent studies — particularly those concerning the case of the random distribution of political positions. See Sintomer (2007), Buchstein (2009).

the rate of its expansion and the extent to which an expanding literature might indicate that the age of sortition is, indeed, upon us.

In section one I outline the corpus of texts included in this review; in section two I turn to the presentation of the descriptive texts on sortition. In section three I describe both the exploratory texts and those that advocate particular schemes that use sortition. Finally, I sketch some conclusions about this bibliography and introduce a research hypothesis concerning the emergence of a new school of political philosophy.

1 Presentation of the corpus

For the purposes of this survey my first task was to identify a body or corpus of work in which sortition receives what I call an 'active mention' — in other words those works where the authors do more than merely mention the subject in passing. In doing so three problems immediately presented themselves. First, the references range from antiquity to the present day. Such an immense span of time made it impossible to be exhaustive. I therefore decided to focus on the post-World War II period, but at the same time to make some reference to the most significant earlier contributions to this field of study, especially those that occurred in standard or classical texts or that were produced by significant writers in the field of political thought. Second, I found it necessary to effect a division between a text 'database' and the 'corpus'. The former is more broadly defined and includes in part 'grey literature', translations and reprints of books and articles and also texts on randomness and statistics. The latter only considers published texts about sortition. For example the database includes three texts from Goodwin; the corpus two only (taking the 2005 re-edition of the book 'Justice by Lottery' aside). Third, I had to limit my research to books written in five languages which are, in decreasing order based on the number of references: English, German, French, Italian and Spanish. Taking these limitations in account, the corpus includes 232 texts and the database 365 texts.[3] In order to present the references in an analytical way I suggest a distinction between three types of texts:

(1) The descriptive texts which explore any past or present use of sortition in an historical or ethnographic manner.

---

3   The collation of works for this paper was made possible by the use of the software 'zotero'. The research concluded on the 25th August 2009. The up-to-date and collaborative database and corpus are to be found on: www.zotero.org/groups/sortition/items. The references can be consulted and imported in local bibliographic tools. The online bibliographical database will be completed by early January 2010 and aims at being a useful, up-to-date tool for scholars working on sortition.

(2) The 'advocative' texts in which actual proposals for the introduction of a sortition scheme in politics are made and defended.

(3) The 'exploratory' texts that would constitute a mixed category because the authors are searching for new political norms and standards—often based on a study of existing/past sortition schemes—but do not necessarily propose the introduction of any particular instrument or institution based on sortition.

Type of text / Type of item		Database	Corpus
Texts about randomness and/or previous to 1945		42	33
Sortition: descriptive		97	65
Sortition: exploratory		84	58
Sortition: advocative	Positions	97	44
	Lots	25	18
	Decision Making	20	14
Subtotal advocative		142	76
Subtotal exploratory and advocative		226	134
Subtotal sortition		323	199
TOTAL		365	232

Figure 1. Overview of the recorded texts

2 Historical and descriptive works about sortition

2.1 Randomness and statistics: the broad field

As noted above, sortition relies on a random mechanism and therefore makes use of randomness and statistics. Hence it is important to present some reference works on the emergence of statistics and the growing comprehension of randomness in relation to the use of sortition schemes, such as that of Bellhouse and Hacking who track down the historical origins of the concept of probability and review the changing perceptions of randomness and how they relate to the shift from a deterministic to a probabilistic conception of events.[4] There is also a review by Thomas on the evolution of the use of divination in European societies.[5] Also worth mentioning are the studies of Chaitin on randomness and its definition in terms of informatics.[6]

2.2 The history of sortition in critical literature

Random selection has been used in many historical contexts and has been presented and commented upon by contemporary as well as later authors. In order to clarify my presentation of the pre-1945 texts and their earlier and later commentators I shall introduce a chronological division centred around five 'moments' and in each case I make a thematic distinction between primary and secondary sources.

2.2.1 The golden age of sortition

The classical Athenian democracy is not only the first well-known example of the wide use of sortition in politics; it is also the most studied one. Virtually all authors in the database mention the Ancient Athenian City State when it comes to sortition. The major primary sources of information on the Athenian sortition are to be found in Aristotle, Herodotus, Plato, Pseudo-Xenophon and Xenophon.[7] Within these texts, the one which is without doubt the most helpful in understanding the use of sortition in the Athenian *polis* is the *Athenian Constitution* found in 1879 and often attributed to Aristotle.[8] Quite interestingly, the first modern secondary work dedicated to election by lot in Athens written by Headlam was published the same year[9] and the content of the Aristotelian text supported Headlam in his opinion that random selection was largely independent of any religious motivation despite what the majority of the

---

4   D. Bellhouse, 'Probability in the Sixteenth and Seventeenth Centuries', *International Statistical Review*, 1988. I. Hacking, *The Emergence of Probability*, 1975. Also see Hacking (1990).

5   K. Thomas, *Religion and the Decline of Magic*, 1991.

6   G.J. Chaitin, 'Randomness and Mathematical Proof', *Scientific American*, 1975. See also Chaitin (1988), (2001). On the broader concept of randomness, see Bork (1967) and Bennett (1998). On the general topic of the procedures of choice, see Thiele (2008).

7   Whereas some of these classical authors spend a central attention to the topic others merely evoke it. Aristotle (*Politics*, books IV, 15 and VI, 2; *Rhetoric*, 1393b3–8; *The Athenian Constitution*, § 43–55 and 63–5), Herodotus (*Histories*, Book III, § 80–4), and Plato (*Politeia*, 557a–558 and 562a–564e; *Nomoi*, 740a, 741b, 745e, 759b–c) would be in the former category. Pseudo-Xenophon (I.2, 10–12 and I.3, 1–3) and Xenophon (*Memorabilia*, I.2.9 and III.9.10) would belong to the second.

8   The text was found in the year 1879 and published for the first time in the year 1891.

9   J.W. Headlam, 1891 : see Headlam (1933) in Bibliography. Headlam had been preparing the book for some years, that is to say without any real knowledge of the content of the *Athenian Constitution*.

contemporary historians still thought.[10] The discovery of the function of the *Kleroterion*, or lottery machine by Dow, which was completed by the work of Bishop, reinforced this vision in the following decades and the majority of the up-to-date reference studies present the Athenian sortition as a central pillar of the democratic practices of the ancients.[11] Bleicken refers to it as the 'safeguarding procedure of the democratic idea' and Hansen judges the hypothesis of a religious based motivation for sortition as 'an exciting but weakly based' theory.[12] Some more papers and studies which are dedicated to the technical details of how sortition was used in Athens or which discuss the role of the *Boulè* are also of value.[13]

In comparison with this profusion of work, there have been few on the other ancient uses of sortition. This is partly because sources are so rare. The two major exceptions are texts on the Judaeo-Christian tradition based on the bible and the Roman empire.[14]

2.2.2 Middle-ages and renaissance

The documentation and discussion of the use of sortition during the European middle-ages and renaissance periods mainly rests on the examples of Venice and Florence. This is not only because of their well-conserved city archives but also because famous contemporary authors were themselves directly part of the ongoing controversies. That is the case of Bruni and later of Guicciardini.[15] The latter gives a very dynamic account of the sharp debates that agitated Florence at this time. These discussions were

10 See Glotz (1907), Ehrenberg (1927). A remarkable exception is Heistebergk who followed Headlams' conclusions as soon as 1896. Heistebergk, *Bestellung der Beamten durch das Los*, 1896.
11 See Dow (1939), Bishop (1970).
12 Bleicken, *Die Athenische Demokratie*, 1995, p. 313. Hansen (1991), p. 51.
13 The *boulè* or Council of 500 was the most powerful random selected body of the *polis*. For the technical aspects see Mabel Lang, 'Allotment by Tokens', *Historia: Zeitschrift für Alte Geschichte* 8, 1959, Nr. 1: 80-89. * Fred Alford, 'The "Iron Law of Oligarchy" in the Athenian Polis', *Canadian Journal of Political Science* 18, 1985, Nr. 2:295-312. See also Kroll (1972). * For the Boulè, Rhodes (1985) and Blackwell, 'The Council', *Demos: Classical Athenian Democracy*, 2003.
14 On the bible: John Lindblom, 'Lot-Casting in the Old Testament', *Vetus Testamentum* 12, 1962, Nr. 2:164-178. J.L. Boursin, *Les dés et les urnes*, Paris: Editions du Seuol 1990. * On the Roman Empire see Meier (1956), Manin (1997). * N. Rosenstein, 'Sorting out the Lot in Republican Rome', *The American Journal of Philology* 116, 1995, Nr. 1:43-75. J-Y. Guillaumin, 'Le tirage au sort dans l'attribution des lots de terre', *Dialogues d'histoire ancienne* 24, 1998, Nr. 1:101-124. Also see Gataker (2008), 1st ed. 1627.
15 Bruni, *Laudatio Florentinae Urbis*, 1421, book V, *Ton florentinon Politeias*, 1439. For Guicciardini, see Guicciardini (1932) (1964) and (1984). * Machiavelli also mentions sortition in his writings — for example it plays a role in his proposal for a new constitution for Florence — but does not really discuss it. See Machiavelli, *History of Florence*, Book V. These few authors are merely the outstanding figures in a general culture of political debate and writing. An exploration of how sortition features in the lesser-known writers of this period would constitute a fertile ground for future research.

reviewed in depth by the later, secondary works of Manin and Dowlen.[16] Both these authors base their analyses on the very detailed work of Najemy concerning Florence, and Lane and Finlay in the case of Venice.[17]

Interestingly, the case of the Realm of Aragon, which represents the other example of wide use of sortition in the renaissance period is almost ignored, although the *insaculación* (the putting of names into bags) was employed at all levels of the political system from at least 1446 and was still in use after the end of the reign of Ferdinand II (in 1515).[18]

Other, more disparate, cases of sortition in the middle-ages and renaissance have also been the subject of specialist studies: these include the case of the allotment of land near Oxford and the distribution of political offices in Switzerland.[19]

2.2.3 The gradual vanishing

From the middle of the seventeenth century and till the end of the nineteenth century, sortition gradually disappeared both from political praxis as well as from literature and research, except in the case of the judicial jury (see infra). Whereas Harrington, Montesquieu and Rousseau still considered the procedure in their work as one of the standard political tools, the progenitors of the liberal revolutions did not regard it as a trustworthy alternative to other methods of selection such as voting (Manin, 1997).[20] There are exceptions. Some North-American colonies made proposals that included sortition,[21] there is also evidence that it was used in election procedures in England (Kishlansky, 1986) and there were a number of proposals to use sortition made during the French revolution.[22]

2.2.4 The case of the judicial jury

As noted above, the judicial jury is a remarkable exception to the progressive elimination of sortition in politics around the turn of the nineteenth

16 See Manin (1997), Dowlen (2008).
17 F.C. Lane, *Venice, A Maritime Republic*, Baltimore: Johns Hopkins University Press 1973. R. Finlay, *Politics in Renaissance Venice*, London: Benn 1980. See Najemy (1982).
18 The most valuable contributions are: T. Bisson, *Història de la corona d'aragó a l'edat mitjana*, Zaragoza: Editorial Crítica 1988. * J. Reglá, *Temas Medievales*, Valencia: Facsimil 1972. * J.A. Sesma Muñoz, *La Diputación del reino de Aragón en la época de Fernando II*, Vol. 24. Tesis doctorales. Zaragoza: Imprenta librería general 1978. J. Vicens, *Els Tràstamares*, Zaragoza: Editorial Vicens y Vives 1980. * More recently, see Weller (2009).
19 Respectively: Gretton, 'Historical Notes on the Lot-Meadow Customs at Yarnton, Oxon', *The Economic Journal*, 1912; Rambert, *Les Alpes suisses. Etudes Historiques et Nationales*, 1889.
20 See Harrington (1977) (1992), Montesquieu (1748), Rousseau (1988).
21 For example, the 'Fundamental Constitutions for the Province of East New Jersey in America of the year 1683'.
22 See Lanthenas (1792), Condorcet (1793), Lesueur (1932).

century. Juries have been studied, criticized and reformed many times since their creation, but the principle of random selection, first applied in the late seventeenth century, has not been abolished and was, on the contrary, enlarged. The jury-principle has also been studied by many democratic theorists as an aspect of citizen paticipation in law making, the question of citizenship or the general concept of democracy.[23] Despite this wide general literature, there seem to be very few studies that concentrate on the random principle itself in respect to jury selection. An exception to this general trend can be found in a small number of articles that discuss whether a jury can be representative.[24]

2.2.5 Other applications

One of the main characteristics of sortition is that it has been 'invented' in many places to answer practical problems of distribution/selection. Some of these uses have been the object of scientific, particularly anthropological, attention over time. These have generated very little, if any, primary written material. One of the most complete attempts to study this diversity on the European scale and from an ethnological point of view is the work directed by Bromberger and Travis, which notably contains papers on the use of lots for the distribution of land.[25] The latter subject was also reviewed by Levy for the case of Greece, Bohanon and Coehlo for the case of the USA and Lobe and Berkes for the Indian tradition of *Padu* (rotation of fishing parcels through sortition).[26]

2.2.6 Two classic commentaries

Modern developments in the study of sortition should not cause us to neglect two authors from the past who produced outstanding works of inquiry into the nature and potential of sortition. In their texts, Aquinas and — almost four centuries later — Gataker present the range of possibilities arising from the deliberate use of randomness as well as their opinions about which forms of sortition should be avoided and which were to

23 G. Jacobsohn, 'Citizen Participation in Policy-Making: The Role of the Jury', *The Journal of Politics* 39, 1977, Nr. 1:73-96; J. Levine, 'The Legislative Role of Juries', *American Bar Foundation Research Journal* 9, 1984, Nr. 3:605-634; M. Constable, *The Law of the Other*, London: University of Chicago Press 1994. See Gobert (1997), Abramson (2000).

24 D. Kairys *et al.*, 'Jury Representativeness: A Mandate for Multiple Source Lists', *California Law Review* 65, 197, Nr. 4: 776-827. * H. Fukurai *et al.* 'Cross-sectional jury representation or systematic jury representation?' *Journal of Criminal Justice* 19, 1991, Nr. 1: 31-48.

25 See Bromberger & Travis (1987).

26 H. Levy, 'Property Distribution by Lot in Present-Day Greece', *Transactions and Proceedings of the American Philological Association* 87, 1956, pp. 42-46. * C. Bohanon and P. Coelho, 'The Costs of Free Land: The Oklahoma Land Rushes', *The Journal of Real Estate Finance and Economics* 16, 1998, Nr. 2:205-221.. * K. Lobe and F. Berkes, 'The Padu System of Community-Based Fisheries Management', *Marine Policy* 28, 2004, Nr. 3: 271-281.

be considered as 'lawfull' (Gataker, 2008).[27] Their contributions belong in this historical section, but in terms of the thoroughness and perspicacity of their arguments they are a challenge to any modern works that seek to present an overview of the subject of sortition.

3 Exploring and advocating sortition

3.1 Classification of the texts

My corpus of works lays a solid foundation on which to present a series of modern authors who have sought to take the subject forward. They have done this not only by presenting past and current sortition schemes but also by surveying the potential and limits of sortition as a selection method. Some authors have gone still further and proposed the (re)introduction of sortition schemes in the political systems of today. Texts that discuss the potential and limits of sortition as a method of distribution, allocation or decision making I call *exploratory*. Texts that are comprised of proposals I call *advocative*. My criteria of classification within these broad categories is based on the nature of the item which is subjected to random distribution. This division rests on three main reasons:

(1) The great majority of the texts concern a specific item. This can be a position, an award (be it good or evil) or a decision. Texts dealing with more than one type of item will be presented in the overview section.

(2) Texts about the random selection of a similar item are often critical responses to each other and therefore build thematic blocs. A good example of it is the case of random distribution of scarce medical resources which produced a large academic discussion in the 70s and 80s, some texts were exploratory, others advocative.

(3) Presenting the advocative and exploratory texts together allows me to show how authors use these two different approaches to tackle what is, for the most part, the same set of problems. Furthermore, many advocative texts rest upon, and include, detailed exploratory studies.

3.2 Overview of works

The first post-war author who presented a theoretical approach to sortition seems to have been Aubert in a text called 'Chance in Social Affairs' in which he defines 'chance devices' as 'institutionalized types of decisions' where the 'chance element is, as in the selection of juries, a manifest characteristic' of the procedure.[28] This seminal paper remained the only eploratory work to

---

27   Aquinas, *De sortibus*. For Gataker, *Of the Nature and Use of Lots*, 1619 see Gataker (2008).
28   See Aubert (1959) p. 2. For a more modern and short definitional work, see Lockard (2003b). For a good and very short pro/contra presentation of sortition, see Wolfle (1970).

give an overview of the potential of lots in politics until 1984, which was—on the contrary—a very productive year in this domain: no less than nine publications tackled the topic of sortition, with two of them giving an overview. The first one made a strong and unwavering endorsement of the use of lotteries in politics in order to achieve more social justice (Goodwin, 1984). In her paper, Goodwin argues that with 'the lottery principle, organized chance, is [...] a necessary part of any mechanism of distribution and any theory of justice' (Goodwin 1984, p.1). The author developed her radical position in the book *Justice by Lottery* which surely represents—together with the 1999 published *Random Selection in Politics*— the most comprehensive advocative work on sortition to have been published so far.[29]

Broome had a comparable goal when he addressed the topic in his paper. He considered 'what justification can be found for selecting randomly and in what circumstances it applies' but without proposing any actual scheme to introduce it in the political system.[30] This exploratory work was later completed by Elster who gave a very complete overview of uses and justifications for sortition with a strong focus on the idea that random selection does not necessarily represent an abnegation of rationality but may in fact be very rational in recognizing the limits of the human mind.[31] During the same years the Social Science Information Review published a series of articles exploring different theoretical aspects of lotteries.[32]

This series of exploratory studies was later rounded off by two major works. On the basis of an extensive and precise historical study of past usages of sortition for political offices, Manin and Dowlen developed a frame of argumentation for the potential of sortition.[33] More recently, Buchstein has delivered one more monograph on the topic with the theoretical purpose of capturing the nature and forms of sortition without necessarily referring to a historical context or a type of item (Buchstein, 2009). Stone has published a series of papers on technical problems with precise questions concerning sortition. These include titles such as 'Vot-

---

29   For Goodwin, 1992, see Goodwin (2005). See Carson & Martin (1999).

30   See Broome (1984) p. 1. On the related topic of the functions of random selection, see Wasserman (1996).

31   J. Elster, 'Taming Chance: Randomization in Individual and Social Decisions' in G. Peterson (ed.), *Tanner Lectures*, Cambridge: University of Utah Press 1987. See also Elster (1988), (1989), (1992). The 1987 reference seems to be the first text that consistently cites other papers on the subject and can be considered as the oldest trace of intertextuality in the corpus.

32   See Kornhauser & Sager (1988), Eckhoff (1989), Engelstad (1989), Hofstee (1990).

33   See Manin (1997) and Dowlen (2008). A first version of the Manin book was published as early as 1993 in Italian under the title *La Democrazia dei Moderni*, but it was not as complete as the 1996 French and 1997 English editions. I decided to ignore this first book in the corpus.

ing, Lotteries and Justice' or 'Why Lotteries Are Just'.[34] The latter paper is
a response to the first exploratory text on the question of random selection
and fairness (Sher, 1980). And lastly, the first attempts have been made to
propose a typology of random selection (Delannoi, 2003) or to present
those authors working on sortition as a school of political philosophy
(Snider, 2007; Vergne, 2009).

3.3 Random distribution of political positions

3.3.1 Proposals for 'Minipopulii' in theory and practice

The idea of a re-introduction of random selection in order to distribute
political positions was developed by no less than forty-four authors since
1970, which is the year of the first post-war proposal made by Dahl in his
book *After the Revolution*: 'I propose that we seriously consider restoring
that ancient democratic device and use it for selecting advisory councils to
every elected official of the giant polyarchy — mayors of large cities, state
governors, members of the US House and Senate, and even the president'.[35] This proposal was clarified with slight modifications in two later
texts: 'I would propose the creation of what might be called a
mini-populus. Its members would be a group of randomly selected citizens who would serve for a limited period.'[36]

Dahl's proposal of the creation of what could be called 'deliberative
power' is interesting because it foresees the creation of a new branch of government in addition to the 'classical' three: legislative, executive and judiciary. This idea was later defended by other authors who wanted the
creation of Deliberative Elections, Citizens Assemblies, a Popular Tribunate
or a People's House.[37] Some more authors were able to take the next step and
succeeded in implementing their proposals. The most famous are Dienel,
Crosby and Fishkin,[38] who respectively and chronologically developed the
Planungszelle (Planning Cell, 1970), the Citizens Jury (1976) and the

---

34   See Stone (2007), (2008), (2009).

35   See Dahl (1970), p. 149. In fact Dahl's proposal is not the first. One proposal was made a year
     before by Vidal-Naquet but involved an executive position and not a deliberative one (see
     infra).

36   See Dahl (1987), p. 205. R.A. Dahl, *Democracy and its Critics*, New Haven: Yale University Press
     1989 is also worth mentioning.

37   Respectively: see Gastil (2000), P. Schmitter and A. Trechsel, *The Future of Democracy in Europe*,
     Strasbourg: Council of Europe Publications 1994. See McCormick (2006), O'Leary (2006).

38   P. Dienel, 'Was heißt und was will Partizipation?', *Der Bürger im Staat* 21, 1971, Nr. 3. For *Die
     Planungszelle*, 1978, see Dienel (2002). For English texts see Dienel (1995). * N. Crosby, *In Search
     for the Competent Citizen*, 1976 (unpublished ms.); N. Crosby et al., 'Citizens Panels: A New
     Approach to Citizen Participation', *Public Administration Review* 46, 1986, Nr, 2: 170-178. See
     Crosby (2003). * J. Fishkin, *Democracy and Deliberation*, New Haven: Yale University Press
     1991. See Fishkin (1995) and Ackerman & Fishkin (2004).

Deliberative Poll (1991), which are three models of participatory democracy based on the random selection of participants.[39]

3.3.2 *Advocating the random selection of legislative bodies*

Concerning the first of the traditional powers, the legislative one, the first proposal was probably made by Mueller [et al.]: 'We would like to propose for consideration the selecting of a national legislature at random from the voting populace.' The main reason put forward for this was the fact that such a system would 'combine the advantages of collecting decentralized information through polling with the efficiency of representation'. Four years later Becker in his 'Un-vote for America' presented almost the same idea but with more polemical arguments. For him a 'Half Random House' would prevent the disadvantages of the elective system and allow a 'true' representation of the people against the 'elite'.[40] This pattern of discourse is very interesting because it represents the core arguments of the majority of those who advocate the re-introduction of sortition for selecting legislative bodies. It can be found in almost all following books and papers which contain such advocacy. It is not possible to give full details of this broad literature here, but instead I present it as a synthesis (see Figure 2), qualfied by the following three remarks:[41]

(1) The majority of the proposals seem to have been formulated independently one from the other.[42]

(2) Some authors advocate the random selection of the legislative body with very aggressive arguments. In their pamphlets they announce the 'death of democracy' or want to 'exile the members of political parties'.[43] These militant texts are not included in the corpus.

(3) Three proposals concerned the election of the members of a legislative body in an indirect way. The first is the *Wählerspezialisierung* (Voter Specialization) proposal by Horn made in 1974 in which the author

---

39 The vast literature on models of participatory democracy based on sortition was not included in the corpus because in the main it does not address the question of sortition specifically. Exceptions were made for the founding texts presenting these models and for the few texts that tackle the use of random selection directly. See for example Coote & Lenaghan (1997) or Carson & Martin (2002).

40 See Müller *et al.* (1972), pp. 50, 57); Becker (1976), pp. 183–5.

41 See Barber (1974), (1984), Becker (1976), Burnheim (1985), Callenbach & Phillips (1985). B. Martin, 'Demarchy. A Democratic Alternative to Electoral Politics', *Kick It Over* 30, Fall 1992: 11-13. M. Schmidt, 'Institutionalizing Fair Democracy', *Futures* 33, 2001, pp. 361-370. D. Steele, 'Why Stop at Term Limits?' *The National Review* 47, 1995, Nr. 17: 38-42. R. Long, 'The Athenian Constitution: Government by Jury and Referendum', *Formulations*, Autumn 1996. See Sutherland (2004), Sintomer (2007). Finally Buchstein and Hein, 'Zufall mit Absicht', *Soziale Welt*, 2009.

42 A. Barnett & P. Carty, *The Athenian Option*, London: Demos 1998. See Barnett & Carty (2008), p.14.

43 F. Amanrich, *La Démocratie est Morte*, Paris: Barre et Dayez 1999, and F. Weyh, *Die Letzte Wahl*, Frankfurt am Main: Eichorn 2007.

proposes to permit electors to apply for and be chosen at random for 'thematic electoral colleges' working and voting on proposals for legislation. The second one is the 1976 'Modest Proposal for Election Reform' by Burton and Settle whose idea is to select a pool of electors randomly in order to 'substantially reduce election costs without appreciably altering the election outcome'. The third one is the proposal of Amar to use 'lottery voting', i.e., a weighted lottery, among the candidates after the elections in order to decide the actual winner.[44]

Author-Year	Name of the proposal	Type of random selected body
Mueller [et al.] 1972	Random Legislature	Lower House of Parliament
Horn 1974	Voters Specialization	Voter Committees
Becker 1976	Half-Random House	USA House of Representatives
Barber 1984	Strong Democracy	Local and state-wide legislative bodies
Amar 1984	Lottery Voting	Choice of the winner after elections. For candidates to the legistlative power
Burnheim 1985	Demarchy	Legislative Committees
Callenbach and Phillips 1985	A Citizen Legislature	USA House of Representatives
Martin 1989	Democracy without Elections	Legislative bodies at all levels of government
Steele 1995	-	Members of Congress
Long 1996	-	Members of all legislative bodies
Barnett and Carty 1998	The Athenian Option	UK House of Lords
Schmidt 2001	Statistical Democracy	Minipublics at the national level
Schmitter and Trechsel 2004	Citizens Assembly National Deliberative	Legislative body at the European level
Sutherland 2004	Legislative Assembly	Legislative body at the UK national level
Sintomer 2007	Senate	French Senate
Buchstein and Hein 2009	(Lot)house	Second house of the European Parliament

Figure 2. Overview of proposals concerning the Legislative Power

44   G-H. Horn 1974.A. Wahlen 2002. *Frankfurter Hefte* 9, Nr. 7: 244-488. See Burton & Settle (1976) p. 45, and Amar (1984). In the Amar proposal, each candidate receives chances proportionally to the number of votes earned in the election.

3.3.3 Proposals concerning executive and judiciary positions

Although the majority of the proposals have been made for the legislature, some authors advocate sortition for judiciary positions. In some cases the authors suggest that sortition could be used to make the existing jury system more representative. In a more radical move Bunting advocates extending the system of juries so that 'state-court judges should be selected by a process similar to that currently used to select trial juries, where the set of possible candidates is now roughly defined as all members of the state bar'.[45]

Eight authors have spoken up for the random selection of executive positions. The first post-war proposal came from Vidal-Naquet who advocated the creation of an *anti-conseil* (anti-council), that is to say a randomly selected administrative council for the *école des hautes études pratiques* in Paris. Later proposals were made by Emery who advocated the use of the jury system for 'determining government service'; by Barber for municipal officials; by Mulgan for executives in organizations like Trade Unions or associations; by Burnheim who called for a radical change in the way all government positions were filled; by Knag for the last step of the presidential election in the USA. In addition Frey and Stutzer call for international organizations to be controlled by a pool of randomly selected citizens who would have the power to recall executives of their respective organizations and Snider argues for the creation of a randomly selected jury to determine election rules and then oversee their implementation.[46]

3.3.4 Exploratory studies about the random distribution of positions

As seen above, the idea of reintroducing sortition for distributing political positions has produced a great variety of advocative texts. Some other theoreticians and writers have, in contrast, limited themselves to exploratory work, following the same distinction between the legislature, the judiciary and 'minipopulii' (Röcke, 2005; Warren & Pearse, 2008).[47]

45 H. Alker *et al.*, 'Jury Selection as a Biased Social Process', *Law & Society Review* 11, 1976, Nr. 9. See Lichtman (1996). Bunting (2006), p. 172.

46 A. Schnapp and P. Vidal-Naquet, *Journal de la Commune Etudiante*, 1969, p. 40. Emery, *The Jury System and Participative Democracy*, 1976. See Barber (1984), Mulgan (1984) p. 555, Knag (1998), Frey & Stutzer (2005). J. Snider, 'Solving a Classic Dilemma of Democratic Politics', *National Civic Review*, Winter 2006. This proposal is based on the Canadian experience of the Citizens' Assemblies of British Columbia and Ontario.

47 On the legislative power see Engelstadt (1989) and Dowlen, *Sorted: Civic Lotteries and the Future of Public Participation*, 2008. On the Judiciary see Pope (1989) and the very complete Duxbury (1999). On deliberative bodies see Röcke (2005), Warren & Pearse (2008).

3.4 Random distribution of awards

In the post-World War II literature, the first proposals for the random distribution of awards were made in the field of medical ethics to solve the problem of how to distribute scarce medical resources. Rescher elaborated a scheme arguing for random distribution, followed by Childress, Katz, Kilner and later Waring. This proposal was criticized for example by Basson or Mavrodes.[48] In the same vein, but going far further, Harris proposed to introduce a 'survival lottery' which gave birth to an important controversy in the field of ethics.[49]

Far from these theoretical developments, actual concrete cases of the distribution of 'evils' are, surprisingly, of little interest to scholars. One exception is the draft lottery for military service. Here sortition was used to select people who could be asked to risk their lives for their country. Unfortunately most contributions on this question are limited to questions of methodology (Fienberg, 1971; Scheirer & Fienberg, 1971).[50] Proposals concerning 'evils' like taxation or punishment after a trial have also been defended under the form of random taxation or the assignment of random punishments.[51]

The distribution of positive awards ('goods') has often been proposed and discussed for specific items like federal grants (Abert, 1972), oil-leases (Haspel, 1985), school admission,[52] jobs (Boyle, 1998), national-

---

48   N. Rescher, 'The Allocation of Exotic Medical Lifesaving Therapy', *Ethics* 79, 1969, Nr. 3: 173-186. J. Childress, 'Who Shall Live When Not All Can Live?', *Soundings* 53, 1970, pp. 333-355. See Katz (1973). J. Kilner, 'A Moral Allocation of Scarce Lifesaving Medical Resources', *The Journal of Religious Ethics* 9, 1981, Nr. 2:245-285. See Waring (1995). Basson, 'Choosing Among Candidates for Scarce Medical Resources, *The Journal of Medicine and Philosophy*, 1979. See Mavrodes (1984). More recently, see Hirose (2007).

49   A short presentation of this survival lottery is made by Hanink, 'On the Survival Lottery', *Philosophy*, 1976, p. 223): 'He asks us to suppose that organ transplant procedures have been perfected. Having supposed this, we are urged to put ourselves in the place of Y and Z. They will die without, respectively, heart and lung transplants. But we have no spare organs in stock. So Harris proposes a no-nonsense reform. We ought not to let Y and Z die; rather we ought to take A's heart and lungs, thus killing A, to save Y and Z. And never mind A's right to bodily integrity. Two for one, after all, is a bargain not to be missed. Moreover, we can quiet most of our moral scruples about this proposal by scientifically selecting A through a national lottery'. On this controversy see Singer (1977). See Harris (1975), (1978). M. Green, 'Harris's Modest Proposal', *Philosophy* 54, 1979, Nr. 209: 400-406. S. Leiman, 'Therapeutic Homicide', *The Journal of Medicine and Philosophy* 8, 1983, Nr 3: 257-267.

50   For a comprehensive historical overview of military draft in the nineteenth century in Europe, see N.S. de Bohigas, 'Some Opinions on Exemption from Military Service in Nineteenth-Century Europe', *Comparative Studies in Society and History* 10, 1968, Nr. 3: 261-289.

51   J. Stiglitz, 'The Case for Random Taxation', *National Bureau of Economic Research Working Paper Series*, 1982, Nr. 694: 1-56. See Lewis (1989).

52   M. Simpson, *Medical education: a critical approach*, London: Butterworth 1972. See Hofstee (1983), Goudappel (1999)..A. O'Hear, 'The Equality Lottery', *Philosophy* 82, 2007, Nr. 2: 209-210. See Saunders (2008). P. Stone, 'What can Lotteries do for Education?', *Theory and Research in Education* 6, 2008, Nr. 3: 267-282.

ity[53] or residency placement.[54] The most complete overview of the distribution of awards by sortition has been done by Boyle.[55]

3.5 Decisions by random

The use of sortition for reaching decisions — tossing a coin to choose whether to go left or right for example — is probably the most widespread of all usages of random selection. It has a long tradition in the act of divination for example.[56] But this is the field which seems to have produced the least number of exploratory and advocative texts. Zeckhauser has been the first post-war author to propose sortition for decisions from the rational-choice viewpoint. For Zeckhauser, decisions by lottery may, under mathematically defined circumstances, be a better method than deliberate choice. This view has been widely discussed among scholars.[57] Random decision making has also been advocated for its fairness and at the same time rejected for its blindness.[58] Random decision making has also been considered and advocated as a mean to resolve cases of difficult choice and also to overcome situations of rent-seeking and corruption; to break some ties; to improve the representativeness of decision making rules in the parliament; to enhance the voting system for the primaries during the US-presidential elections; or to make daily decisions in cases in which the cost of information gathering supersedes the gain of a preference-based choice.[59]

---

53   See Grötzinger (1998). The author proposes to create a 'second nationality' which would be randomly allocated. Each human being would so have a double nationality with some of the rights and obligations it creates. This could include, for example the obligation to give three per cent of one's income to the second country of nationality.

54   T. Murphy, 'Justice in Residency Placement', *Cambridge Quarterly of Healthcare Ethics* 12, Nr. 1: 66-77.

55   Conall Boyle, *Who Gets the Prize: the Case for Random Distribution in Non-Market Allocation*, (unpublished ms. 2005). See Greely (1977), Szaniawski (1991) which are older but still provide reference texts.

56   W. Silverman and I. Chalmers, 'Casting and Drawing Lots: A Time Honoured Way of Dealing with Uncertainty and Ensuring Fairness, *British Medical Journal* 323, 2001, Nr. 7327:1467-68.

57   See Zeckhauser (1969). K. Shepsle, 'A Note on Zeckhauser's "Majority Rule with Lotteries on Alternatives"', *The Quarterly Journal of Economics* 84, 1970, Nr. 4: 705-709. See Fishburn & Gehrlein (1972). M. Intriligator, 'A Probabilistic Model of Social Choice', *The Review of Economic Studies* 40, 1973, Nr. 4:553-560. S. Nitzan, 'Social Preference Ordering in a Probabilistic Voting Model', *Public Choice* 24, 1975, Nr. 1: 93-100. See Fishburn (1977), (1978). A. Gibbard, 'Manipulation of Schemes that Mix Voting with Chance', *Econometrica* 45, 1977, pp. 665-681. P. Pattanaik and B. Peleg, 'Distribution of Power under Stochastic Social Choice Rules', *Econometrica* 54, 1986, Nr. 4:909-921. J. Ledyard and T. Palfrey, 'Voting and Lottery Drafts as Efficient Public Goods Mechanisms', *The Review of Economic Studies* 61, 1994, Nr. 2: 327-355.

58   J. Taurek, 'Should the Numbers Count?' *Philosophy and Public Affairs* 6, 1977, Nr. 4: 293-316, defends the fairness of Random Selection. See Boyce (1994). F.M. Kamm, *Morality, Mortality*, New York: Oxford University Press 1998, and Broome (1998) criticize this view.

59   On difficult decisions: C. Sunstein and E. Ullmann-Margalit, 'Second-Order Decisions', *Ethics* 110, October 1999: 5-31. V. Schmidt, 'Das Los des Loses', *Leviathan* 28, 2000, Nr. 3: 363-377. On

4 Concluding remarks

The corpus of texts about sortition presented here has proved to be relatively large and very diverse. Keeping this overview in mind and within
the limits of the bibliographic research, I shall now try to answer the questions formulated at the beginning of the chapter. The first was about the
quantity of literature and the second was about its quality.

4.1 A clear quantitative growth in the interest in sortition

A quantitative look at the database and the corpus makes it clear that
there has been a growing interest in sortition. Since 1956, when the first
post-war text was written there have been more than 350 writings produced on the subject which are included in the database. Of these 199 of
them can be considered to form a corpus. Half of these texts were published between 1956 and 1989 (over thirty-four years) and half in the last
twenty years; no less than thirty per cent of them were published in the
last ten years. These figures are even more impressive when taking into
account the whole database: fifty per cent of the texts were produced in
the first thirty-eight years and fifty per cent in the last fifteen years; forty
per cent in the last ten.

Independently from this evolution, publication cycles of five to eight
years seem to exist: in 1976, 1984, 1991, 1998, 2003 and 2008 more than
seven texts were published (see Figure 4). On the contrary, in other years
there was merely one (for example in 1980 and 1993).[60]

4.2 A new school of political philosophy?

A closer look at these figures makes it possible to formulate a hypothesis:
the evolution of the exploratory and advocative corpus since the end of
the World War II permits the identification of the emegence of a new
school of political philosophy which deals with and advocates the use of
random selection in politics. Four elements appear to corroborate this
hypothesis:

---

rent-seeking and corruption see Lockard (2003a). Antoine Vergne, *The Fight against
International Corruption through the Use of Random Selection* (unpublishe ms, 2006). See
Delannoi (2008). On Tie-Breaking see Elster (1988), Duxbury (1999). On decision making rules:
Holler, 'Strict Proportional Power in Voting Bodies', *Theory and Decision*, 1985. See Berg &
Holler (1986). On presidential Elections see Gangale (2004), Tolbert, Redlawsk & Bowen
(2009). On information and decision: R.P. Wolff, In *Defense of Anarchism*, New York: Harper &
Row 1998.

60   The existence of such peaks may be explained as follows: the 1976 peak could have been
     generated by two debates, the first concerned the 'survival lottery' proposed by Harris in
     1975, the second was in responses to Intriligator and Zeckhauser's work in the field of rational
     choice theory. By contrast in 1998 none of the papers published between 1997 and 1999
     correlate in terms of topic or cross reference.

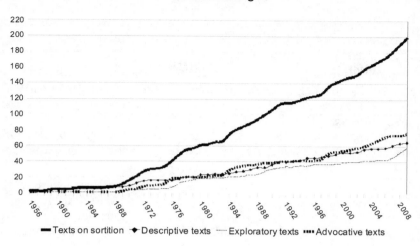

Figure 3. Publications on random selection in politics (stapled)

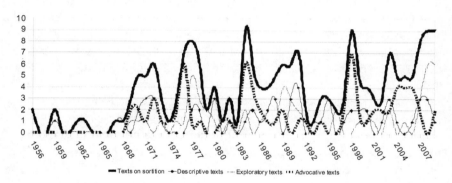

Figure 4. Publications on random selection in politics (not-stapled)

(1) Almost seventy per cent of the texts comprised in the database and sixty-seven per cent of those in the corpus are exploratory or advocative: their authors are convinced of the appropriateness of the procedure for the actual political system even if they do not propose an actual scheme.

(2) Fifty per cent of the exploratory and advocative texts of the database were produced in the last thirteen years which represents an average addition of nine texts a year. A trend that is remarkable in the texts of the corpus too, with fifty per cent of the texts produced in the twenty last years and seventy-five in the last thirty-one years.

(3) In the last ten years a growing number of advocative books and texts
    have been re-published such as in the case of the 'Sortition in Public
    Policy' series from Imprint Academic.[61]

(4) From a more qualitative perspective the intertextuality within the cor-
    pus is rapidly growing. As noted above, the older texts on sortition
    were relatively isolated and the idea of random selection was re-cre-
    ated independently. But in the last twenty years the authors started to
    learn from each other and progressively began to build their
    argumentation one on another, creating a strongly intertextual net-
    work of texts.

(5) The authors and scholars themselves are starting to act as a network.
    Four from the five recorded academic events on the topic took place in
    the last four years. Simultaneously a communication structure is
    emerging. The 'Kleroterion Mailing List', which had nine members in
    the year 2004 has now more than thirty recipients.[62]

In addition to this increasing activity, authors writing on sortition seem
to share a common textual ground. Indeed, the great majority of them use
a similar pattern of argument, albeit not always presented in the same
manner or order. Some start by exploring past/actual uses of sortition
and use this to show the potential of random selection in politics; they
sometimes go further by proposing some new sortition scheme. Other
authors start with a statement about the prevailing procedure for
distributing positions, allocating awards or making decisions which they
judge unsatisfactory (undemocratic, unjust, unfair, non-transparent, etc).
Sortition is then proposed as a possible solution, usually on the grounds
of actual (historical or current) experience of the procedure.[63]

Beyond the common argumentative pattern, advocative authors also
formulate comparable proposals, often without learning from each other.
Such an evolution points to the fact that the appearance of this topic is not
the creation of a pre-existing 'lobby of sortitionists' but seems on the contrary to be a sign of an evolution in the comprehension and appreciation
of sortition as a legitimate procedure for distributing positions, allocating
awards or reaching decisions.

4.3 Outlook

The bibliographic research presented in this chapter has shown — in spite
of its limitations — that 'the age of random selection' is *not* 'clearly upon

---

61 See Goodwin (2005), Barnett & Carty (2008), Callenbach & Phillips (2008), Gataker (2008),
    Sutherland (2008).

62 This list was created by Conall Boyle who was one of the first scholars to write about sortition
    for awards.

63 It is interesting to notice that all proposals concerning positions take Athens as a 'best practice'
    example.

us'. Around 200 texts published in more than fifty years cannot be considered enough to advance such a hypothesis; at least not concerning the literature.

Nonetheless, the interest in sortition is growing. This can be interpreted as the mere emergence of a new field of research and academics. But it can also be seen as the tip of a more important movement. Indeed, it may not be a coincidence that the first theoretical proposals were made at the same time as the first practical experiences of randomly selected deliberative bodies in Germany and in the United States were organized. In the last decade, moreover, we have not only witnessed an acceleration of the interest in sortition in the literature but also an acceleration of its use in such diverse cases as school entry selection, distribution of social housing and of course deliberative and participatory democracy. In this sense the growing bibliography can also be interpreted as the reflection of a trend in political practice. Far from being in an 'age of sortition' it would be more accurate to see the present sate of affairs as a period of tentative experiments in the practice of random selection accompanied by the first steps in the development of a broader, more comprehensive understanding of the subject in theory.

Part II

New Perspectives Connecting Theory and Practice

5 Gerhard Göhler

Controlling Politics by Sortition

It will be argued that sortition can be a means of controlling politics. With this purpose, I will first sketch out the current debate on controlling. This provides me with a starting point for understanding sortition as a means of controlling, because both controlling and sortition involve the exercise of political power. I will then identify sortition as a means of controlling democratic politics, specifically as a mode of 'soft' controlling. If, in this way, sortition turns out to be an important instrument for control in democracies, then sortition will move into the mainstream of the current discussion on effective and efficient forms of democratic governance.

1 Introduction: sortition and controlling

My following considerations are not concerned with the advantages and disadvantages of sortition compared to other democratic procedures in politics. They are even less about the question of where sortition is practically and realistically applicable. I simply presuppose that such procedures do exist and can, in theory, be used. What I am interested in is to ask if schemes involving sortition are, or may be, an instrument of governance: for controlling politics. This may sound strange at first. At first glance sortition appears to have nothing to do with controlling. As we currently understand it, control in politics is the making and implementing of binding, directed decisions concerning the state and its citizens by a sovereign power. Apart from the fact that this idea of controlling is becoming increasingly obsolete in the modern and post-modern state, and independent from questions of how far controlling is still possible or actually happening, sortition in principle seems to be the opposite of controlling. With sortition there is no indication which way a decision might go — indeed the great advantage of using sortition is that it is the perfect mechanism for ensuring that no influence of any sort can be brought to bear on the decision-making process.

On closer inspection, however, sortition can indeed be a means of controlling. To understand this, though, we need a suitable idea of controlling and the first task of this paper is to propose and develop such an idea. Once this has been achieved, I present my basic argument that if we can bring the discussion on sortition into the discussion on controlling, and if sortition turns out to be an important instrument for control in democracies, then sortition will move into the mainstream of the current discussion on effective and efficient forms of democratic governance. First I will sketch out the current debate on controlling and note its shortcomings. This provides me with a starting point for understanding sortition as a means of controlling. I define this starting point as the power-oriented idea of controlling (2). I will then identify sortition as a means of controlling democratic politics, specifically as a mode of 'soft' controlling (3). Finally, I will return to my initial thesis in a brief résumé (4).

2 The current discussion on controlling

Since the discussion on controlling politics seems to be a very German concern (without thereby losing its meaning, in my opinion), I have to elaborate a little.[1] Because it is not easy to give a definition of controlling that really fits with current political problems, the discussion revolves around finding a suitable concept of political controlling

The classical idea of controlling mostly refers to the state and follows the Platonic pattern of 'the ship's pilot steers his ship'.[2] It is the statesman as the sovereign pilot of the state's affairs who shows the 'state ship' the right way by suitable means. In the sense of this metaphor and especially since it is connected to the idea of a powerful sovereign state, this model of controlling has become increasingly problematic. This is completely understandable, and especially so because the developments such as European integration and the effects of globalization, of which we are increasingly aware, make it obvious that the classic concept of controlling, which in the end relies on command and obedience, does not meet the problems and problem solving possibilities of modern politics. Luhmann's sharp critique of the classic concept of controlling has

---

1   In its theoretical form the debate on controlling is mostly limited to the German speaking world. In the USA, where there is no tradition of a strong state in theory or in practice, the discussion is strongly influenced by principles of self-administration and social self-control See Renate, Mayntz, 'Politische Steuerung: Aufstieg, Niedergang und Transformation einer Theorie', 1996, in Mayntz (ed.) *Soziale Dynamik und Politische Steuerung. Theoretische und methodologische Überlegungen* (Frankfurt a.M., New York: Campus, 1997), p. 269. Generally, English texts take a more practical approach.

2   Plato, *Republic*, 551c.

expressed the aporiae poignantly.[3] Indeed, the idea of purely top-down controlling on the level of the nation state has become inadequate. Processes of controlling are becoming horizontal as well as vertical and are entwined across state borders. In the course of these developments the difficulties already existing on the level of the nation state have increased dramatically. It is therefore obvious that the classic concept of controlling does not suffice any more — and it is not surprising that controlling is now being reconsidered and the whole concept questioned. Thus in more recent discussions the classic concept is almost rendered obsolete. Either the term is completely removed or the definition is substantially extended.

(1) A primarily terminological but contextually far-reaching innovation is the step-by-step replacement of the term *political controlling* by the term *governance*. Mayntz considers governance as 'the entity of all coexisting forms of collective regulation of social issues'.[4] However, it remains unclear whether the concept of controlling is replaced or just pushed aside.[5] While some authors now use 'governance' as a synonym for 'controlling', Mayntz is concerned with a different perspective opened up by the governance approach.[6] The term governance is not directed at actions but at structures. Instead of focussing on actions like controlling, governance turns to structures of regulation in which public and private, hierarchical and network-shaped forms are combined.[7] It is nonetheless questionable whether this change in perspective actually solves the problem of controlling. How can governance control without controlling? It seems more reasonable to ask whether there might be other forms of controlling with mechanisms that do not follow the pattern of the pilot metaphor, but which can, nonetheless, be considered as modes of action of governance.

(2) Where the concept of controlling was not abandoned, it was expanded. Next to direct forms of hierarchical controlling by command and obedience, more indirect forms of controlling have been included in the discourse such as controlling by incentive and controlling by institutionalized self-regulation. When *controlling by incentive,*

---

3   Niklas Luhmann, 'Politische Steuerung: Ein Diskussionsbeitrag', *Politische Vierteljahresschrift*, 30 (1989), no. 1, pp. 4–9.

4   Renate Mayntz, 'Governance im modernen Staat', in Arthur Benz (ed.), *Governance – Regieren in komplexen Regelsystemen. Eine Einführung* (Wiesbaden: VS-Verlag, 2004), pp. 63–76.

5   Gerhard Göhler, 'Neue Perspektiven politischer Steuerung', *Aus Politik und Zeitgeschichte*, no. 2–3/2010, p. 35.

6   Dietmar Braun and Oliver Giraud, 'Steuerungsinstrumente', in Schubert and Bandelow (eds) *Lehrbuch der Politikfeldanalyse* (München, Wien: Oldenbourg, 2003), pp. 147–70.

7   Renate Mayntz, 'Governance Theory als fortentwickelte Steuerungstheorie?', In Gunnar Folke Schuppert (ed.): *Governance-Forschung. Vergewisserung über Stand und Entwicklungslinien* (Baden-Baden: Nomos, 2004), pp. 11–20.

the success of controlling does not depend on the avoidance of sanctions but on the receipt of advantages. Controlling relies on the expectation that addressees wish to receive the advantages offered to them when conforming to the aims of the controller.[8] Controlling through the *institutionalization of self-regulation* is even more indirect. There is no immediate way in which the subject of controlling, the state for example, can influence the addressees either in a negative or a positive sense in the pursuit of its aims. Instead, a framework is set up in the form of a context or a structure by which self-regulation is institutionalized. Within this framework, the parties perform the tasks that are assigned to them — so to speak — horizontally. These are networks or systems of negotiation or competition that are expected to be more successful and suitable in complex social problems through their internal horizontal co-ordination of actions than schemes that rely on the immediate influence of a super-ordinate authority.[9] At the same time, the remaining 'shadow of hierarchy' can always counteract unwanted developments by changing or dissolving the form of institutionalization.[10] Indirect controlling is horizontal and vertical at the same time.

Finally, purely horizontal controlling has also become increasingly relevant. 'Horizontal' means that there is no strict and unchangeable 'top' or 'bottom' in the relationship between actors and addressees of controlling.[11] Controlling can be achieved completely without hierarchies. This is the case with, for example, campaigns of NGOs, which explicitly turn against hierarchical settings, and in areas of limited statehood, where the apparatus of the state has lost most of its influence. Thus these forms were an alternative to hierarchical controlling. They are forms of *soft controlling*. The form of action of controlling, which was first expanded from direct to indirect controlling, is now extended further to horizontal mechanisms, and because these forms generally do not influence formally and unam-

---

8   Gunnar Folke Schuppert, 'Grenzen und Alternativen zur Steuerung durch Recht', in Dieter Grimm (ed.), *Wachsende Staatsaufgaben* (Baden-Baden: Nomos, 1990), pp. 217–49. * Renate Mayntz, 'Politische Steuerung und gesellschaftliche Steuerungsprobleme', in Renate Mayntz (ed.) *Soziale Dynamik und politische Steuerung. Theoretische und methodologische Überlegungen* (Frankfurt a.M., New York: Campus, 1997), p. 196.

9   See recent works: Hans-Heinrich Trute, Wolfgang Denkhaus and Doris Kühlers, 'Governance in der Verwaltungswissenschaft' in *Die Verwaltung* 37: 4 (2004), pp. 451–75. * Gunnar Folke Schuppert, 'Verwaltungsorganisation und Verwaltungsrecht als Steuerungsfaktoren' in Hoffmann-Riem, Schmidt-Aßmann and Vosskuhle (eds), *Grundlagen des Verwaltungsrechts*, Bd. 1 (München, Wien: Oldenbourg, 2006), pp. 995–1081. * Thomas Risse, 'Regieren' in *Räumen begrenzter Staatlichkeit: Zur Reisefähigkeit des Governance-Konzepts*, SFB-Governance Working Paper Series, no. 5, DFG-Sonderforschungsbereich 700 (Berlin, April 2007).

10 Fritz Scharpf, *Interaktionsformen. Akteurzentrierter Institutionalismus in der Politikforschung* (Wiesbaden: VS-Verlag, 2000), p. 323.

11 Gerhard Göhler, Ulrike Höppner and Sybille De La Rosa (eds) *Weiche Steuerung. Studien zur Steuerung durch diskursive Praktiken, Argumente und Symbole* (Baden-Baden: Nomos, 2009), p. 15-19.

biguously from the top through a chain of command and obedience, they are therefore considered to be 'soft'.

In recent literature the term 'soft controlling' is used increasingly to identify alternative controlling mechanisms, but a systematic study of mechanisms of soft controlling is still to be conducted.[12] It is the subject of a research project I am currently carrying out on 'Soft Control' at the Berlin Research Center: 'Governance in Areas of Limited Statehood: New Forms of Governance?'[13]

Altogether, the range of forms of controlling reaches from hierarchical through indirect forms to soft controlling. It is this differentiation that allows us to continue using the concept of controlling while questioning the state's role in that controlling. This seems to me to be urgently necessary. It is obvious that — as Scharpf justly points out against Luhmann — a concept of political controlling cannot be abandoned for functional reasons.[14] The critique of the hierarchical concept of controlling can be countered by advocating the use of a whole variety of forms of controlling. Anyway, politics *must* be controlling. Politics, void of its controlling ability in the realization of its intentions, could not perform its function of creating binding commitments for the community. For these reasons the debate should not be about whether we replace the concept of controlling with different concepts but about how we differentiate between different types of controlling and how we define controlling anew as new problems present themselves.

How can controlling now be defined to account for this necessary complexity — not the least in a way that will enable us to discuss sortition as a means of controlling? I propose to situate the concept of controlling systematically within the framework of power theory. This opens up a broad perspective. As we have seen, too narrow a concept of controlling would make it difficult to talk realistically about controlling in politics. We can solve this problem on a theoretical and conceptual level by placing controlling within the framework of power theory ̄because power theory offers different perspectives. Basically, controlling is one form of exercising power. Power in its broadest sense is a social relation that structures

---

12 Braun and Giraud, op. cit., 2003, p. 170. * Axel Görlitz and Hans-Peter Burth, *Politische Steuerung* (Opladen: Leske & Budrich, 1998), p. 32. * Nicolai Dose, 'Trends und Herausforderungen der politischen Steuerungstheorie', in Grande and Prätorius (eds), *Politische Steuerung und neue Staatlichkeit* (Baden-Baden: Nomos, 2003), p. 29.

13 See Gerhard Göhler, 'Weiche Steuerung: Regieren ohne Staat aus machttheoretischer Perspektive', in Risse and Lehmkuhl (eds), *Regieren ohne Staat? Governance in Räumen begrenzter Staatlichkeit* (Baden-Baden, 20070, pp. 87-108. * Göhler, Höppner and De La Rosa, op. cit., 2009. Further texts are in preparation.

14 Fritz Scharpf, 'Politische Steuerung und Politische Institutionen', *Politische Vierteljahresschrift* 30 (1989), no. 1, pp. 10-21. * Luhmann, op. cit., 1989.

the options for action.[15] The addressee of power's space of action is limited, directed, or widened in a certain direction (where new options to act are offered) by those exercising power. As with power in general, controlling in particular *limits, directs or widens actions in the way they are projected from actor to addressee.* Compared to power, controlling is always *intentional.* Controlling always has a particular aim; it is a category of action theory. A controlling actor attempts to structure the addressees' options for action according to his own sense of what these should be. Controlling is intentionally exercised power in an assignable social relationship.[16]

Situating controlling within the discussion of power therefore offers significant advantages. First, it brings the factor 'power' back into the concept of governance. The loss of this factor to a discussion that seems to be drifting more and more in a technocratic direction has been noted and lamented.[17] We should not seek to remedy this solely by remembering the existence of power and adding the idea into the debate ('there seemed to be something like power ... ') but use the concept as a systematic starting point for analysis and critique. Second, and for the same systematic reasons, referring to power allows us to reconceptualize the notion of controlling itself. The use of power is as vertical as it is horizontal. Referring to power helps to resolve the limitations suffered by the concept of controlling when it is restricted to describing the conditions of traditional, hierarchically organized statehood. As long as it is based upon classic ideas of sovereignty it is, as we have seen, only partially useful. It cannot, however, be completely abandoned because controlling based on power is indispensable for any form of political order. The way in which power is used for political control even when hierarchical options to sanction no longer exist or are not adequately available still remains to be analysed.

Thus consideration of sortition as a means of controlling should be based on a power-oriented concept. Only this makes it possible to integrate sortition into the theory of controlling, and to understand it as an instrument controlling politics. In a second step it allows us to classify

15 Gerhard Göhler, Art. 'Macht', in Göhler, Iser and Kerner (eds), *Politische Theorie. 22 Umkämpfte Begriffe zur Einführung* (Wiesbaden: VS-Verlag, 2004), pp. 250–67. * Gerhard Göhler, '"Power to" and "Power over"', in Clegg and Haugaard (eds), *The Sage Handbook of Power* (London: Sage, 2009), pp. 27–39.

16 Controlling is thus only a specific form of power relations, namely intentional exercise of power. Power itself does not have to be intentional. The discussion of power recognizes directly and consciously exercised power along with structural and discursive forms where no directed aim can be diagnosed. In contrast, controlling without intention is impossible, since controlling always has an aim. Mechanisms of power become mechanisms of controlling politics if they are 'intended' in this sense.

17 Renate Mayntz, 'Zur Selektivität der steuerungstheoretischen Perspektive', in Burth and Görlitz (eds), *Politische Steuerung in Theorie und Praxis* (Baden-Baden: Nomos, 2001), pp. 17–27. * Renate Mayntz, 'Governance im modernen Staat', in Arthur Benz, (ed.), op. cit., 2004, p. 74.

sortition within a range of different modes of controlling. One extreme in this range would be *hierarchical* or 'hard' controlling. This encompasses mechanisms that are designed to create wished-for actions by a process of command and obedience. Hard controlling happens in vertical, mostly hierarchically structured, relationships. It is based on the normative force of institutions to generate co-operation, and it is marked by an imbalance of power. Hard power is mostly formalized, in other words institutionalized towards set procedures. The other extreme is *soft* power. This encompasses mechanisms by which controlling instances purposefully structure the addressee's options to act without needing a 'top' or a 'bottom'. Soft controlling does not happen through hierarchical authority but on the horizontal level of social relations, informally and without set procedures. It is the *intentional and horizontal exercise of power*. In soft control situations either the sanctioning potential of institutions is not used willingly or it cannot be used because it does not exist in sufficient amounts. It is therefore important to see that soft controlling does not generate strict causal relationships. These are relationships in which the result can be seen as a consequence necessary consequence of the action. Soft controlling only offers a chance for addressees to orient themselves according to the intentions of the actors. In its power structure, however, soft controlling controls just as much as its antipole, hierarchical controlling.

I will now argue that sortition with its mechanism of random selection can be an instrument of controlling democratic politics. In controlling theory, it can only be recognized and identified when considered as soft controlling. The first assumption is not immediately obvious, as I mentioned in the beginning, and the second needs much more explanation. A significant outcome of mounting a convincing argument along these lines could be the inclusion of discussion of sortition within the debate on controlling.

3 Controlling by sortition

I need not discuss sortition too broadly here.[18] Sortition is — in life as in politics — always applied when the result is supposed to be open. Either a material decision is selected randomly; in which case the final option is picked by random selection from several alternatives; or a certain position or function is to be filled by sortition, then only the group of people from which the selection is to be made is determined in advance and the choice of the particular person is by random selection. Another use of random selection is the distribution of material benefits where the recipients are selected by lottery. The last option is less important for politics because

18   See Goodwin (2005), Manin (1997), Sintomer (2007), Delannoi (in this volume), Dowlen (2008), Buchstein (2009) in Bibliography.

political controlling should be focussed on the first two options. The question is whether sortition can fulfil certain functions in politics best, or at least as well as other procedures. Functions are here defined as useful capacities for the overall system. We may now ask which of the capacities that a democratic community depends on should be delivered by sortition and how far these capacities can be politically controlled by this means. If such capacities can be identified, sortition could be seen as an important, maybe even a highly welcome, element in the rational control of democratic politics.

But which functions of a democratic state are best carried out by sortition? Since I am concerned with controlling, I will present a summary of recent attempts to list the functions of sortition.[19] I do so under three headings: prohibitive effect, increase in rationality and integration.

(1) The basic function of sortition in politics is negative. Provided the procedure is performed correctly, there are no external influences — especially lobbying or corruption — on a decision made by random selection. In the face of simple and easily verifiable rules there are no differences in transparency between the options — there is only the intransparency of chance, which is the same for all concerned. In this way, sortition has first and foremost a *prohibitive effect*.

(2) There is also a positive function of sortition in politics. First, sortition can support an increase in technical or participatory rationality. The *technical rationality* of decisions is increased by sortition if it is used as a last means — an *ultima ratio* so to speak — to find a solution all parties involved can respect. If forms of sortition are agreed upon as an ultima ratio, they often increase the pressure to find a compromise in such a way they do not even have to be used any more.[20] In the first instance this is true for decisions on substantive matters that partners have to agree upon, but personnel decisions can also become more efficient through this use of sortition. Here the main saving is on transaction costs. When, for instance, a selection is made randomly out of a pool of principally eligible candidates (as in the selection of juries) there are no drawn-out election campaigns or other tedious selection procedures. In both cases the technical rationality of sortition ensures that differences in content are superimposed by a neutralizing procedure insofar as a solution is provided by the principle of chance.

The neutralizing procedure can also create prior conditions for the formation of a representative body for making material decisions.

---

19   There are vast differences. With the same focus, but from differing perspectives, Buchstein and Delannoi (inthis volume) are much more detailed.

20   Hubertus Buchstein and Michael Hein, 'Zufall mit Absicht. Das Losverfahren als Instrument einer reformierten Europäischen Union', in *Soziale Welt*, Sonderheft 18, 2009.

Compared to representative democracy in general, which depends on the election of representatives, here representativeness is achieved by random procedures. Committees formed in this way statistically picture the whole society; they consult and decide in its place (e.g., in planning cells). They thereby increase *participatory rationality* because, on the one hand, they are independent from interests and power structures; in the sense that they are not bound by instructions or need to consider the interests of their voting district. On the other hand, they still represent the whole society, and they have a chance to exchange their arguments in a quasi 'authority-free discourse' and condense their opinions into reasonable positions. [21]

(3) Last but not least using sortition can facilitate *integration*. This is often overlooked in existing typologies.[22] Here, integration is not understood as the technical unification of rules but — following the German constitutional law scholar — as an orientation of meaning, as the mental alignment of the citizens to their community.[23] If the citizens identify themselves with the values of their community, and if the fundamental values of the community offer orientation in all general affairs to and on behalf of the citizens, only then can the community become stable and alive. Rudolf Smend has emphasized that the constitution's function is to integrate the citizens into the community. But the task of political integration is not limited to the constitution. All political institutions must perform this function — and this includes the procedures used for their recruitment of personnel just as much as in their other modes of operation. In this respect as well sortition may prove to be an important component — or even an essential element — of democratic politics.

How can sortition integrate citizens into democracy? Crucial here is the aspect of equality expressed in the form of neutrality. Common affairs can in principle only be dealt with by all citizens regardless of their political

---

21 These committees only really become politically relevant when they consult and decide, rather than merely giving recommendations. On participatory rationality see Goodwin (2005). In contrast, Sintomer (2007) argues that participation always and fundamentally requires the decision by voting of all citizens. I don't think that both requirements are incompatible (see note 27.) It is moreover remarkable and worth further discussion that sortition is much closer to the classical idea of representation that was defined by Siéyès, incorporated into the French constitution of 1791, and became the prototype for all later continental constitutions, than to the current understanding of representation. Even though article 38 of the German Basic Law (GG) specifies that representatives should be independent, this independence exists neither factually nor even theoretically because of the partisan tensions within the modern party state (article 21 GG).

22 Since this is an aspect outside hard procedures, it is neither discussed by Buchstein (2009) nor by Delannoi (2008), and this seems to me to be quite typical for actual research in this respect. I argue strongly for the explicit inclusion of the aspect of integration into the discussion on sortition. See Delannoi's reply in Chapter 1 of the present book.

23 Rudolf Smend, 'Verfassung und Verfassungsrecht', in Smend, *Staatsrechtliche Abhandlungen* (1st edn. 1928), Berlin: Dunker & Humblot, 2nd edn. 1968, pp. 119–276.

weight—this is a basic credo of democracy. General elections are an expression of this principle, but they decide—at best—on some candidates and only on general lines of policy. In a representative system what is actually decided upon, concerning persons or matters, is beyond the scope of the individual vote, which only operates at the beginning of electoral term. Reality also shows that all decisions voted on by the electorate are—more or less obviously—structured in advance through the many channels of influence of dominant interest groups. Citizens may accept this because experience tells them that a mass democracy cannot aggregate interests for decision making in any other way. It is, however, difficult to expect them to accept the results if they clash with their own interests. This problem of integration can be found in any representative democracy.[24] Its formal procedures are seen to be neutral but it is difficult to recognize the 'one man, one vote' principle immediately from its results. Within the structure of representative democracy there is so much going on between the vote and the result that the neutrality of the democratic procedures themselves would appear to be compromised. All this is not the case with sortition. If, with sortition, democratic decision making really remains open until the decision is made, it remains neutral in respect to the different interests in the field and the principle of equality remains unharmed. This is especially true for randomly selected committees like juries or the planning cells in Germany. Since they have been randomly selected from all citizens they symbolize equality based on the completely neutral selection of special participation within the whole citizenry. This has integrative results. I assume that a visible expansion of the model of planning cells might substantially reduce the growing reluctance of citizens to get involved in politics because every citizen could then participate meaningfully on equal terms.

The use of sortition in such functions is—this is my point—a mode of *political controlling*. As I acknowledged in the beginning, this supposition may sound strange since sortition prevents what controlling stresses: reaching a set goal or realizing a hidden intention. Still, sortition can be grasped as political controlling and is therefore an important candidate when searching for optimized forms of governance in democracy. I advance this claim in two steps. First I discuss how far sortition can be controlling at all. Then I will try to show that sortition can only be consid-

---

24   I have been pointing out this problem for a while (Gerhard Göhler, 'Der Zusammenhang von Institution, Macht und Repräsentation', in Göhler u.a., *Institution–Macht–Repräsentation* [Baden-Baden: Nomos, 1997], pp. 11-62.). I have argued that symbolic representation of common values in institutions and in the actions of its members is fundamental for all procedures of representative democracy. The use of sortition, where it may be possible, is another way to strengthen integration.

ered as controlling when assigned to a system of soft controlling. However, this is no disadvantage but an advantage. As soft controlling becomes increasingly important within governance, sortition can become an important element in a new debate on controlling and in this way prove to be an effective and efficient instrument for democratic politics.

(1) Controlling, I had stated, cannot simply be seen as 'the pilot steers his ship' — as an immediate causal realization of the aim of the controlling actor. This definition is far too narrow and the pilot model fits politics at best only within the theory of classic sovereignty. Instead, controlling must be considered in much broader terms: as a form of power. It is the intentional exercising of power that limits, directs or extends the addressees' options to act in an intended way. This can be done in an immediately causal way like steering a ship, but many other variations are also possible. Sortition is one of them. No doubt sortition purposefully limits the involved parties' options to act — either by only allowing one alternative in reaching a decision or by radically limiting and minimizing the group of people allowed to consult and decide in advance. However, sortition leaves the result of the decision to chance, either directly, by drawing lots, or indirectly, by randomly selecting the group of decision makers whose decision can neither be influenced nor predicted. Thus, with sortition, the intention of controlling cannot be directed at the *result*. Nonetheless, the *installation* of such procedures is an important form of controlling. It decides *how* the results of political decision making are reached and which consequences are connected to this. Where procedures of random selection are installed the options of the addressees to act become strictly limited. Outside influences like corruption or lobbying are generally impossible, and are therefore not worth considering. In these circumstances, assuming that the political actors have some level of normative controlling intention, the technical and participatory rationality of democratic procedures increases drastically. Finally — and this seems to me to be the crucial effect — the installation and practice of random selection is one of the few possibilities we have of strengthening the integration of citizens into the political process and countering the reluctance of citizens to engage in politics. To the degree to which sortition can believably, that is, transparently, exclude outside influences on political decisions, trust can grow in the idea that politics is not guided by dominant interests but by the common good. In a community that is directed towards the common good all citizens can find and identify themselves as equals. The controlling function then becomes that of installing and practicing random selection schemes within a body of politically integrated citizens. I assume that this is going to be more and more necessary in the future.

(2) This controlling by sortition, however, is not carried out hierarchically but horizontally. This means that if controlling is only considered in its hierarchical sense, the use of random selection cannot be seen as controlling and therefore it cannot become a meaningful element in the debate about effective and efficient forms of governance in democracies. This is only possible if a broader concept of controlling is used and sortition is considered as a mode of *soft controlling*.[25] At first glance, sortition as described here seems to be a mode of hard, hierarchical controlling. This would certainly seem the case if we consider the installation rather than the results of any scheme. A parliament or government could decide to use sortition in the future and could realize this decision against opposition and resistance. This would be hierarchical. But, as when we considered the question of controlling and sortition as a whole, the first glance deceives us. Sortition is, in its basic intention, the instrument *per se* to reach alternatives to 'Herrschaft' ('authority' or 'domination' in the sense of Max Weber) in the form of the hierarchical execution of power.[26] At a closer look this is not only true for the results but also for the installment and practice of any scheme of sortition.

The practice of sortition can be installed by agreement between all parties involved. This is a case of controlling by common consensus. Here a sortition scheme controls the procedures practiced by all participants and asks them to recognize the binding nature of the outcome. This is 'reflexive' controlling. Alternatively sortition schemes can be installed and practiced by institutions. This variation is also non-hierarchical, as it does not function according to a pattern of command and obedience. Those in authority explicitly give up their right of command in respect to certain decision-making processes — they actually use their authority in order to give it up at the same time. The precondition is of course that the results of sortition are deemed binding in advance. They cannot be disregarded or changed at the whim of the political authorities. [27] In cases where active

25   I will present a theoretical discussion of to the consequences of this in the résumé.

26   'Domination is the probability that a command with a given specific content will be obeyed by a given group of persons.' Max Weber, *Economy and Society*, p. 53, § 16, ed. Guenther and Wittich (Berkeley, Los Angeles & London: University of California Press, 1978) [1st edn 1922].

27   Unlike controlling by incentive or by structuring, therefore, sortition is a mode of soft controlling because undesirable results cannot be altered by anyone in political authority. This also means that modern forms of sortition like planning cells can only really become instruments of soft controlling when it is impossible for their results to be hierarchically suspended in this way. In fact, because planning cells can currently only consult, they are a mixture of hierarchical and non-hierarchical controlling. As long as this remains the case, sortition in the case of planning cells cannot be purely horizontal controlling, and planning cells cannot become a really powerful constitutional form. Sortition is only an effective means of controlling politics if it leads to binding decisions, even if, and while, it works horizontally. This seems to be inconsistent with the principle of participation in our democracies. See Sintomer (2007). But in the case of soft control there is no inconsistency of this kind. Modern

participation is needed (sortition of offices, or planning cells) it is also necessary that those randomly selected are permanently willing to play an
active role in the decision-making process. In both cases the controlling is
soft because it is horizontal: in the practice of sortition there can be no
'top' and 'bottom'.[28]

4 Résumé

The considerations presented here have two intentions. *First*, based on the
introduction into the (predominantly German) debate on controlling, I
have tried to show that sortition can be considered as a mode of political
controlling. Sortition does not stand apart from the question of identifying the most effective, efficient and therefore the most legitimate forms of
governance in modern democracies. Rather, it is an important and even
possibly — at least normatively considered — a necessary component. In
any case it would be wrong to exclude it from the discussion. *Second*, I
have tried to show that sortition in politics can only be considered as controlling if the concept of controlling includes soft, horizontal controlling.
At a closer look, hierarchical controlling and sortition exclude each other.

The results of my argument lead to two conclusions that merit further
consideration:

(1) If it can be demonstrated that political controlling by sortition is possible, we should recognize that this is not controlling directed at certain
results. Only the *installation* of procedures of sortition is a controlling
process — and we should further recognize the importance of this element in respect to the procedure as a whole. But sortition itself
remains a form of indirect controlling because it enforces the criterion
of strict equality. No community, no democracy, can, however, rely
on indirect controlling alone. Even if sortition is introduced as far as
possible, there will always be a need for direct controlling in a democracy, be it hierarchical and vertical or soft and horizontal, or a mixture
of both. As can be seen very clearly when considering the aspect of
controlling, sortition can only supplement other forms of governance
in a democracy.

---

democracies are organized on the basis of representation. Institutions created by sortition are
without any doubt representative ones. So, in order to be representative in a strict sense, they
must be independent from any political authority. Independence from hierarchies does not
exclude the possibility that institutions created by sortition could appeal to the decision of the
people in case of essential questions. This course of action, however, would have to be an
autonomous decision.

28 The expression 'soft controlling' can be misunderstood when 'soft' is interpreted as 'random'.
Successful controlling leads to intended aims, not to random ones; it is 'soft' because it is not
hierarchical but horizontal. This is the paradox of soft controlling: if it is successful, its results
are *as if* there had been achieved by hierarchical controlling.

(2) If sortition and soft controlling are taken together to form a combined research programme, this could provide a means of evaluating the practice of sortition as well as improving the concept of soft controlling. Sortition, on the one side, can only enter the mainstream of the debate on forms of governance once it can be identified as a mode of controlling. Soft controlling, on the other side, is often perceived intuitively but rarely analyzed systematically. More often, however, the concept of controlling is given up altogether in the face of new problems. Unfortunately, as many researchers also recognize, this leads to an exclusion of the power component from the political discourse. As an alternative, identifying sortition as a mode of soft controlling helps us to apply a broader concept of controlling and to achieve a better understanding of possible new forms of governance in democracies.

Lotteries, Markets and Fair Competition

This chapter asks whether allocative lotteries combined with markets could play a useful role in promoting fair competition. It also considers whether 'markets plus lotteries' could be a useful tool for regulatory agencies — for example, the regulators of privatised utilities. I argue that the use of lotteries could assist borderline competitors in a competition to win a lucrative contract and that it could also combat tendencies to collusion and oligopoly in procurement processes.

1 Introduction

The first question I shall address in this chapter is whether allocative lotteries combined with markets can play a useful role in promoting fair competition. The second question I consider is whether 'markets plus lotteries' could be a useful tool for *regulatory* agencies — for example, the regulators of privately-owned utilities and the regulators of communications networks, whose remit is to ensure competitive pricing and adequate investment.

When might a 'market plus lottery' be appropriate?

I am dealing here with two sorts of market transaction:

(1) where companies compete to sell goods or services to another company or organisation, and

(2) where companies compete for a franchise to be awarded by a government agency or by a regulator.

The regular retail 'market-place', where suppliers sell goods directly to customers, is not under consideration.

I shall argue that, in the context of (1) and (2) there are three reasons why it could be valuable and would be practical to combine an element of allocation by lottery with the competitive bidding which typifies the market process. These reasons are:

(a) To assist the borderline competitors, the companies who would not normally have the chance of being awarded a contract, against more powerful or more established competitors. (The definition of 'borderline' will be discussed in Section 4.)

The purpose would be to promote the development of new or innovative companies by giving them the chance to compete with the major players in the market.

(b) To counter oligopoly and collusion in a particular market. The existence of free and fair competition and the prevention of various forms of oligopoly (cartels, collusion, price-fixing and so on) are axiomatic in economic theories of the market; in practice, they are the central objectives of the European Union. Successful prevention of market flaws promotes fairness to companies and should ultimately provide best value for customers. The promotion of new entrants to the market, as suggested in (i) above, also militates against collusion.

(c) In order to pursue non-economic objectives in the allocation process in situations where fair competition is not the only or overriding consideration because other important principles are at stake.

2 The generic advantages of lottery allocation and lottery selection

These advantages, or virtues, can be classified variously as normative or practical.

Normative advantages

(1) Fairness: lotteries promote fairness between candidates or competitors; they offer equal chances of success in the competition (where everyone has same number of `tickets') or proportional chances (where competitors have different numbers of tickets in proportion to their merit, or experience, or wealth, etc.). The latter are called *weighted lotteries.*

(2) Impartiality: lotteries avoid the possible partiality of a human agent choosing between competitors. They are proof against prejudice, bribery, corruption and unforeseen irrationality on the part of the chooser (lotteries themselves are a-rational, not irrational).

Fairness and impartiality are, of course, essential to the theory and practice of competition.

Practical advantages

(1) Efficiency and practicality: random selection or allocation can solve some practical problems which would otherwise confront the chooser. A selection lottery saves the agent from having to make a

choice where the competitors are 'not significantly different' and where a *rational* choice is therefore impossible.[1] It prevents the 'Buridan's Ass' problem of being unable to choose between incommensurable goods (or, again, goods too similar for rational choice). Making a choice can also be time-consuming while random selection or allocation is swift and decisive.

3 Bids, pitches and choices: saving time and cost

In general, the process of competing for a contract involves all the competitors in preparing elaborate tenders, bids or 'pitches' (a marketing term). The process is expensive in terms of time and money for the competitors. Rather than preparing full-scale bids they might prefer to submit light-touch bids and to have the selection process determined randomly.

The full contracting process imposes costs on the purchasing company as well on the competitors; it has to attend lengthy pitches and evaluate the bids. Therefore, one reason why the purchasing company in a bidding process might also prefer to select a bidding company by lottery is that it would be saved the cost of evaluating fine distinctions between the different bids in order to come to a decision.

There may therefore be purely practical reasons for the purchasing company to decide by lottery which company to hire. Additionally, it can claim that the random selection process is both fair and impartial.

4 Using lotteries to enhance competition

I now return to the questions raised in the introduction.

Borderline cases

In order to explain the idea of the 'borderline competitor' and to justify my argument that such competitors deserve at least some chance of winning, I will utilise two examples from the field of education where random selection could be used to the benefit of borderline candidates:

(1) classifying degrees
(2) allocating places to good state schools. (I am indebted to Conall Boyle for these examples.)

Degree classification

In British universities, undergraduate degrees (BAs, BScs) are classified according to the grades achieved as First, Upper Second, Lower Second, Third, Pass, Fail. The class of degree achieved is important for the stu-

---

1   See in Bibliography: Boyle (1998), p.295.

dent's future career; employers may specify a degree class, e.g., 'Upper Second or better'.

In an 1888 paper, the economist Edgeworth argued that at Cambridge University the process of degree classification contained an element of lottery: there was always a probability that an individual student would be allocated to the wrong class. He suggested borderline cases could be decided by lotteries (drawn by the Fellows of the Colleges). This promoted some lively debate (although it was not put into practice) and in 1890 Edgeworth proposed another, similar, use of a lottery. He analysed civil service entrance examinations (these exams determined who should start work on the fast-track higher grades in public service). He argued that the rigid cut-off point between those who fail and those who succeed 'impose[s] hardship on those just outside the gates of Paradise' because failing the examination meant a lower income and a (permanently) lower position in the civil service hierarchy.[2] To avoid the inflexibility and rigidity of this system, Edgeworth proposed a light-touch examination, instead of the intensive and exhausting entrances examinations of that time. There would then be a lottery for entrance to the civil service's higher grades, with candidates being allocated tickets in proportion to their marks in the exam. In the long run, Edgeworth asserted, the same proportion of worthy candidates would be appointed.

The British 'eleven- plus' examination for entry to state schools

An examination introduced after the second world war which was taken by children at the age of eleven, the eleven-plus determined whether they should go to 'grammar schools' with high academic standards or to 'secondary modern schools'. These were more practically or vocationally orientated and would usually have lower standards and attract less able teachers. Only about twenty-five per cent of children went to grammar schools so the system was markedly elitist. The eleven-plus has been phased out in a lot of areas although some education authorities still use it as a selection procedure.

Conall Boyle discusses how a graduated lottery for eleven-plus candidates in the 'border zone' could have been used to advantage.[3] His reasoning is similar to Edgeworth's concerning the civil service examination: stakes for 11-year-old pupils are very high. An abrupt cut-off point is unfair and actually counterproductive, argues Boyle. It is counterproductive in the sense that the purpose of education is to ensure that pupils get an education corresponding to their ability; a rigid cut-off does not guar-

2   Edgeworth, as cited in Boyle (1998), p. 292.
3   See Boyle (1998).

antee this. Rejected candidates who could nonetheless benefit from a grammar school education occupy a 'fuzzy zone' just below the cut-off point. A lottery for school places among the candidates in the borderline zone would have given at least some of them a chance of the standard of education for which they were sufficiently equipped.

I will argue that, just as in these examples of competitive allocation, in the context of competitive bidding for contracts there is normally a penumbra of borderline candidates who could do very well if they won the contract. The proposal is that the use of lotteries would enhance competition and make it fairer, giving these marginal companies the chance to break into a market and succeed. I will illustrate this through a example based on a real market situation.

Ecohelp is a global environmental consultancy, one of the 'Big Five' players in that field. Suppose that a large company, *Mines'R'Us*, wishes to contract for a company to advise it about environmental issues. *Ecohelp* and the other four companies wish to bid; they must expend time, money and other resources to make their pitches, while *Mines'R'Us* must also incur costs on attending the pitches and judging between them. What advantage would be gained by using a lottery to choose between the rival consultancy firms, rather than by evaluating bids, tenders and pitches? Who would benefit? The Big Five would benefit: they could spend less time on preparing their pitch since they know that they have an equal chance with the others of succeeding which will not be enhanced by more elaborate pitches or more extravagant claims. *Mines'R'Us* also benefits by saving time and money on choosing between bids and drawing fine distinctions. If this practice were generally adopted, over time the 'Big Five' would continue to receive an approximately equal number of contracts from purchasing companies since each would have an equal probability of being randomly awarded the contract.

A more extended lottery

Suppose we now extend the lottery to firms outside the Big Five which meet certain threshold requirements for entry into the competition. Importantly for the argument of this chapter, once the lottery is not confined to the Big Five any borderline company that only had the resources to make a minor pitch and could not compete with the major pitchers would get some chance to win the contract. Who benefits in this situation?

(1) The competitive process itself benefits because the system is less 'cosy' and there is less likely to be a 'Buggins' turn' arrangement between the major players. It is therefore still competitive but on a much fairer basis.

(2) It is beneficial and fairer to smaller or newer companies which might be able to offer a comparable service but under current practice would never get the chance. Because entry costs have been greatly reduced, they could enter the competition with a chance of breaking into the charmed circle of the Big Five and gaining experience of top-level work.

(3) The contracting company, *Mines'R'Us*, retains the benefits noted above (economy of time and resources) but it may also benefit from employing a fresh, innovative but lesser-known company as its environmental consultant.

Applied generally, the combination of lottery selection and (light-touch) competitive bidding for contracts — which will be referred to as *market-plus*-lottery — would counteract the oligopolistic situation prevailing in many markets where the major players always get most of the contracts. Such a situation is obviously conducive to price-fixing or to collusion or to a 'Buggins' turn' system and unconducive to new entrants to the market who may have much to offer.

Some caveats are needed: obviously, companies admitted to the lottery process would have to fulfil certain criteria stipulated by the purchasing company — threshold criteria and other pre-requisites — to prove that they had sufficient resources, experience and skilled personnel to deliver the required product or service.

An example of the use of lottery combined with a market is the oil lease lottery introduced in the USA in 1959 by the Bureau of Land Management to dispose of tracts of state-owned land whose previous lessees had not renewed their leases. Ordinary citizens could, for a modest sum, buy a lottery ticket to win the lease on a parcel of land of unknown or unpromising oil-extraction potential. While land with *known* oil reserves was sold to commercial companies through a normal competitive bidding process these unpromising parcels of land were won in the lease-lottery by citizens who could (and did) re-sell the leases for large sums if oil was discovered. Citizens could buy only one ticket each so everyone had an equal chance of winning — even so, various loopholes were quickly discovered and exploited by companies hoping to acquire more land leases, or simply to make a profit out of the new system and people's gullibility. Under this system the lottery and the competitive market run in tandem, the lottery being used only for land which would not attract competitive bids — so the case is not strictly parallel to what is being proposed here for a market-plus-lottery. But, interestingly, Haspel argues that:

> the present lottery, irrational though it may seem at first glance, is not so easy to dismiss. Moreover, so long as there is a competitive private after-market that will ultimately deliver each tract to the party who values

it most, the lottery will be more socially efficient than a public competitive sale requiring costly and slow fair-market-value determinations across the board. It will also raise more revenues for the government and do so faster. Finally, it will lead to higher energy production.[4]

So here is a case where a lottery plus an after-market is preferable to a straightforward market.

5 Using lotteries to assist regulation

The growth of regulation

In Britain, in the 1980s and 1990s, Conservative governments undertook extensive privatisation of publicly owned companies (telephone, energy, water, transport). In many instances, this process led naturally to the creation of private monopolies - for example, British Telecom had a monopoly on telephone landlines, exchanges, and the telecommunications network. This monopoly was actually guaranteed by the government to last for a number of years before competitors could enter the market. In the case of regional water companies, geography guaranteed them a natural monopoly.

To ensure that these private monopolies did not exploit their position to charge excessive prices for their products or services, the government created regulatory bodies such as 'Ofcom' (the Office of Communications, regulating broadcasting and telecommunications), Ofwat (the water services regulation authority), Ofrail (the Office of Rail Regulation, which grants operators' licences) and Ofgem (the Office of the Gas and Electricity Markets).

Lotteries in aid of regulation

A market-plus-lottery combination where companies pay for the chance to be selected for a contract (i.e., a ticket, or tickets, in the draw), seems particularly applicable in two contexts where the state regulates business:

(1) where regulators are involved because public interest is at stake and pure competition should not reign (e.g., the highest bidder may not be the most suitable choice)

(2) where regulators are involved because the nature of the business itself makes proper competition less likely, e.g., a quasi-monopoly situation.

Suitable applications in the British context might be:

4   See Haspel (1985), p. 30.

The award of television franchises

Such franchises award a monopoly on broadcasting to particular regions of the country. Competing companies would have to buy tickets in the allocation lottery; the more marginal companies could afford fewer tickets but would still have a chance of being selected. A threshold condition for entering the lottery would be that the company's bid fulfilled certain criteria such as a promise to broadcast a certain percentage of current affairs and news or a guarantee of a certain percentage of 'public interest' broadcasting. (Companies entering the current competitive tender process have to give such undertakings.)

The award of rail franchises

Here, similar principles could apply. Because running the train service in a particular geographical region usually means having a monopoly on the use of train lines, stations and other facilities, the regulators must ensure that the competition to buy a virtual monopoly must be fair. Here again, the big players and the borderline companies should be given the chance to compete in a franchise lottery, either by having an equal number of tickets in the lottery or alternatively by purchasing tickets according to their resources. In either case the competing companies would need to meet a threshold requirement in order to enter the lottery. They might initially have to prove that they could deliver the required service, i.e., had the necessary capital (this is particularly relevant in the case of railways where they must be able to afford the 'rolling stock' — carriages, locomotives etc. — to run the service) as well as the relevant experience and personnel.

Contracting out

Lotteries might also be relevant to the public-sector 'contracting-out' of services, a process which has occurred in Britain for almost twenty years. Local authorities, civil service agencies and the National Health Service have been required by central government to put various functions (e.g., the payroll function, cleaning, and waste collection) out to tender, rather than supplying these services in-house. The purpose and justification was (and is) cost-cutting or, looked at another way, increased efficiency. Thus, their activities are regulated by law (rather than a regulatory agency) — but are regulated nonetheless.

For companies competing for the work, the process of preparing a bid for these contracts is time-consuming and costly and has to be regularly repeated since the contracts must be put out to tender again every three or five years. As well as efficiency benefits the public sector organisation also incurs the costs associated with drawing up specifications for the work and choosing between companies. Local authorities have often had to bear *the additional cost of competing for their own contracts*! In the case of waste collection and the maintenance of parks and roads, for example, local authorities generally formed separate companies from their in-house workforces. These then put in bids and were frequently success-ful in landing the new contracts — another wasteful cost.

As in the *Ecohelp* and *Mines'R'Us* example, some of these costs and pro-cesses could be short-circuited by a lottery, provided that the competing companies had the necessary pre-requisites and could satisfy the public interest aspect of the service. In the private provision of public housing, for instance, the houses would have to be inexpensive to build, affordable to rent and would have to meet certain building regulations and standards.

The use of lotteries in the allocation of franchises, licences and contracts is particularly appropriate for regulatory and contracting out processes because taxpayers' money is involved. In these contexts it is imperative that those awarding the contracts are seen to be fair, free of influence and immune from corruption.

6 Other possible applications

I have examined the use of lottery allocation as a regulatory device because in the regulated industries there is a greater risk of monopolies, of prejudice to the public interest, and also, perhaps, of collusion or price-fixing. But does the principle apply more widely, to 'private' mar-kets where public interest is not directly involved? Suppose that a govern-ment adopted the market-plus-lottery principle for the allocation of contracts in the regulated industries, why might it also decide to make the system compulsory for other industries?

It may at first seem unjustifiable for a government to interfere in a 'pri-vate' market and to dictate the principles on which transactions are con-ducted. But is there such a thing as a private sphere where business and industry can operate without regulation? The era of laissez-faire is long past. Most companies are, after all, *public* companies. In return for the ben-efits of limited liability and the legal enforceability of their contracts, they have to pay taxes, submit to audit, observe safety legislation and conform to myriad rules and regulations. Beyond this, there may be industry-specific interventions. In the UK, for example, the Competition Commis-sion intervenes in 'private' markets to prevent mergers or takeovers that might create a monopoly interest and to investigate collusion and price fixing. In the interest of fair competition and of promoting the development of new or innovative companies, it would be possible for the Commission to require that business transactions, such as the awarding of contracts, incorporate a lottery element.

Lottery allocation where competition is not the main priority

In the introduction it was suggested that a lottery might be appropriate where an agent wishes to pursue objectives other than the maximisation of profit in an allocation process. In Dartmouth University (USA), student housing is allocated by lottery rather than by price-rationing. The objective is to get a diverse mixture of students living side-by-side in the accommodation. The universities could simply charge higher rents for the most desirable rooms or flats, thus maximising its income but a higher priority is to achieve social, class and ethnic mixing among the students from the start.[5] This is a case of a lottery *instead of* a market but it could easily be converted to a market-plus-lottery system if the college needed to increase its income from housing.

In general, a combination of market and lottery in an allocation process would also achieve 'psychological' objectives such as allowing everyone who enters the bidding process to feel that they have a chance of winning the 'prize' (the contract) and ensuring that the losers do not feel that they have been judged to be deficient. It would have the virtue of retaining the efficiency-inducing competitive element while widening the range of those able to compete. It would also guarantee the fairness, impartiality and incorruptibility of the allocation process. The system is versatile and the two allocative principles could be combined in different ways: there could be a higher or lower entry charge or higher or lower threshold requirements. Competitors could be limited to just one ticket or permitted to buy as many as they wished; although a weighted lottery will always favour the larger and wealthier competitors it still gives hope and incentive to those on the margins.

7 Critiques of the lottery-market principle

From the perspective of economists, the market-plus-lottery principle may appear plain perverse because it undermines the workings of the market. In this section I summarise some of the criticisms offered and questions raised when I presented a version of this discussion to a group

---

5   Conall Boyle, Draft PhD on the use of lotteries in non-market distribution, Department of
     Economics, University of Wales, Swansea, 2006. Website: www.conallboyle.com

of economists.[6] I also attempt to rebut their objections although some of them are quite convincing!

The threshold or pre-qualification for entry

All are agreed that some threshold or pre-qualification (resources, expertise, pricing policy etc.) would be necessary to enter a lottery-market process or a pure lottery process for the allocation of contracts (procurement). The company allocating the contract would need to be satisfied that, whichever bidding company was randomly selected, the outcome would be satisfactory (i.e., the 'winner' would do the work to an adequate standard.) *However*, there would be a risk of tacit collusion by competitors to show that they all had the necessary pre-qualifications to enter the lottery. I agree that this could be a risk but this scenario suggests that a degree of oligopoly already exists—in which case I would argue that any normal market allocation procedure would also be subject to the same prejudices and pressures.

Competitive pricing?

Would the process of bidding for a ticket in the lottery to procure a contract cause the competing company to lower its prices? If so this would benefit the customer. But one would need to weigh this against the cost of the bid, which would be passed on to the customer indirectly. The problem with this objection is that it can be argued against any bidding or tendering process, not just the market-plus-lottery. As noted in earlier sections, preparing specifications for contracts and preparing pitches or bids is generally costly. The purpose of the lottery would be to reduce these costs by allowing 'light-touch' bids.

Transferability?

Would the winning company be able to sell the contract to another company? In principle, I think it would. If the purchasing company is satisfied that all those in the competition had the necessary pre-qualification it should not matter which of the companies in the lottery eventually carries out the work. But transferring the contract to a company *not* in the original lottery would need to be prohibited since companies outside the lottery might not have the necessary pre-qualifications or meet the entry threshold.

---

6   One economist offered some interesting lottery-market examples: taxi licences in Hungary are distributed randomly (among those who have qualified as taxi drivers). Also, in Yellow Pages (the advertising directory) the position of an advertisement on the page is allocated randomly, i.e.,the advertiser pays for the size of advertisement required but cannot buy a prominent position—an excellent example of market-plus-lottery. He also suggested there should be a lottery for time slots at airports, which seems an excellent idea.

Competition *for* the market and competition *within* the market

Encouraging 'competition for' by requiring competing companies to attain the necessary pre-qualifications could prevent 'competition within' the market by those eligible for the contract. Once they had obtained `tickets' in the process they would have no further incentive to compete since the outcome would be determined randomly. This seems a fair point but, in order to be sure, one would need to examine in each case whether competition to enter the market would be as exacting as competition within the market in the bidding or 'pitching' process. It has been argued that the 'light-touch' approach would save competing companies wasted costs. It could also be argued that the market-plus-lottery procedure merely moves competition to an earlier stage but does not change the quality of the competition.

Worst scenario not too bad (a point in favour of the proposal)

Using the example of *Mines'R'Us* choosing an environmental consultant randomly between the 'Big Five' competitors it was agreed that, whichever competitor won the contract, the outcome should be satisfactory for the purchasing company even if the lottery 'made a mistake'. The cost of the mistake would be small compared with the cost incurred in running the full competitive bidding procedure.

Excessive entry costs

The argument here is that the lottery-market could be inefficient in that *too many companies* would incur the fixed costs of entry (e.g., preparing initial bids, or getting the necessary pre-qualifications) and a number of bids — the losers' bids — would be wasted. But surely this also applies to a normal market-bidding process where each company has to prepare a bid and the losers bear those costs without the compensating prize of the contract? The economists' point is, however, that the more borderline companies enter the lottery, the more entry costs (costs of meeting the pre-requirements) would be wasted. This would need to be weighed against virtuous effect of the lottery element in reducing the time and costs of those few companies that otherwise would have had to prepare full bids.

Disincentive effect

Because the final choice would be made by lottery the competitors work less hard and do not strive to compete with each other. By contrast, a pure market system favours those who work hard and are innovatory. I discuss this point in my conclusion, below.

A number of the economists' arguments naturally turned on the cost of the proposed system. It was suggested that if the competing company had to pay a high price for the chance to enter the lottery it could reduce its performance when it won the contract. This leads us to a new area of discussion — so far the focus has been on the threshold which competitors must cross to obtain a ticket for the lottery. The purchasing company must be satisfied with the adequacy of the competitors before it would be willing to allocate by lottery. Passing the threshold may already be costly. An additional requirement to *buy* a ticket (or tickets) would price some competitors out of the market at the second stage. The argument in this chapter has been that lottery allocation would reduce costs both to the purchasing company and the competitors but this may ultimately be a question to be investigated empirically in every instance.

In this connection, the economist John R. Boyce has argued that lotteries are not always conducive to fairness of allocation and that they are actually a way of increasing income for the company which is allocating the goods:

> Participation fees are almost always charged and they are often discriminatory. In addition, goods ... allocated by lotteries are usually not transferable. Both lottery participation fees and restrictions on transferability reduce rent-seeking from speculators. Each feature increases the rents to the primary user groups relative to the rents attainable from alternative mechanisms such as auctions, queues or merit allocations.

This contrasts with Haspel's argument, summarised earlier, that the oil-lease lotteries maximised income to the state or federal government despite the low ticket price and the fact that the leases were transferable. It appears that there is no decisive economic case either for or against.

8 Conclusion

I have advocated the use of lotteries in conjunction with a market process to achieve three objectives:

(1) to ensure that the allocation of a contract (i.e., selection of a contractor) is free from partiality, 'cosiness' (a polite term for some degree of collusion between the competing companies or between the contracting company and one or more of the competitors), and any element of corruption or other imperfections which might damage the competitive process.

(2) to give borderline companies the chance to enter, and win, a competitive bidding process, thus enhancing competition. This would tend to prevent oligopoly or collusion between the major players in the market and should have the added benefit of ensuring the market equiva-

lent of Pareto's 'circulation of elites'. It would mean that the same companies did not carry off the prizes every time.

(3) to enhance the efficiency and practicality of the competitive bidding process by saving time and costs while ensuring that competitors are sufficiently competent too undertake the work.

I suggest that (1) and (2) are compelling reasons for the regulator of an industry to require that some or all contracts should be awarded randomly among competing companies. The Competition Commission might make the same requirement for similar reasons.

An underlying assumption of the argument has been that the differences between the best and the worst competitor in the lottery are not so significant that the purchasing company will suffer — this is the purpose of the threshold requirement.

The main practical disadvantage of using a lottery in the final allocation of contracts is that it might act as a disincentive to competitive endeavour by those in the 'pool'. My argument is that because competitors have to make considerable efforts to enter the pool in the first place (i.e., to reach and cross the threshold), competition still takes place but at an earlier stage. Also, the increase in new entrants to the pool (the borderline companies) shold ensure that the major players continue to compete and innovate. The borderline companies would not bother to compete for a lucrative contract if they were sure that one of the 'Big Five' would always get it, but the lottery gives them a chance of winning and an incentive to reach the threshold.

Finally, would it improve the market-plus-lottery allocation system if some companies were to buy more tickets in the lottery than others? If wealthier companies could buy more chances, the virtue of the lottery would diminish and it could be objected that a straightforward market system would be preferable. The counter-argument, for preferring a weighted lottery to a regular market, is that the market alone would exclude smaller companies from any chance of getting the sought-after contract and would thus discourage competition. The case is parallel to the examples of the civil service examinations and the eleven-plus examination discussed in Section 4 — borderline candidates and companies should have a chance, even if it is a smaller chance than the best examinees or big players. The general principle in both weighted and unweighted lotteries is that even those fated to lose should have some hope of winning. Although there are threshold costs, this hope stimulates competition and acts as a barrier to monopoly and oligopoly.

7 Hubertus Buchstein and Michael Hein

Randomizing Europe

The Lottery as a Political Instrument for a Reformed European Union

In this paper we argue for the introduction of lotteries as a decision pro-cedure for policy making in modern democracies. Our suggestions are focused on the political system of the EU. We start our line of argument by bringing to attention the recent renaissance of the lottery in demo-cratic practices and political theory. Next we follow the rich body of lit-erature on policy making in the EU and identify three aspects of the European political system, which are normatively problematic. In the last sections of the paper we suggest dealing with these problems by the implementation of decisions by lot. Our reform agenda includes: (1) a weighted lottery in order to distribute a reduced number of positions within the European Commission among the EU member states; (2) the drawing of lots for the members, the chairpersons and the rapporteurs of the European Parliament's committees; and finally (3) the introduc-tion of a second chamber of the European Parliament whose members are chosen by lottery among all EU citizens.

1 Introduction

Today, the political system of the European Union (EU) is facing its most serious challenge since the early 1970s. On the one hand, the reactions to the financial and economic crisis demonstrate the lack of ability of the European political system to reach strong and mutually binding policy decisions. On the other hand, the Irish vote against the Lisbon Treaty in the summer of 2008 has left European politicians confused about the future of the EU. Both the necessity to come to terms with the financial cri-sis and the Irish veto have made it evident that the EU needs to reconsider its reform agenda and its further development as a political system. Times of crisis are also times when fresh new visions of the future can be developed. Our paper was written with the intention to contribute to this debate, because, in our view, now is the time to develop a vision of a future European political system that is more acceptable to its citizens.

The suggestion we are going to outline is based on the idea of using the productive and democratic potential of lotteries for the political system of a reformed EU. Political scientists have been observing the institutional development of the EU closely and critically for years. For them the attempt to create a post-national mode of democracy is an ideal case to study. The problems faced by the EU in realising its intentions have caused some observers to suggest that the democratic standards necessary to legitimate the European political project should simply be reduced. Others, however, call for further reforms in order to turn the EU into a role model for future forms of supra- and transnational democracies.[1] Despite all talk about 'multi-level-systems' and 'comitology', both sides in this debate still adhere to the traditional institutional model of the modern democratic nation state. Our article intends to step in at this point of the current debate. To do this we temporarily put our familiar ideas about how a democracy should be organised to one side. Instead, we perform an institutional thought experiment and consider how the (once common) lottery could provide a viable political instrument with which to address these problems.

Since early antiquity the normative core of 'democracy' has been defined as a political order based on the political equality of its members in the collective decision-making process. Such a minimal definition, however, reveals no information about the procedures at work or about the design of democratic institutions. Both the procedures and the designs have varied considerably since the emergence of the first governmental systems which carried the name 'democracy' and both have since been the subject of intense debates and disputes. An historical review, however, reveals a basic pattern. In first generation democracies ancient city states like the *polis* of Athens made use of the instrument of direct voting in the legislative process in the popular assembly and used the instrument of lotteries to fill offices, seats on committees or offices in the courts. After the fall of the Greek *poleis*, 'democracy' became a term of invective for nearly two millennia. Only since the end of the eighteenth century, have newly emerging political systems in North America and Western Europe

---

1   See for the first point of view: Andrew Moravcsik, 'In Defence of the "Democratic Deficit": Reassessing Legitimacy in the European Union', *Journal of Common Market Studies*, 40, 2002, p.603–24, and also see Glyn Morgan, *The Idea of a European Superstate: Public Justification and European Integration*, Princeton University Press, 2005. * For the second point of view see Jürgen Habermas, *The Divided West*, Polity, Cambridge 2006.

claimed the ancient name of 'democracy' again. Their proponents could do so successfully because they performed a first territorial transformation of the democratic concept by adapting the former institutional systems — which suited the small scope of the ancient city state — to larger states on a national level. The new democracies belong to the *second generation* of mass democracies. Their democratic features include parliaments (instead of popular assemblies), the extension of the separation of powers (instead of the sovereignty of the *ecclesia*), as well as the election of representatives and other office holders (instead of decisions by lot). Our understanding of 'democracy' is still shaped by these institutional and procedural patterns.

From the point of view of such a general historical perspective, the emergence of supranational regimes like the EU raises the question whether a *second territorial transformation* of democracy to the post-national constellation will succeed and, if so, what kind of change in its institutional patterns will be required to effect this transformation. With respect to the prospects of a fully democratically constituted EU, it can be argued against all skeptics and pessimists that crucial socio-cultural preconditions for such a democratic transformation already exist, namely economic networks, the changed lifestyle of the younger generations and the opportunities provided by new communication technologies. In comparison to these aspects, the adaptation of political institutions still lags behind. Neither the former proposal of a 'constitution' nor the currently suggested 'contract' of the European Union is sufficient to fill this institutional gap.

At this point our proposal comes into play. It is based on the idea of reintroducing the lottery as a democratic decision-making procedure. We suggest deploying the instrument of decision by lot at three crucial institutional levels within the political system of the EU. Our attempt to implement chance mechanisms intentionally in the realm of politics may seem irritating or even absurd at first glance since our modern common sense associates decision making by lot with irrationality or the admission of helplessness. From a theoretical point of view, however, things appear to be much more complex because both systems theory and rational-choice theory discovered the virtues of randomness for modern societies some twenty years ago. From the point of view of systems theory, Niklas Luhmann recommended to 'take advantage of the application of chances to create structures in more and more complex societies'.[2] And in the camp of rational-choice theorists, Jon Elster reconstructed the use of lot-

---

2   Niklas Luhmann, 'Vom Zufall verwöhnt. Eine Rede über Kreativität', *Frankfurter Allgemeine Zeitung*, 10 July, 1987.

teries under certain circumstances as a 'second order rationality'.[3] Supported by such constructive views of the potentially rational effects of lotteries, we will present the arguments supporting our case in the following discussion. In particular we want to argue that an intentional implementation of chance in certain institutional features of the political system of the EU has the potential to address the democratic deficit and deal successfully with the problems of inefficiency and the lack of transparency that currently exists within the European institutional system.

Our arguments will be outlined in four major steps. First, we want to indicate that we can already discover a renaissance of the lottery in some political practices of modern democracies (2). Next, we identify three well-known aspects of the current political system of the EU that are problematic from a perspective of any normative democratic theory: the inefficiency of the European Commission, the hotly debated 'democratic deficit' and finally the lack of transparency in politics in the EU (3). In the third step we will outline when, where and to what extent the implementation of random mechanisms could deal with these deficiencies. In particular, we advocate a weighted lottery to distribute a reduced number of positions within the European Commission among the EU member states; the drawing of lots for the members, the chairpersons and the rapporteurs of the European Parliament's committees; and finally the introduction of a second chamber of the European Parliament made up of members chosen by lottery from all EU citizens (4). In the final section we will defend our suggestions against some potential objections and try to place our reform agenda in a broader framework. Facing the necessity of undergoing a second territorial transformation in a global age, modern democracies are at a decisive turning point. They will either turn into post-democracies or they will be able to catch up with the post-national realities by turning into *democracies of a third generation*. In our view, a clever mix of electoral and randomizing procedures can successfully meet the challenge of institutionalizing trans- and supranational forms of democracy. A reform agenda that complements electoral procedures with a selective implementation of lotteries may even constitute a paradigmatic contribution to the successful second territorial transformation of democracy (5).

2 The lottery as a political instrument today

After an interruption of nearly two hundred years, we can observe a new renaissance of the lot as an instrument in the political toolkit.[4] The out-

---

3   See Elster (1989) in Bibliography, pp. 36–122.
4   For a more detailed history of the lot see Manin (1997) and Buchstein (2009).

come of the debate on the recruitment of jury members in trials in the
United States in the 1960s was crucial for this rediscovery.[5] The traditional ways of picking or choosing members of the juries were discrimi-
nating against minorities. The Federal Law of 1968 provided that new
jury members had to be picked among all citizens of the concerned juridi-
cal district by drawing lots. The judicial sphere became the starting point
of an expansion of lottery practices to other politically relevant spheres.
The 'Harvard Study Group' around John Rawls and other academics proposed the employment of a lottery to determine the recruits among the
draftees for the war in Vietnam. This was introduced in 1970.[6] Furthermore, lotteries were beginning to be advocated as a means of distributing
scarce goods such as medicines.[7] Finally, with Robert A. Dahl's suggestion to appoint members of committees on the level of local politics by
drawing lots, mechanisms of chance re-entered the stage of democratic
theory.[8]

Since then the lottery has become the main issue in a new wave of theoretical work of social scientists, political philosophers and democratic theorists as well as those who are interested in practical issues concerning the
application of lotteries. Four strands may be distinguished in the recent
theoretical and practical discussions on the pros and cons of the lot in
politics:

In the field of decision theory, the work of Jon Elster and Frederick
Engelstad summarizes the debates of a 'second order rationality' of the lot
by emphasizing the rational potential of chance mechanisms in certain
constellations.[9]

In the field of political philosophy, researchers have focused on the fairness of the distribution of goods and offices via lotteries.[10]

Third, the lottery has recently attracted the attention of scientists in the
field of the history of political ideas.[11]

---

5   See Abramson (1994). Also see Akhil R. Amar and Adam Hirsch, *For the People. What the Constitution Really Says about Your Rights*, Free Press, New York, 2006.

6   See Harvard Study Group, 'On the Draft', *The Public Interest*, 9, 1967, pp. 93–9. Also see Fienberg (1971), pp. 255–61.

7   See John F. Kilner, *Who Lives? Who Dies? Ethical Criteria in Patient Selection*, Yale University Press, New Haven, 1990, pp. 192–207 * Also see Claudia Wiesemann and Nikola Biller-Andorno, *Medizinethik. Für die neue AO*, Thieme, Stuttgart/New York, 2007, p. 65.

8   See Dahl (1970), p. 149.

9   See Greely (1977), pp. 113–41; Fishburn (1978), pp. 133–52; Elster (1989); Duxbury (1999); Engelstad (1989), pp. 23–50.

10   See Harris (1975); Sher (1980), pp. 203–16; Broome (1984), pp. 38–55; Goodwin (2005); Stone (2007), pp. 276–95; Saunders (2008), pp. 359–72.

11   See Mulgan (1984), pp. 539–60; Manin (1997); Dowlen (2008); Buchstein (2009).

The final and latest strand is outlined in the work of James F. Fishkin
and others in the area of democratic theory and practical pilot projects.
Under headings such as 'Deliberative Opinion Poll', 'Citizen Jury' or
'Planning Cell', they promote the idea of including randomly picked citizens in the political process.[12]

All in all, these debates give rise to the general question about the future
role of lotteries within the political system of modern democracies. A
closer look at current practices indicates that the lot once again has succeeded in playing a certain role in modern politics. If we analyze these
practices from a functionalist point of view, three main functions of the lot
can be distinguished: first, as a technique to regulate cases of political
indifference (2.1); second, as a tool to enforce political deliberation and
compromise (2.2); and third, as an instrument to include more strata of
society in the processes of political deliberation (2.3).

2.1 Regulation of indifference

The drawing of the lot is a classical instrument when attempting to handle
situations of indifference. In a situation of indifference a rational decision
cannot be taken because none of the existing choices convey any noticeable distinction upon which to base a preference (like two identical copies
of a book on the shelf of a store). Jon Elster refers to such cases as cases of
'absolute indifference'. According to him, the employment of random
mechanisms to come to a decision in such situations is a matter of a 'second order rationality'.[13]

The alternative to drawing the lot would be to come to no decision at all.
In order to avoid such an impasse, a lottery technique, such as tossing a
coin or drawing a piece of wood, serves as *the* classical tie breaker. When
employed to solve situations of indifference, the lottery is used to decide

---

12   See Fishkin (1995) and by the same author, 'Beyond Polling Alone: The Quest for an Informed
     Public', *Critical Review*, 18, 2006, pp. 157–66. * Also see Carson & Martin (1999); Dienel (1995);
     Röcke (2005). * Graham Smith and Corinne Wales, 'Citizens' Jurys and Deliberative
     Democracy' in Passerin d'Entrèves ed., *Democracy as Public Deliberation*, Transaction Publ.
     New Brunswick, 2006, pp. 157–77. * Mark B. Brown, 'Citizen Panels and the Concept of
     Representation', *The Journal of Political Philosophy*, 14, 2006, pp. 203–25. * Joan Font and Ismael
     Blanco, 'Procedural Legitimacy and Political Trust. The Case of Citizen Juries in Spain',
     European Journal of Political Research, 40, 2007, pp. 557–89.

13   Elster presents a list of four situational settings in which the second order rationality of
     decisions by chance comes into play. First the above mentioned situation of 'absolute
     indifference', second situations of 'indeterminacy within limits' (imagine for example a
     multitude of applicants for a job, who are equally qualified in all relevant aspects. In this case
     further research to determine qualitative differences between them would be more costly than
     the goods they might produce). Third, cases of complete 'uncertainty', i.e., when it is
     impossible to base one's decision on any considerable information due to a lack of
     information. The final group of cases includes incommensurable goods or preference orders
     which are incomparable. See Elster (1989), p. 38ff.

among options that are all supported by the same number of good reasons or, are backed up by an equal number of votes — a fact that may be of more practical relevance. As a tie breaker the lot is not employed until all other political procedures like deliberation or the casting of votes have been applied to the decision-making process without achieving a decisive outcome.

In modern democracies, the relevance of the lot as a tie breaker is closely connected to the rules of parliamentarism.[14] To start out with some German examples, the standing orders of the electoral body for the German president, the Federal Assembly (Bundesversammlung), specify that lot should be used to decide between the final two candidates in case of a tie between the two opposing factions. In addition, the lot comes into play in cases in which political parties are equally represented in a State Parliament (Landtag) and are therefore entitled to the same number of seats in the Federal Assembly. At the moment this is the case in three German States (Berlin, Hessen, Lower Saxonia). Hence for the next presidential election in May 2009 three seats of the Federal Assembly have to be drawn by lot.[15] Decisions by lot are also included in the standing orders of the Bundestag. If, in the election of the Speaker, no candidate is able to rally a simple majority of the votes after three ballots, the lot — drawn by the oldest member of the House — is to be used to decide which one of the two candidates who received the most votes is to be chosen.[16] The lot is also used to determine the order of the distribution of committee members of the parliament in cases where there are two eligible parliamentary groups of equal size.[17] A similar provision can be found in most State parliaments. In the State of Bavaria, the provisions even include the use of the lot in case of a tie between rival candidates for the office of Prime Minister.[18]

A comparative overview of twenty-one European countries by Björn Erik Rasch reveals the extent to which the lot is incorporated in parliamentarian procedures.[19] As in Germany, in most countries the election

14 The application of the lot in rules of procedures in modern parliaments was inspired by Jeremy Bentham's reflections on the internal organization of parliaments in his 'political tactics'. See Jeremy Bentham, *Political Tactics* [1st edn 1791], Oxford University Press, Oxford, 1999.

15 According to the law on the Federal President's election (Art. 4, paragraph 3), the number of seats taken on by each State (Bundesland) are decided upon individually in each of the States according to the system of d'Hondt. It reads as follows: 'The decision on the distribution of the last seat will be taken by lot if there is a tie. The lot will be drawn by the Speaker of the State parliament' [our own translation].

16 See rules of procedure of the German Bundestag from 26 September 2006 (Art. 2, paragraph 2).

17 Ibid., Art. 11, paragraph 2.

18 See rules of procedure of the Bavarian Landtag from 9 July 2003 (Art. 45).

19 In the case of a tie the lot is employed in the election of the President of parliaments in Austria, Denmark, Finland, Germany, Iceland, the Netherlands, Norway and Sweden. See Björn Erik

regulations provide for the use of the lot in the case of an electoral tie among candidates for a seat in the parliament. There are practical aspects to consider when evaluating such provisions. Recently, in an election in the Philippines in May 2007 the tie between two candidates in the municipal elections led to a debate whether it was better to draw straws or to toss a coin (the candidates chose the second option).[20] In the United States, a tie at a caucus between the two candidates Barack Obama and Hillary Clinton during the Democratic primaries in the State of Nevada was decided in Las Vegas by drawing a poker card.[21]

In Sweden, between 1973 and 1976 the government and the opposition had exactly the same number of seats in parliament. During this three-year period the parliament used lot to determine policy issues every time a vote resulted in a tie between the two sides.[22]

2.2 Enforcing political compromises

The second function of lotteries in modern political systems is based on the logic of making a decision 'in the shadow of a lottery'.[23] Here, the role of the lot is quite different from the cases mentioned in the section above. 'In the shadow of a lottery' is a metaphor for the strategy that proposes lotteries in order to force participants in the decision making processes to come to terms with each other *in order to avoid* a decision by lot. The lot itself and the associated risk of losing by chance is a threat that motivates conflicting parties to look for a compromise. If no compromise can be found within a certain limit of time, the conflict will be solved by chance instead of reason. This kind of mechanism has been practiced in Scandinavian family courts; and in rare instances, it has recently been applied to standing orders in the political sphere as well. [24]

Again, an example from Germany may illustrate the functional potential of the lot. When the liberal FDP and the social-democratic SPD formed a coalition in the State of Rhineland-Palatinate in 1996, they included a rule in their coalition contract stipulating that when no agreement or compromise could be reached regarding their State's vote in the Second

---

Rasch, 'Parliamentary Voting Procedures' in Döhring ed., *Parliaments and Majority Rule in Western Europe*, Campus, Frankfurt/Main, New York, 1995, pp. 488–527, p. 500.

20   See 'Coin toss decides Philippine poll',
www.news.bbc.co.uk/2/hi/asia-pacific/6674373.stm>, 2008/10/05.

21   See 'Clinton wins precinct tie with queen of hearts', in CNN Political Ticker, 19 January 2008, www.politicalticker.blogs.cnn.com/2008/01/19/clinton-wins-precinct-tie-with-queen-of-hearts>, 2008/11/12.

22   See Detlef Jahn, 'Das politische System Schwedens' in Ismayr ed., *Politische Systeme in Westeuropa*, Leske & Budrich, Opladen, 2003, pp. 93–130, p. 101.

23   See Duxbury (1999), p. 161.

24   See Duxbury (1999), p. 161–5.

Chamber on the federal level (Bundesrat), a lottery should be held to decide which party's view should prevail.[25] Following the statement of the liberal politician Peter Caesar who invented this part of the agreement, the lot was never intended to be utilized in practice. Instead, the agreement was intended to increase the pressure on the coalition parties to create political compromises in due time so as to avoid submitting themselves to the principle of pure chance.[26] And as a matter of fact, the lot was never employed during the term of the coalition between 1996 and 2001. Political analysts have dubbed the agreement as a 'smart solution' to come to terms with quarrelsome coalition partners and praised its hidden rationality. They particularly suggested including such agreements in the coalition contracts of contentious coalitions.[27]

2.3 Bringing all social strata back into the political process

Recently, the lot has begun to fulfill a third function. It is now being employed in a new generation of deliberative institutions. Most pilot projects like the so-called 'Deliberative Opinion Poll', the 'Planning Cell' or the 'Citizen Jury' rely on a random mode of recruitment. Prominent among these projects are James S. Fishkin's Deliberative Opinion Polls. These pick up an idea from Robert A. Dahl, which suggests asking groups of citizens chosen at random among the community members to deliberate policy issues with officials.[28] Based on this idea, Fishkin developed a conceptual framework for a Deliberative Opinion Poll. Instead of creating an opinion poll by simply asking citizens about their opinions on political issues, Fishkin's formula gives citizens the opportunity to discuss these issues among each other during a weekend conference and to get additional information before expressing their opinion. A growing number of political scientists around the globe have conducted more than a hundred 'Deliberative Opinion Polls' in the last couple of years.[29]

Although these projects differ in some details, they basically follow the same pattern: a group of citizens who are representative for a region or a country are invited to meet for a couple of days to discuss a certain political issue. In order to create a socially representative group, the participants are picked by a random mechanism. All participants are free to

25 See Sabine Kropp, *Regieren in Koalitionen. Handlungsmuster und Entscheidungsbildung in deutschen Länderregierungen*, Westdeutscher Verlag, Wiesbaden, 2001, p. 145f.
26 See 'Bei Streit soll das Los entscheiden', *Die Welt*, 29 April 1996, p. 5.
27 See Kropp, op.cit., p. 45; also see F. Pappi, A. Becker and A. Herzog, 'Regierungsbildung in Mehrebenensystemen. Zur Erklärung der Koalitionsbildung in deutschen Bundesländern', *Politische Vierteljahresschrift*, 46, 2005, pp. 432–58, p. 435.
28 See Dahl (1970), pp. 148–51.
29 The original framework is described in James S. Fishkin, *Democracy and Deliberation. New Directions for Democratic Reform*, Yale University Press, New Haven, 1991, pp. 81–103.

collect additional information in advance and receive a considerable remuneration for their engagement. During the meetings of the group participants are encouraged to discuss different policy options with each other in different deliberative settings and are responsible for working out a general policy recommendation.[30]

The empirical evaluation indicates that, for the most part, these projects live up to the intentions of their creators.[31] As the participants are chosen with the help of the lottery system, the deliberative bodies in the Deliberative Opinion Polls closely resemble the social characteristics of the population in general. Even though the selected groups do not perfectly match the social statistical cross-section of the population — which is never perfectly possible — they nevertheless show a much higher degree of social heterogeneity than the members of all other institutions within the political system.[32] More important from the point of view of a demanding normative approach of deliberative democracy is the fact that the participants of Deliberative Opinion Polls did indeed change their political opinions in the course of the deliberations towards much more informed and reflective policy recommendations. Deliberate Opinion Polls initiate a process of 'political learning'[33] which is, at least to some extent, a result of the social heterogeneity of the deliberative settings produced by the random selection mechanism.[34] The positive results of the projects that

30   Topics of some of the workshops carried out in the past concerned a great variety of issues such as family policies (USA), the abolition of monarchy (Australia), tax policies (Great Britain) or the introduction of the Euro (Denmark). The Danish government has been arranging these 'Consensus Conventions' regularly for more than twenty years. Some of the topics discussed in the past are: green gene technology (in 1987), air pollution (in 1990), the limits of fertility techniques for humans (in 1993), electronic surveillance of the public sphere (in 2000) or financing public roads (in 2002).

31   For an overview of the empirical evidence from the point of view of Fishkin and his group see Bruce A. Ackerman and James S. Fishkin, *Deliberation Day*, New Haven: Yale University Press, New Haven, 2004. * Also see James S. Fishkin and Cynthia Farrar, 'Deliberative Polling. From Experience to Community Resource' in Gastil and Levine eds, *The Deliberative Handbook*, Wiley & Sons, San Francisco, 2005, pp. 68–79. * For the evaluation of other projects see Lyn Carson and Brian Martin, 'Random Selection of Citizens for Technological Decision Making', *Science and Public Policy*, 29, 2002, pp. 105–113. * David M. Ryfe, 'The Practice of Deliberative Democracy. A Study of 16 Deliberative Organizations', *Political Communication*, 19, 2002, pp. 359–77. * Carolyn M. Hendriks, 'Consensus Conferences and Planning Cells' in Gastil and Levine eds, *The Deliberative Democracy Handbook*, Wiley & Sons, San Francisco, 2004, pp. 80–110. * Eva J. Schweitzer, *Deliberative Polling. Ein demoskopischer Ausweg aus der Krise der politischen Kommunikation?* Deutscher Universitätsverlag, Wiesbaden, 2004. * Smith and Wales, op. cit., 2006 (see note 12).

32   See Carson and Martin, op. cit., 2002, pp. 109–12; Brown, op. cit., 2006 (see note 12).

33   See Fishkin and Farrar, op. cit., 2005, p. 76 (see note 31).

34   The evaluation of expressed preferences shows that they are based on more factual knowledge and are logically more consistent than before the deliberative process. In addition, they take the complexity of the given problems more seriously into account. For empirical evidence of these findings see Carson and Martin, op. cit, 2002, pp. 112–25. * Also see James S.

have been carried out so far permit a more general conclusion: the use of lot in order to create deliberative political institutions offers a promising opportunity to breach the gap between the demanding participatory and epistemic norms of deliberate democratic theory.

2.4 The multiple functions of the lot

The recent comeback of the lot in the political realm could be interpreted as a starting point for thinking more seriously about the functional capacity of decisions by lot within the institutional system of modern democracies. The practices and experiences with political lotteries mentioned in the sections above demonstrate that decisions by lot are supposed to fulfill specific functions. In addition, the instrument of the lottery can be adapted to different institutional contexts. This finding is in line with the historical fact that the lot has fulfilled more purposes than simply serving as a tool in radical democracies. Both in democratic and aristocratic Athens the lot was introduced as a kind of 'anti-corruptivum' for the distribution of offices that were highly susceptible to bribes (like the courts or the decision to place construction orders).[35] In the Northern Italian city republics lotteries fulfilled the function of neutralizing the power struggle between the competing elites and served to defend the aristocracy against the lower orders.[36]

The acknowledgment of such a variety of functions has recently evoked the idea among political scientists and economists that there may be additional ways for modern democracies to profit from the merits of chance mechanisms. Whereas in some contributions to this discussion lotteries have a rather heuristic status, other authors are more serious in their intentions.[37] The list of practical suggestions includes the following ideas: drawing of lots to determine the dates of re-election (within a certain time span) in order to minimize the negative effects of the political business cir-

Fishkin and R.C. Luskin, 'Experimenting with a Democratic Ideal: Deliberative Polling and Public Opinion', *Acta Politica*, 40, 2005, pp. 284–98, pp. 292–6. * Vibeke Normann Andersen and Kasper M. Hansen, 'How Deliberation Makes Better Citizens. The Danish Deliberative Poll on the Euro', *European Journal of Political Research*, 46, 2007, pp. 531–56.

35   See Hansen (1991).

36   See Machiavelli, *History of Florence and of the Affairs of Italy. From the Earliest Times to the Death of Lorenzo the Magnificent* [1525], Harper and Row, New York, 1960. * Also see Najemy (1982), p. 124–8.

37   See the discussion on a so-called 'Queen for a Day' lottery by David Estlund in his epistemic democracy theory: David Estlund, 'Beyond Fairness and Deliberation. The Epistemic Dimension of Democratic Authority' in Bohman and Regh eds, *Deliberative Democracy*, MIT Press Cambridge, Mass., 1997, pp. 173–204. * Another 'heuristic proposal' was recently presented by John McCormick: he suggests to draw lots in order to fill a 'tribunate assembly' as an additional chamber in the US-legislative with full veto power in order to counter the influence of 'big money': see John S. McCormick, *The European Union. Politics and Policies*, Westview Press, Boulder, 2008, p. 159.

cle;[38] combining the casting of votes with the participation in lottery-jack-pots in order to encourage voter turnout;[39] composing electoral districts by lot;[40] distributing the elected members of parliament among the parliamentary committees by lot;[41] introducing a 'plebiscite chamber' of five per cent of the population, which is responsible for deciding upon national referenda for a time span of one year;[42] selecting the order of primaries in the US by a random mechanism;[43] the introduction of lottery chambers to consult politicians on the local level or even to act as decision making bodies;[44] or the idea of combining a first round of elections for members of parliament with a lottery for the final selection in order to increase the influence of minorities.[45] Some reform proposals already refer to the level of the European Union. A 2004 European Council Green Paper by Philippe Schmitter and Alexander Trechsel suggested that, to encourage participation, voters for European Parliamentary elections should be given tickets to a lottery. The winners would not receive any money, however, but would have the right to allocate certain state funds to beneficial causes of their choice.[46] Finally we would like to mention the suggestion by Gerd Grötzinger who suggests introducing a lottery among the member states of the EU in order to distribute the positions of the EU commissioners.[47]

38 See Victor Ginsburgh and Philippe Michel, 'Random Timing of Elections and the Political Business Circle', *Public Choice*, 40, 1983, pp. 155–64 * Florian Felix Weyh, *Die letzte Wahl. Therapien für die leidende Demokratie*, Eichborn, Frankfurt/Main, 2007 p. 219f.

39 See Hubertus Buchstein, 'Das Verschwinden der armen Wahlhelfer', *Leviathan*, 32, 2004, pp. 309–18. This idea was exercised during the parliamental elections in Bulgaria in 2005. However, even though a car, DVD-players and cell phones were raffled off, the turnout dropped to a historical low of 55.8%; see 'Bulgaria's Election Lottery', *BBC-News*, 25 June 2005, www.news.bbc.co.uk/2/low/programmes>, 2008/01/25.

40 See Klaus Schweinsberg, *Demokratiereform*, Shaker, Aachen, 2003, pp. 276–8.

41 See Richard Thaler, 'The Mirages of Public Policy', *Public Interest*, 73, 1983, pp. 61–74, p. 72 * Also see Weyh op.cit., (note 38), pp. 217–19.

42 See Marcus Schmidt, 'Institutionalizing fair Democracy. The Theory of Minipopulous', *Futures*, 33, 2001, pp. 361–70.

43 See William G. Mayer, 'An Incremental Approach to Presidential Nomination Reform', *PS: Political Science and Politics*, 42, no.1, 2009, pp. 65-9.

44 See Weyh, op. cit., 2007, pp. 198–211. Also see Burnheim (1985).

45 See Akhil R. Amar, 'Voting Rights and Elections. Lottery Voting — A Thought Experiment', paper presented to the University of Chicago Legal Forum, 1995.

46 See Philippe Schmitter and Alexander Trechsel, *The Future of Democracy in Europe. A Green Paper for the Council of Europe*, Council of Europe, Strasbourg, 2004. www.coe.int/t/e/integrated_projects/democracy/Green%20Paper.doc>, 2008/01/28, p. 88.

47 See Gerd Grötzinger, 'Die Vereinigten Parlamente von Europa und weitere Überlegungen zur subsidiären Demokratie' in Offe ed., *Demokratisierung der Demokratie. Diagnosen und Reformvorschläge*, Campus, Frankfurt/Main, New York, 2003, pp. 211-31, p. 219f.

We do not want to address the pros and cons of the suggestions on this list in detail here.[48] This list in itself already illustrates that the set of ideas for reforming modern democracies is changing: the lottery *per se* is not taboo anymore and has risen from its long lasting oblivion to take its place within the modern political toolkit. Picking up on this new tendency, we want to outline ways that lotteries could be used to cope with some of the crucial problems of the EU political system.

3 A critical diagnosis of the EU: democratic deficit, inefficiency and non-transparency

The politics of European integration on the level of the EU have already been in a serious crisis before the financial crisis. The Irish vote against the Lisbon Treaty in the summer of 2008 and the, at least temporary, reluctance of the Czech and Polish parliaments to sign the treaty have put the EU in a sort of waiting-room. From a democratic point of view, the result of the Irish vote has to be considered a total disaster: the only country where the citizens had the opportunity to vote directly on these substantial changes of the European political order, failed to produce democratic support for the measures. Since then, the reform process of the EU has been stuck in a deadlock and will only recover from its agonizing rebuttal if a new and promising political perspective emerges. Such a solution not only needs to cope with the problem of the so-called 'democratic deficit'. It also needs to consider the problems of European inefficiency and non-transparency as well. This is exactly the point where our proposal to bring the lottery back into the procedures of modern politics comes into play.

But before presenting our reform propositions in more detail, we will take a closer look at the critical debates on the recent democratic state of the political system of the EU. Armin Schäfer suggests that we distinguish between four main positions within the masses of literature:[49] (a) First, the *optimists*, who argue that a democratization of the Union is desirable and feasible. They want to model the reform agenda for the European institutions on the model of the nation state.[50] (b) Second, the *pessimists*, who argue that even though the democratization of the European institutions

48 A detailed discussion of the different proposals can be found in Buchstein (2009).
49 See Armin Schäfer, 'Nach dem permissiven Konsens. Das Demokratiedefizit der Europäischen Union, *Leviathan*, 34, 2006, pp. 350–76.
50 See Andreas Follesdal and Simon Hix, 'Why There is a Democratic Deficit in the EU: A Response to Majone and Moravcsik', *European Governance Papers (EUROGOV)*, 2005, no. C-05-02, www.connex-network.org/eurogov/pdf/egp-connex-C-05-02.pdf>, 2007/12/06. * Also see Hauke Brunkhorst, 'Unbezähmbare Öffentlichkeit—Europa zwischen transnationaler Klassenherrschaft und egalitärer Konstitutionalisierung', *Leviathan*, 35, 2007, pp. 12–29.

may be worthwhile it is at the same time impossible. They name the following deficiencies: the lack of a common European identity, the lack of solidarity and the lack of a European public sphere that includes its organizational structures. According to their view, these deficiencies would remain even after the institutional settings were reformed. Based on this assumption they critically argue that the attempt to democratize the EU would not only miss its target, but in addition would undermine democracy in the individual national states.[51] (c) Third, the *apologists* of the status quo consider a European democratization possible, but nonetheless they do not believe that it is worthwhile because the Union would lose its present capacity to act and produce policies efficiently.[52] (d) Finally, the *fatalists* who do not think that a European democratization is desirable at all, and do not even consider it to be a feasible option. In their view more political participation in a corporatist system of interest groups and policy networks not only misses the point of any normatively demanding concept of democratization, but also jeopardizes the stability and efficiency of the EU.[53]

Schäfer's typology provides an overview of the different camps within the complex debates about the European Union and its democratic quality and future. However, it systematically excludes one additional position within this debate. This is the one we take: namely that democratization is a desirable goal, but that such a goal cannot be fulfilled if we simply try to transfer the features of our national political institutions to the level of the EU. Starting out with the diagnosis of the *pessimists'* view, we want to give it a more constructive twist. In particular we agree with their statement that the main obstacle to the democratization of the EU so far is the lack of a common European identity and public sphere. However, we disagree with their pessimistic view of the potential reform options.

The lack of a common language, deficiencies with respect to a European mass media system and European political parties as well as the persistence of national identities cannot be moderated by simply strengthening the role of the European Parliament within the political system of the EU.

---

51   See Dieter Grimm, 'Does Europe Need a Constitution?', *European Law Journal*, 1, 1995, pp. 282–302. * Peter Graf Kielmansegg, 'Integration und Demokratie' in Kohler-Koch and Jachtenfuchs eds, *Europäische Integration*, Leske und Budrich, Opladen, 2nd edn, 2003, p. 49–83.

52   See Moravcsik, op. cit., 2002 (see note 1). Also see Peter Mair, 'Popular Democracy and the European Union Polity', *European Governance Papers (EUROGOV)*, 2005, no. C-05-03, www.connex-network.org/eurogov/pdf/egp-connex-C-05-03.pdf>, 2007/10/19. Also see Morgan, op.cit., 2005 (note 1).

53   See Matthew J. Gabel, 'The Endurance of Supranational Governance: A Consociational Interpretation of the European Union', *Comparative Politics*, 30, 1998, pp. 463–75.

It is most likely that this would have the opposite effect: the national executives would be strengthened compared to their national parliaments.
The proposed solution of the *apologists* does not lead to any improvement
of the deficit either. The radius of the output legitimacy of European politics is limited and cannot solve the problem, since such a form of legitimacy only functions in cases of non-redistributive policy decisions and
most of the EU-decisions are distributive and do not fall into this category.[54] Nor does the realization of the idea to install a president of the EU
provide for a higher level of democratization.[55]

Thus, current suggestions to cope with the democratic deficit of the EU,
such as presidentialization, parliamentarization and output legitimacy
still refer to the model of a nation state as their conceptual framework.
These suggestions do not consider the option of looking for institutional
designs that go beyond this traditional model. In our view the democratization of the EU can only be achieved by *developing new institutional
forms* – and at this point our plea to contemplate the potential of the lottery as a political instrument comes back in. We want to argue that the
implementation of decisions by lot in the political system of the EU not
only has the potential to reduce the democratic deficit but could also serve
to redress problems of non-transparency and inefficiency. Before we can
present specific lottery schemes as possible responses to the institutional
problems of the EU, however, we have to understand those problems in
greater detail. We will start with the issue of the growing inefficiency of
the executive branch, the European Commission (3.1). Second, we will
address the issue of non-transparency and the deficient democratization
of the institutional networks within the EU (3.2). Finally we will discuss
the problems concerning the definition and change of the contractual and
constitutional foundations of the EU (3.3).

3.1 The European Commission

Together with the Council of the EU and the European Parliament (EP),
the European Commission is one of the three main institutions in the
political system of the EU. The Commission has crucial authority over

54 See Fritz W. Scharpf, 'Legitimationskonzepte jenseits des Nationalstaats' in Schuppert,
    Pernice & Haltern eds, *Europawissenschaft*, Nomos, Baden-Baden, 2005, pp. 705–41, p. 714.
    According to Schäfer, op. cit., 2006, p. 371 (see note 49), Scharpf's conclusion is confirmed by
    an analysis of Eurobarometer surveys: 'From the perspective of EU citizens, the democratic
    deficit cannot be overcome by improving the problem solving capacity (= improving the
    output). In the EU, legitimacy depends on the possibility of citizens exerting influence and on
    the fact that decisions by the representatives of the electorate are not disconnected from the
    public opinion making process' [our own translation].
55 For such a suggestion see Frank Decker, 'Parlamentarisch oder präsidentiell?
    Entwicklungspfade des europäischen Regierungssystems nach dem Verfassungsvertrag',
    Zeitschrift für Staats – und Europawissenschaften, 5, 2007, pp. 181–202.

European legislation and has the competence to initiate it.[56] The president of the Commission is in charge for a period of five years. In order to be elected into office, he first needs a qualified majority of the Council for his nomination. Next he needs the absolute majority of the votes of the EP. The Commissioners of the EU are elected according to the same procedure by the EP — but they need to be recommended by both the new Commission's president and the Council beforehand.

The EU Commission has grown due to the enlargement of the EU based on the old founding era principle that every member state should be represented on the highest European political level. Currently, the number of twenty-seven Commissioners equals the number of the member states. It is common knowledge among observers of the EU that such a large number of commissioners is hardly efficient. This was evident once again after Bulgaria and Romania became members of the EU in 2007. It was nearly impossible to find new political task fields for the two new commissioners Meglena Kuneva and Leonard Orban. The problem was solved by extracting responsibility for consumer protection and multilingualism from the competencies of other commissioners and turning them into separate European tasks. Two problems follow from this model of enlarging the Commission. One is the question of the efficiency of such a division of political tasks, which has resulted in the creation of small and overlapping fields of competence. The other is the internal organization of such a big Commission, which has become increasingly complicated and inefficient over the last couple of years. To make things even more complicated, the traditional rule of 'one member state, one Commissioner' violates one of the normative kernels of the idea of the European Integration, because according to the contracts which were signed officially, the Commissioners are supposed to represent the entire European citizenry and not their national interests.[57]

Hence, the reduction of the number of Commissioners has become an obvious political necessity. The goal to reduce the Commission is even part of the modifications in the new European contracts. The enlargement protocol of the Treaty of Nice in 2001 already included the introduction of 'equal rotation' among the member states, even though the exact procedure of this rotation was not laid out in more detail. According to the protocol, the number of EU commissioners was to be reduced as soon as the EU welcomed its 27th member state so as to be smaller than the number of

---

56 McCormick, op. cit., 2008, pp. 245–62 (see note 37).
57 See Frank R. Pfetsch, *Die Europäische Union. Geschichte, Institutionen, Prozesse*, W. Fink, 3rd edn, München, 2005, p. 68.

member states.[58] However, as already mentioned above, a commissioner from both Bulgaria and Romania was appointed and the announced procedure of an 'equal rotation' was not put into practice after all. Some plans went even further. The draft of the 'Constitution for Europe' in 2003 even included a suggestion to reduce the number of Commissioners to only fifteen. In the draft, an 'equal rotation' principle was suggested as well (once again, without being laid out in detail).[59] The finalized 'Constitution for Europe' and again the 'Treaty of Lisbon', which has been ratified with legally binding effect by twenty-two of the twenty-seven member states so far, even go further as they entail a profound reduction in the number of commissioners. Beginning with the second Commission elected under the new rules, the Commission will be composed of Commissioners from only two-thirds of the member states. In order to determine the composition, 'a system of strictly equal rotation' is to be created in the future, in which 'the demographic and geographical range of all the Member States' is expressed.[60] However, the European Council has retained its right to revoke the rotation principle at any time it deems it to be necessary.

Considering all these developments, it remains to be seen whether the inefficiency problem in the Commission will be solved based on the regulations envisaged in the Lisbon Treaty. Most likely, once again, some single member states will feel at a disadvantage. And since the rotation procedure has to be passed unanimously, every member state has a veto position. Even if such a decision should ever be taken, one can imagine exhaustive negotiation processes because the rotation procedure has to be redrawn again every five years. Under such circumstances, the Commission's expectation to find a more efficient way to distribute the political tasks within the Commission and to find an adequate way to fill the offices among the member states should not be too high. Our suggestion in section 4 of this paper provides a way out of this stalemate by outlining a certain kind of lottery system for the Commission.

58 *Protocol on the Enlargement of the European Union*, Art. 4,
www.europa.eu/eur-lex/en/treaties/dat/C_2002325EN.016301.html>, 2008/11/14.

59 However, the President of the Commission was supposed to appoint additional Commissioners from all other member states to the Commission. These Commissioners would not have had the right to vote but at least all of the member states would have had a seat in the Commission. See *Draft Treaty establishing a Constitution for Europe*, Art. 25, www.european-convention.eu.int/docs/Treaty/cv00850.en03.pdf >, 2008/11/14.

60 *Treaty of Lisbon* amending *Treaty on European Union*, Art. 9a, Paragraph 5,
www.eur-lex.europa.eu/JOHtml.do?uri=OJ%3AC%3A2007%3A306%3ASOM%3AEN%3A
HTML>, 2008/11/14.

3.2 European policy making

Decisions on EU policies are divided into three so-called 'pillars'. The first pillar includes directives and regulations as the main form of supranational European legislation. They are the main instruments to regulate the areas of agriculture, economy, social and environmental policies. All three main institutions of the EU — the Commission, the Council and the Parliament — are involved in different ways to produce this legislation, mostly in the *co-decision* or the *co-operation* procedure.[61] However, not only are these procedures highly complicated, they are also non-transparent. They hardly allow for institutional accountability. This mode of legislation is also problematic from a normative point of view due to the tremendous influence of lobby groups on this legislation in areas such as the Committees of the European Parliament.[62]

The gradual increase in the political influence of the European Parliament has not led to any change in this problematic situation. Even though the EP is almost equal to the Council in the first pillar of the EU in terms of power, and even though the Commission now needs the consent of the EP during the entire term, the parliamentarization of the EU has only had a small impact on the problems mentioned above. According to Andreas Maurer, this critical diagnosis is based on three reasons:[63] first, the EP is not the central institution in the drafting of European legislation. The classical functions of a parliament — designing policies and political structures — are still weak (the EP has no competence to initiate bills and does not take part in all political matters of the EU). Second, within the EP there is no clear political distinction between government and opposition. The EP only serves a negative elective function regarding the election of the members of the Commission, i.e., the appointment of the Commissioners is subject to approval by the EP, and its power to check the Commission is limited. Thus it is not surprising that the EP does not develop political agendas of its own but acts more like an opponent to the Commission and

---

61   See Andreas Maurer, 'Das Europäische Parlament in der Gesetzgebung' in Maurer and Nickel eds, *Das Europäische Parlament. Supranationalität, Repräsentation und Legitimation*, Nomos, Baden-Baden, 2005, pp. 93–119. * Also see Andreas Maurer and Wolfgang Wessels, *Das Europäische Parlament nach Amsterdam und Nizza: Akteur, Arena oder Alibi?* Nomos, Baden-Baden, 2003.

62   On the other hand, the rather popular thesis of the increased inefficiency of designing policies in the EU cannot be confirmed: cf. Marcus Höreth, 'Entscheidungsfindung nach Nizza — die Europäische Kommission' in Zervakis and Cullen eds, *The Post-Nice Process: Towards a European Constitution*, Nomos, Baden-Baden, 2002, pp. 85–102. The opposite seems to be the case. The co-decision procedure takes less time than other procedures. The average amount of time for co-decision procedure decreases and procedures which take more than the average time are carried out by the Council. * Also see Andreas Maurer in Maurer and Nickel, op. cit., 2005, p. 110 (see note 61).

63   See Maurer, ibid., pp. 95–9.

the Council. Third, interaction *with* the EP and interest articulation *by* the EP are only weakly developed. Even though the political importance of the EP has grown over the last decades, voter turnout has continually fallen from sixty-three per cent in 1979 down to 45.5% in the last election in 2004. The members of the European Parliament are relatively unknown to their voters and the political interest for the European Parliament among the European citizenry increases cyclically before an election only to decrease again afterwards. This insignificance of the European Parliament in the eyes of the general public turns the egalitarian legitimacy principle of the EU into a pseudo-legitimacy. European Parliamentarism, according to a variation recently coined by Hauke Brunkhorst of a famous saying by Max Weber about the political constitution of the German Empire, is a *'strong parliamentarism without democracy'*.[64] So far, the vague definition of the 'qualified majority' in the Council of the EU, which is necessary in many realms of European legislation, has made things even less transparent. Nowadays, a 'qualified majority' comprises three features: first an absolute majority of member states (currently fourteen out of twenty-seven member states), second, and in addition, seventy-four percent of the assessed votes, and third, any member state may request verification that the votes cast in favor represent at least sixty-two per cent of the total EU population. This complex set of internal regulations needed to define a 'qualified majority' is supposed to be reformed by the Treaty of Lisbon, but the new rule is only supposed to be applied from 2017. The new qualified majority will be based on a double majority of fifty-five percent of all member states accounting for sixty-five per cent of the EU's population.

The second pillar consists of common foreign policy and security policy and the third of police and judicial co-operation in criminal matters. So far decisions taken within these pillars are based on the intergovernmental procedure. In the Treaty of Lisbon, the member states have agreed to retain this policy decision-making procedure for the time being. Member states can only decide unanimously on these issues and the EP has, at best a marginal influence on them. The fact that national executives are making decisions behind closed doors without being supervised by national parliaments or the EP is the main problem of political legitimacy in these areas. Since these policies include matters that are sensitive for member states, the parliamentarization of these fields is not to be expected in the near future. Thus the main opportunity to introduce reforms that would make political decisions more transparent lies in the area covered by the

---

64   Hauke Brunkhorst, op.cit., 2007, p. 25 (see note 50).

first pillar: the drafting and issuing of directives and regulations. In section 4, our proposals to introduce the lottery refer to this fact.

3.3 Designing the political system of the European Union

Nothing pointed out the democratic deficit of the European Union more than the failure of the referenda in France and the Netherlands on the Constitutional Treaty in 2005 and the subsequent political reactions to these failures. Instead of reacting to the reasons for the rejection by the majority of the people in those countries by making substantial changes to the treaty, European polity-makers have chosen to simply ignore the negative responses to their plans. The new 'Treaty of Lisbon' basically contains the old content of the European Constitution Contract and integrates it into the non-transparent and complicated contractual structure of the European Union. According to the former French President Valery Giscard d'Estaing the new attempt successfully reduces the danger of referenda with negative outcomes by avoiding any vocabulary which might implicitly or explicitly refer to the constitution.[65] So instead of proposing an innovative solution that would allow the fundamental order of the European Union to be decided democratically by the European Citizenry, representatives of the member states retreated behind closed doors – only to emerge with a new formula that was remarkably similar to the old one. It is not surprising that the new treaty was rejected by the only EU member where a new referendum was held in the summer of 2008. Before the Irish vote finally stopped the planned agenda, we were not faced with a *democratic deficit* with respect to the question of designing the political system of the EU but simply with the *absence of democracy*. In order to go against this tendency, our proposal in the next section includes a suggestion to use lotteries as an instrument to include the citizenry of the EU in policy issues.

4 A new role for sortition in the political system of the EU

We will now introduce an agenda to reform the political system of the EU that builds upon some of the functional potentials of lotteries displayed in the first two sections. In particular, our proposal includes three reform steps: a revised distribution of the seats in the EU Commission by a weighted lottery among all member states (4.1), the implementation of drawing lots to determine the members, the chairpersons and the rapporteurs for the committees of the European Parliament (4.2), and finally the

---

65   See Valery Giscard d'Estaing, 'The EU Treaty is the same as the Constitution', *The Independent*, 2007, 30 October.

installation of a 'House of Lots', a second chamber of the European Parliament consisting of EU citizens drawn by a weighted lottery (4.3).

4.1 The selection of countries appointing EU Commissioners via lottery

Following the intention of the Treaty Establishing a Constitution for Europe, we propose to reduce the number of Commissioners in the European Commission to fifteen members and to use a lottery to pick the countries of origin of the Commissioners among all member states.[66] The distribution of these fifteen offices should be carried out as a weighted lottery among all member states (currently twenty-seven) every five years at the beginning of a new term. The procedure by lottery guarantees fairness towards every member state. The basic criterion for the assessment of the weight in the lottery is the number of EU citizens of each country. In strict analogy to the elections of the EP, we further propose to apply the principle of *degressive proportionality* in order to calculate the exact quotas for the weighted lottery. Degressive proportionality was introduced by the Treaty of Lisbon in order to minimize the number of Parliamentarians in the European Parliament to 750 members. The degressive proportionality goes along with a slight under-representation of the larger member states like Germany (at max. twenty-three per cent) and an almost 900% over-representation of the smallest members like Malta or Luxemburg (see Table 1, columns 4–6).[67] According to such a formula even the smallest member states would have a noticeable influence in the EP, whereas the weight of the larger states would be weakened.[68]

Every five years, the weighted lottery would give every member state a chance to gain *one* seat in the Commission. The lottery could take place as a public ceremony, performed after the election to the EP, in which the

66   As mentioned above, the first part of our reform proposal refers to a suggestion by Gerd Grötzinger, op. cit, 2003, p. 229 (see note 47).

67   The definition by the European Parliament says 'that the principle of degressive proportionality means that the ratio between the population and the number of seats of each Member State must vary in relation to their respective populations in such a way that each Member from a more populous Member State represents more citizens than each Member from a less populous Member State and conversely, but also that no less populous Member State has more seats than a more populous Member State' (Report on the composition of the European Parliament, www.europarl.europa.eu/sides/getDoc.do?pubRef=-//EP//TEXT+REPORT+A6-2007-035 1+0+DOC+XML+V0//EN>, 2008/11/14; cf. ibid for details regarding the calculations). Nevertheless, this clear-cut definition was not fully employed in the treaty because Italy refused to have one seat less than the UK in the EP (although Italy has 1.8 million less inhabitants). Thus the EP is supposed to have 751 seats and the speaker is supposed to renounce his right to vote.

68   With a rigid proportionality, none of the 750 mandates would go exclusively to Malta or Luxemburg.

names of the member states for the new term of the Commission would be drawn from a lottery box. Apart from this change in procedure, there would be no change in the process of appointing the Commission's President and the Commissioners. The lot should not be introduced in order to depoliticize the process of determining the composition of the Commission and its internal division of responsibilities. In comparison to the current routine, the only, but nevertheless crucial, difference lies in downsizing the number of member states who gain the opportunity to nominate their candidate for a particular office among the Commissioners. Thanks to the chance mechanism of the lottery, every member state would have at least some opportunity to be among those who may present a candidate. Its chance of success would depend on its degressive proportional weight. While the large member states with proportionately large quotas would be very likely to be represented in every Commission they could still not be sure that they would be drawn. On the other hand, every small country would actually have a chance of appointing one of the Commissioners. Under this system, moreover, the Commissioners would have real political power and influence because the reduction of the number of Commissioners would also be accompanied by an elimination of the less important commissionerships such as the Commissioner for multilingualism. Therefore even smaller countries would have an incentive to opt for such a lottery, because it offers them a chance to appoint a commissioner with some real political power.

According to this formula, every member state would participate in the lotteries every new term. If necessary, the quotas would have to be adapted from time to time due to changing numbers of inhabitants in Europe. According to the rationale of such a lottery, the statistical 'law of great numbers' would lead to a distribution of the chances to nominate a Commissioner that would be closely related to the degressive proportionality quotas in the long run. Thus the political representation would also be comparable to that in the European Parliament.

Such a procedure could fulfil the requirements of the Treaty of Lisbon, which strives to take the demographic and geographic range of all member states into account. This use of the lottery would also have the crucial functional advantage of eliminating the time-consuming stalemates, irritations and potential conflicts that would arise if a process of collective bargaining were used to decide how to nominate a new, smaller, group of Commissioners. The lottery provides a comparatively easy way to generate a smaller Commission with efficiently organized fields of political responsibility and with better capacities to act politically. With the weighted lottery, not all of the member states would be represented in every Commission at any given point in time. However, each member state would still have an equal chance of getting one of the offices.

4.2 Selection of the members, chairpersons and rapporteurs of the committees of the European Parliament by lottery

As in national parliaments, the main work of the European Parliament does not take place in the plenary assembly but in the committees. As the political competence of the EP has increased, the committees have become more important and they have now taken over most of the work of the plenary assembly.[69] Members of Parliament are appointed to the respective committees on the basis of their specialist knowledge. Because every representative has a specialist area within their respective party, he or she will strive to become a member of the committee that coincides with this interest. Two consequences arise from this.

First, this system produces a high degree of continuity in the personnel making up the committees. This leads to an increase in the members' professional knowledge and experience on the one hand — but, on the other hand, it establishes long-lasting power structures and these begin to affect the nature of fundamental policy decisions. Due to lower re-election rates in the EP this effect is less distinctive than in some of the member states. However, according to the recent 'MEP Survey' the members of the EP chose their committee affiliation with respect to the following criteria: personal political interest (54.7%), occupational qualifications (53.9%), general political relevance of the issues dealt with in the committees (50.2%), and relevance of the issues dealt with in the committees to their own voters (34.5%).[70]

Second, such a system of allocation of the committee memberships is particularly susceptible to the influence of lobbyists. In the political decision-making process on the level of the EU, lobbying often takes place in a grey zone between legitimate practice and illegitimate political corruption. The influence of certain lobby groups is a serious matter of concern in public debates and has caused European citizens to lose confidence in their political representatives. However, lobbying should not always be viewed negatively. Lobbying is a legitimate form of representing interests. It provides special and technical knowledge and it also

---

69 See Virginie Mamadouh and Tapio Raunio, 'The Committee System: Powers, Appointments and Report Allocation', *Journal of Common Market Studies*, 41, 2003, pp. 333–51, p. 334.

70 See David Farrell *et al.*, 'A Survey of MEPs in the 2004–09 European Parliament', Paper presented to the Annual Conference of the American Political Science Association, Philadelphia, 31.08.–03.09.2006 www.lse.ac.uk/collections/EPRG/pdf/farrell_et_al_eprg_2006_MEP_survey.pdf>, 2007/12/04, p. 20.

gives decision-makers an advance indication of the potential success of
their decision. This kind of information can be of great value for good legislation. Thus lobbying may serve to assist in the communication between
society and politics. But despite these functional advantages, lobbyists
first and foremost try to influence decision-makers to push through their
particular political interests. To avoid being misunderstood, we would
like to point out that we do not want to repeat the populist and anti-plu-
ralist accusations against the system of interest groups in modern democracies. We would prefer to draw attention to the well-known fact that the
influence of interest groups varies between different groups and constituencies in society, and that the political influence that operates through
these channels is invariably uneven due to the differing abilities of these
groups to apply political pressure.[71]

How, then, can we diminish these political inequalities on the level of
European policy making? Over the past couple of years, empirical
research has indicated that — even when compared to the much higher
levels of pressure exerted on the Commission by lobbyists — lobbying has
now become an eminent factor in the decision making process of the EP. It
comes as no surprise that the degree of lobbyism has increased in parallel
with the increase of the political power of the EP, especially after the introduction of the co-decision procedure in the first pillar in 1993.[72] Today,
'national' interests (like the protection of domestic industry) and 'European' interests (like consumer protection) play an almost equal role in
influencing the policy options of the EP.[73] However, this contradicts the
intended functional differentiation between the European institutions.
Whereas the Council of the EU is supposed to represent the different
national interests of its member states, the Commission and the Parliament are supposed to design politics according to the common good from
a European perspective. Although, in the past, the EP has also cam-
paigned for some of the common interests which are difficult to organize
in lobby groups like those of consumers, the environment or the protection of personal data — special interest lobbyists' and policy-networks'

71   See as classical references for this point Mancur Olson, *The Logic of Collective Action*, Harvard
     University Press, Cambridge Mass., 1965. * Claus Offe, 'Politische Herrschaft und
     Klassenstrukturen. Zur Analyse spätkapitalistischer Gesellschaftssysteme' in Offe ed.,
     *Herausforderungen der Demokratie. Zur Integrations- und Leistungsfähigkeit politischer
     Institutionen*, Campus, Frankfurt/Main, New York, 2003, pp. 11–41.

72   See Miroslaw Matyja, 'Interessenverbände im Entscheidungsprozess der Europäischen
     Union' in Kleinfeld, Zimmer and Willems eds, VS Verlag für Sozialwissenschaften,
     Wiesbaden, 2007, pp. 148–68, pp. 162–4.

73   See Arndt Wonka, 'Lobbying des Europäischen Parlaments' in Maurer and Nickel eds, *Das
     Europäische Parlament. Supranationalität, Repräsentation und Legitimation*, Nomos,
     Baden-Baden, 2005, pp. 165–72, pp. 169–73.

activities remain a serious factor in influencing the decision-making process of the EP.

Previous attempts to limit the political influence of these policy networks have not been very successful so far. They are based on the idea of generating more transparency by increasing publicity and passing agreements on ethical codes for the Members of Parliament. Even though this process has just begun, an additional provision — based on an idea originally mentioned briefly in an article by Richard Thaler — could be introduced: the appointment of the Members of Parliament to the committees via lottery.[74] Although this procedure would entail a serious disadvantage due to the fact that the new members would not necessarily have as much knowledge and experience as the previous ones, there are also positive aspects to this process. The main advantage of such a lottery is the fact that established policy networks between lobbyists and Members of Parliament would be disbanded. In addition, newly appointed committee members would be likely to take on different and new perspectives when debating political issues. And finally, such a mechanism would force politicians to strive to fulfil the role model of a political representative who has a reservoir of general knowledge on different political issues and who is able to become familiar with a whole range of new issues. Opponents to our proposal may argue that the representatives selected via lottery have to become acquainted with so many new and unfamiliar topics that they become extremely vulnerable to the external influence of lobby groups and other political actors. However, this objection is much weaker than it seems at first glance: Members of Parliament already rely on the knowledge and competence of their staff and it is part of the job of any Member of Parliament to learn to choose relatively quickly between different policy options presented by experts.

Considering the committee structure of the European Parliament in detail, we believe that the lottery system can be implemented successfully in three areas:

First, concerning the members of the committees, certainly, the number and proportion of seats allocated to the parties in the committees should approximate to the strength of the elected parties or parliamentary groups. The lot is employed in order to distribute the seats among the members of the parties and groups. Furthermore, we would suggest that committee members should not be re-appointed to the same committee in consecutive legislative periods.

Second, each committee's chairperson should be elected by lot. Currently, these influential offices are usually distributed according to the

74   See Richard Thaler, op. cit., 1983, p. 72 (see note 41).

rule of seniority. It is not surprising, therefore, that conservative attitudes and traditional problem perceptions prevail in the committee work.

Third, the most far-reaching consequences could probably be achieved if the rapporteurs were drawn by lot as well. The rapporteurs present the final report on the legislation projects to their committee and—as the empirical research about policy formation in the European Parliament indicates—they have an immense influence on policy projects. Thus it is not surprising that they are the ones who are most exposed to lobbying.[75]

In particular the last proposal concerning the office of the rapporteur seems to be prone to counter-arguments against the employment of the lot because this position necessitates a high degree of political expertise. However, a second look reveals that the lot may actually serve to increase the competence of the office holders because of the deficiencies of the current proceedings. Currently, the seats of the rapporteurs and the chairpersons are not distributed according to the policy qualifications of the representatives, but are awarded on the basis of proportional representation of the parties. According to research by Karlheinz Neunreither the main interest of parties in the EP

> is not to make sure that the best qualified committee member becomes rapporteur [...] but to get a fair share for themselves out of the total number of rapporteurships. [...] The objective is always to get an agreed percentage for your own group. As one can imagine, the actual proposal for appointment will be influenced by many factors, including the one of 'justice'—that is, to give a fair chance to all members, at least to the more active ones, to become a rapporteur.

'Such systems', Neunreither concludes, 'do not maximise the expertise of the average rapporteur—quite the contrary'.[76]

Some of these committees work with so-called 'point systems' which rate the importance of reports. Upon deciding who is going to write the 'big' reports, smaller parties are systematically discriminated against compared with the bigger parties.[77] In addition, the reports are spread unequally among the committee members. The third legislative period (1989–1994) presents an extreme example: 174 delegates did not write a single report while the Italian delegate Antonio la Pergola produced

75 See Mamadouh and Raunio, op. cit., 2003, p. 344 (see note 69); Matyja op. cit., 2007, p. 163 (see note 72).
76 Karlheinz Neunreither, 'Elected Legislators and their Unelected Assistants in the European Parliament', *The Journal of Legislative Studies*, 8/4, 2002, pp. 40–60, p. 45.
77 The committee of budgetary affairs already distributes all of the reports at the beginning of every legislative period; cf. Mamadouh and Raunio, op. cit., 2003, p. 340ff.

forty-three reports.[78] Taking these disproportions into account, it comes as less of a surprise that the rapporteurs selected their assistants less and less from the General Management II (Internal Policy Affairs) of the EP in the past years, while the importance of 'interest groups that have appeared on the scene as voluntary legislative assistants' increased at the same time.[79]

Hence, we would expect professional qualifications and political independence of the rapporteurs to improve with the introduction of the lot. If this position is awarded on short-term notice and based on chance, this will raise the probability that the concerned delegates will rely more on the politically neutral and well-equipped General Management II of the EP instead of well-established policy networks with their lobbyists. A lottery system for committee members, committee chairpersons and the rapporteurs would disturb long-term relationships between lobbyists and certain political representatives at the European level. In our view, such a procedure would have two additional advantages. First, it would lead to a higher degree of democracy because it would reaffirm the political equality of the Members of Parliament. And second, it might foster a process of further integration in the European party structures because the lottery for committees would not take the national aspect of proportional representation into account.

4.3 A European 'house of lots'

While our second proposal — which was aimed at reforming the Committees — is mainly defensive, we take a more offensive strategy with our third which is designed to address the problems of the democratic deficit and non-transparency in the decision making processes of the EU. Some aspects of the current debate about the democratic deficit at the level of the EU are located in a field of conflicting democratic goals — a subject that has been debated among democratic theorists since the emergence of modern democracy two hundred years ago. The unanimity principle in the European Council generates a high degree of legitimacy for its political decisions. At the same time, it turns decision making in the EU into a slow process with a lack of democratic control. In contrast, the majority principle in the Council and the Parliament generates quick decisions and is able to overcome political deadlocks, but it contains the risk of creating structural minorities and majorities. This diminishes the legitimacy of decisions made by both Council and Parliament. Up to now, practical

---

78   See Mamadouh and Raunio, op. cit., 2003, p. 344. The idea that rapporteurs who have already been drawn should have the possibility of refusing another report if they have already been responsible for two or three others should be added to our proposal.

79   Neunreither, op. cit., 2002, p. 49 (see note 76).

efforts to deal with this conflict of interests have looked to the idea of transforming the EU according to the model of the traditional nation state and they have thus been caught in the old field of conflicting democratic goals. The Irish vote against the Lisbon Treaty in the summer of 2008, however, reaffirmed Armin Schäfer's diagnosis of two years earlier: that while European integration could no longer continue as an elite project, the way to turn the EU into a mass democracy was nonetheless blocked.[80]

At this point, the idea of an additional chamber of the EP drawn by a lottery may be able to cut this Gordian knot. The idea of a lottery chamber was first introduced in the modern debate on democratic theory in the book *After the Revolution* by Robert A. Dahl (which we mentioned above) and was later picked up by other political theorists and economists. Whereas Dahl suggested the employment of the lot as a device for selecting advisory councils to elected officials like majors of large cities, state governors or members of the U.S. House and Senate,[81] the idea of the lottery chamber was picked up by others to promote their respective reform agendas. Dennis M. Mueller proposed to carry out a lottery to determine the 435 delegates of the U.S. House of Representatives in order to avoid extensive expenses for election campaigns.[82] As opposed to this neo-liberal use of the lot, radical democrats from the left like John Burnheim, Ernest Callenbach and Michael Phillips, as well as Barbara Goodwin, Anthony Barnett and Peter Carty suggested using the lottery in order to fulfil the so-called 'mirror-concept' of political representation.[83] They all refer to the famous dictum of John Adams, who describes the legislator as an 'exact portrait in miniature of the people at large [...] as it should think, feel, reason and act like them'.[84]

In contrast to the neo-liberal and the radical-democratic interpretation of a lottery chamber, we would like to consider the idea of political representatives drawn by a lottery by referring to the deliberative democratic theory mentioned in section 2 and to the empirical findings on the deliberative qualities of the 'Deliberative Opinion Polls', the 'Consensus Conventions' and the 'Citizen Juries'. In particular we can build on the evidence about the following deliberative qualities: 1) the problem of polarization in elected parliaments is alleviated by employing the ran-

80 See Schäfer op. cit., 2006, p. 373 (see note 49).
81 See Dahl (1970), pp. 148–51 and later in his concept of a consultative 'Minipopulus'; see Robert A. Dahl, *Democracy and Its Critics*, Yale University Press, New-Haven, 1989, pp. 338–42.
82 See Dennis C. Mueller, Robert Tollison and Thomas D. Willett, 'Representative Democracy via Random Selection' in Mueller ed., *The Economic Approach to Public Policy*, Cornell University Press, Ithaca, 1976, pp. 381–93.
83 See Burnheim (2005); Callenbach & Phillips (1985); Goodwin (2005); Barnett & Carty (2008).
84 Quoted in Callenbach & Phillips (1985), p. 31.

dom mechanism as it ensures group heterogeneity; 2) the strategical exploitations of arguments, which characterizes the communication between the government and the opposition in classical parliamentarism, decreases drastically due to the fact that randomly drawn actors are independent from political clients and lobbyists.[85] In addition, 3) the findings indicate that randomly-picked members show a serious reluctance to invest their time in non-binding political talks. This apathy was reduced when the participatory-deliberative procedures led to binding political decisions, rather than those that were merely recommendations.[86]

On the European level, the introduction of a lottery chamber to preside over serious decision-making power within the European political system, would have the potential to increase both the deliberative and the participatory aspects of democracy. Such a chamber would represent the interests, problems and perceptions of a statistically representative sample of all EU citizens. We plead for the implementation of a lottery-based chamber in the political system of the EU not as a substitute for the elected EP, but as a second chamber of the EP. Such a European 'House of lots' (Barbara Goodwin has coined this term to describe a similar institution on the national level) should ideally consist of 200 members. This chamber should represent the citizens — in analogy to the current elected chamber of the EP — according to the principle of degressive proportionality (see Table 1, columns 7 and 8). The members should be picked every two-and-a-half years in accordance with the election cycle of the EP (every five years). Every EU citizen may hold a mandate in the lottery chamber only once in his or her life. The remuneration of a lottery-representative should be equal to that of the elected representatives. We think that it should be obligatory for all EU citizens to take part in such a lottery because a voluntary model would only lead to an over-representation of political activists. The goal of our suggestion — to achieve a statistically representative sample of EU citizens — will only be fulfilled if participation were made mandatory. Thus legitimate reasons for rejecting a mandate should be narrowly defined.

---

85 See David Ryfe, op. cit., 2002, pp. 264–6 (see note 31); John Gastil, 'Adult Civic Education Through the National Issues Forum: A Study of How Adults Develop Civil Skills and Dispositions Through Public Deliberation', *Adult Education Quarterly*, 54, 2004, pp. 308–28, pp. 317–19.

86 See Thomas Saretzki, 'TA als diskursiver Prozess' in Bröchler, Simonis and Sundermann eds, *Handbuch Technikfolgenabschätzung 2*, Edition Sigma, Berlin, 1999, pp. 641–53, p. 648. * Georg Simonis, 'Die TA-Landschaft in Deutschland — Potenziale reflexiver Techniksteuerung' in Simonis, Martinsen and Saretzki eds, *Politik und Technik*, Westdeutscher Verlag, Wiesbaden, 2000, pp. 425–56, p. 449. * See as well the findings about 'Deliberative Opinion Polls' by David Ryfe, op. cit., 2002, pp. 366–8; Joan Font and Ismael Blanco, op. cit., 2007, pp. 579–81 (see note 12).

The lottery chamber should be able to contribute to the political decision-making process of the EU in a productive manner. Basically, the lottery chamber should only be involved in the legislative realm, i.e., it should not be permitted to control the executive EU Council and the Commission.

On the level of *supranational policy making* we suggest the following political responsibilities:

First, the second chamber should be able to make legislative recommendations to the first chamber, the Commission and the Council.

Second, the chamber should have absolute veto power within a certain procedure: there should be a fourteen day period between the decision and decree of all legislative bills, during which the second chamber has the right to intervene in order to scrutinize all bills. If the chamber decides to carry out such an examination, the objection time during which the chamber can reject the bill extends to ninety days.

Finally, the chamber should be able to initiate legislation. If the chamber makes use of this right, there should be a shorter legislative period with lower majority quotas, because the chamber has a higher degree of deliberative and participatory quality than the other EU organs. After the Commission has issued its statement on a legislative initiative of the lottery chamber, it would then seem to be sufficient to have only one reading of the bill in the EU Council and in the elected EP. In each location approval would require an absolute majority. The deadlines should be one month for the Commission and three months for the first chamber of the EP as well as for the Council.

The normative rationale behind these three procedural elements is to exert a higher degree of deliberative pressure on the European Council. However, the Council would maintain its superiority and would preserve the integrative and stabilizing advantages of qualified majority and the need for unanimity in all areas in which the lottery chamber was not involved.

Provided that our line of reasoning is correct, one should consider applying the two intervention measurements, namely the right to recommend legislative acts and the veto right (not the right to initiate legislation, though), in the other two pillars of the EU — the Common Foreign and Security Policy as well as the Police and Judicial Co-operation in Criminal Matters — in which the Council decides upon intergovernmental matters. So far these matters are beyond any democratic control. Once the reforms have been introduced, they would finally be the subject to a deliberative and participatory democratic supervision.[87] Again, the aim of this

---

87 The same should apply to areas of 'intensified co-operation', where only some of the EU members take part in a deeper process of EU integration, e.g., the monetary union. It remains

division of competences is supposed to put intergovernmental decision-making under deliberative pressure, without abolishing the advantages of intergovernmentalism.

Concerning the *design of the political system* the second chamber should not only have a veto right, but it should be required to vote on *all* changes in the legislation in order for them to be legally binding. This way, the decisions concerning the institutional foundations of the EU would be democratized effectively and it would be impossible to decide upon them without public debates. In addition, one might consider introducing a right for the second chamber to initiate proposals to change treaties in a manner that maintains the other rules of procedure (especially the compliance of all member states). The accession of new EU states should also be dependent on the approval of the lottery chamber. This way, the EU would not simply rhetorically but effectively be obliged to force potential member states to abide by certain well defined criteria. This would also force the EU to carry out the accession proceedings for new members correctly right from the start.[88]

With regard to the organization of the daily work routines of the second chamber, the following additional aspects should be mentioned: first, topics should not be discussed exclusively in the plenary chamber, they should also be debated in detail in smaller working groups (comprising fifteen to thirty people). The members of these working groups should be chosen via lottery; the representatives could then deliberate and develop drafts for the plenary session. In addition, the second chamber ought to have an apparatus of policy experts who could compete with the respective organisations of the other European institutions. Finally, the lottery chamber should be in charge of a petition department of its own to which European citizens, as well as members of the elected EP, the Council of the Union and the Commission, could make political suggestions.

Financing a lottery chamber is not a serious challenge. It seems to be sensible to locate the two chambers in the two existing parliamentary locations in Brussels and Strasbourg. At the same time this would put a stop to the convoy of parliamentarians travelling back and forth between the two locations of parliament. Putting an end to this situation alone would cover most of the costs for the maintenance of the second chamber. Ideally, the elected chamber of the Parliament should be closely incorpo-

---

to be discussed whether only the members of the second chamber from the respective countries involved should be allowed to vote in such cases.

88   For a discussion of this problem see Tina Olteanu and Christian Autengruber, 'Wie ernst meint es die EU mit der Demokratie? Standardsetzung am Beispiel der EU-Beitrittsvorbereitungen mit Bulgarien und Rumänien', *Österreichische Zeitschrift für Politikwissenschaft*, 36, 2007, pp. 81–94.

rated within other EU institutions and should move to Brussels, whereas the lottery chamber should be located separately in Strasbourg.

The following four main objections may be raised against the lottery chamber.

First, it may be argued that citizens who were drawn by the lottery would not have any incentive to take the views of their fellow citizens into account because they would not have a chance to be re-elected. However, there is no reason to assume that members of the lottery chamber should be less responsive than members of the first chamber are today. In addition, it would not be the primary goal of lottery members to be responsive to voters. Rather, they would be asked to bring their own experience and political views to bear in the political process.

Another argument against a lottery chamber might be that its members may be susceptible to corruption. Supposedly, the lot, which has traditionally been considered to serve as an anti-corruption measure, would promote corruption because the lottery representatives would know that they would not serve a second term. In addition to passing anti-corruption laws, one could circumvent this problem by introducing secret ballots in the lottery chamber. While it is an essential part for the voters of elected bodies to know how their representatives voted, this would not be the case in lottery-determined chambers.

Third, one could argue against our proposal by saying that the efficiency of the EP would decrease if an additional chamber were introduced. Most likely, the opposite would be the case: according to the logic of the lottery chamber, it would not be obliged to intervene in every political decision. Rather, it would exert deliberative pressure on the members of the other institutions by hanging over them like the sword of Damocles.

Nevertheless, we agree with a final objection, but only on a temporary basis. Momentarily, most European citizens do not think much of lotteries as a political device. Thus, a newly introduced lottery chamber would probably suffer from low acceptance and would hardly have any assertiveness regarding its decisions. The lottery chamber would gain in democratic legitimacy only if the political culture changed, in such a way as to recognise the rational potential of the lot. Currently, such a cultural transformation is unlikely; however, we know from the history of political ideas that even elections were not regarded as instrument of democracy from the start.[89] With the growing acceptance of random mechanisms in different spheres of modern societies, there is reason to expect that the lottery will gain acceptance in politics as well.

---

89   See Manin (1997).

Recent experiments with Fishkin's model of 'Deliberative Opinion Polls' on the European level may be seen as an indication for a changing perception of the role of lotteries in the EU. In February and March 2007, so-called 'citizen consultations' were conducted in the EU member states which dealt with the European future after the first failure of the European constitution in 2005. The consultations were performed according to the following format: In every state, 28 to 200 citizens were identified in a weighted lottery (based on gender and other criteria). They were invited to join a two-day workshop to discuss the most crucial issues that are at stake for the further development of the EU. In the end, all groups were encouraged to present a 'citizen declaration'. In May 2007, group members combined the twenty-seven declarations into a single 'European declaration' that listed both the agreements and disagreements of the respective national perspectives.[90]

The political impetus of these recommendations is remarkable because the twenty-seven national declarations express a consensus among European citizens on many central issues of EU policy making: the declarations 'nearly unanimously ask for the EU to play a substantial role in virtually all social policy issues, and actively create a "social Europe"'.[91] Furthermore, most of the national consultations 'put the "family as a high value" [...] firmly on the European agenda'.[92] In addition, the declarations reflect a common demand for a common European agenda in the policy fields of energy and environmental politics, which should include fiscal incentives. Finally, eleven out of the twenty-seven citizenries 'express a wish to increase opportunities for a "more active participation of Europe's citizens"'.[93] These recommendations highlight two things. First, they indicate that the political preferences of European citizens, obtained with the help of 'Deliberative Opinion Polls', do converge on central issues. Second, that the demands of European citizens as revealed by the declarations share a vision of a democratic and social Europe which stands in contrast to the policy of the European political elites over the last couple of years.

---

90 European Citizens' Consultations, 2007, *European citizens' perspective on the future of Europe*, www.european-citizens-consultations.eu/fileadmin/user_upload/ECC_Fin_Con_Media/E CC_Fin_Con_Perspectives_FINAL_1_.pdf>, 2008/03/25. See the critical review on the German citizen consultation by Heike Haarhoff, 'Gefühlte Teilhabe', *Die Tageszeitung*, 2007, 27 February,
www.taz.de/index.php?id=archivseite&dig=2007/02/27/a0153>, 2008/01/15.
91 European Citizen's Consultations (see note 90), p. 3, emphasis deleted.
92 Ibid., p. 4, emphasis deleted.
93 Ibid., p. 13, emphasis deleted.

5 Conclusion: sortition and the second territorial transformation of democracy

We do not claim that our proposal will solve all of the current constitutional and political problems of the EU. Nonetheless, we have plausibly argued that the application of lotteries in certain areas may contribute to the alleviation of the democratic deficit of the EU and that lotteries can be applied to problems of inefficiency, non-transparency (including the negative aspects of lobbying) as well as an appropriate representation mechanism of the member states in the Commission. The functional potential of the lot, which we outlined in the first sections of the paper, has not yet been exhausted in modern democracies.

We consider our proposal for the EU to be a starting point for a debate that takes the general problem of democracy in the post-national constellation into account. Many observers consider the process of European integration to be *the* most relevant test case for the possibility of democracy to survive in post national contexts. Two hundred years ago, advocates of democracy in North America were confronted with a similar situation. For them, 'democracy' was a form of government that was only feasible in small city states. Some of them like the authors of the Federalist Papers put aside the term 'democracy' and chose 'republic' to describe their political project. Others, however, succeeded in transforming 'democracy' from small states to large territories by adapting procedures and institutions that had no place in the ancient understanding of democracy. Thomas Paine proudly proclaimed that the new political systems came into existence 'by ingrafting representation upon democracy,'[94] and went further by stating 'what Athens was in miniature America will be in magnitude.' The introduction of a system based on representation and the addition of elections were the main institutional changes that 'updated' democracy and enabled it to transfer from small city-states to a larger territorial entity. The conceptual changes by Paine and others 200 years ago laid the ideological foundation for democracy as a political project suitable for mass societies on a national level in the following decades.

Today, democracy's geographical frame of reference is once again outgrowing its institutional setting. The era of mass democracy in a sovereign nation state, which started its career in the 1820s in North America, has come to an end. It is now an open question to politicians, citizens and political scientists whether future procedures of global governance will be democratic at all. To put the question differently: *will the upcoming second territorial transfor-*

---

94   Thomas Paine, *Rights of Man, Common Sense and other Writings* [1st edn 1792], Oxford University Press, Oxford, 1995. For Paine's democratic theory theory see Nadia Urbinati, *Representative Democracy,* Chicago University Press, Chicago, 2007.

mation of democracy be successful? In case of a negative answer, we already have the option to apply the concept of 'post- democracy'.[95]

If, however, we continue to address the question of what procedures and institutions are appropriate for a democracy in the post-national sphere, all swansongs to democracy will prove to be premature. In the current debate on 'global democracy' we are confronted with a continuing and growing call for more institutional creativity, imagination and innovation. At this point, the rich store of the history of political ideas might provide further intellectual stimuli. This is apparent if we compare the beginning of the first territorial transformation of democracy with our current situation. Paine and his democratically inspired contemporaries found themselves in a situation somewhat similar to the current state of affairs. Ironically, their answer to the new challenge was so innovative because, at first glance, it looked anything but innovative to their contemporaries. Instead of searching for completely new ways to solve their problem with democracy, they referred to old sources of information about political procedures. Paine came up with the traditional institution of a representative body, the contract-theory-tradition of political trust, elections as a means of institutionalising a trust-based relationship and the old doctrine of the division of political powers. Paine did not invent new procedures or institutions. He simply reinterpreted old formulas in the context of the constitutional necessities of his time. Our strategy to cope with the constitutional problems of the EU resembles Paine's approach in the sense that the upcoming second territorial transformation of democracy could also profit from an older idea that was part of the pool of traditional political procedures before its anachronistic image caused it to be ignored or forgotten. This is the idea of the lottery.

In our reform proposal, the positive aspects of lotteries come into play only in combination with other procedures of appointment and allocation. Such a strategy overcomes the fruitless confrontation of elections versus lotteries which has been the topic of many debates. Whereas Plato and Aristotle interpreted the lot as a 'democratic 'tool and considered elections to be 'aristocratic', later on elections became the central feature of democracy. At the same time, lotteries disappeared from the political stage and its use in Venice and Florence became associated with the corrupt aristocracy. It is time to rearrange these paradigms again and to profit from the co-existence of elections and lotteries in order to strengthen modern democracy in the post-national constellation.

---

95 See Colin Crouch, *Post-Democracy*, Polity, Cambridge, 2004.

Country	Population		Degressive Proportionality	Over- & Under-representation	Commission: Assessed Lots	European Parliament: Seats	
	inhabitants (in mil.)	share in EU-27 (in %)	vote share (in %)	1 = representation	1 = not assessed	1st chamber (elected)	2nd chamber (lottery)
Germany	82.3	16.62	12.80	0.77	3.46	96	26
France	63.4	12.80	9.87	0.77	2.66	74	20
United Kingdom	60.9	12.29	9.73	0.79	2.63	73	19
Italy	59.1	11.94	9.60	0.80	2.59	72	19
Spain	44.5	8.98	7.20	0.80	1.94	54	14
Poland	38.1	7.70	6.80	0.88	1.84	51	14
Romania	21.6	4.36	4.40	1.01	1.19	33	9
Netherlands	16.4	3.30	3.47	1.05	0.94	26	7
Greece	11.2	2.26	2.93	1.30	0.97	22	6
Portugal	10.6	2.14	2.93	1.37	0.79	22	6
Belgium	10.6	2.14	2.93	1.37	0.79	22	6
Czech Republic	10.3	2.08	2.93	1.41	0.79	22	6
Hungary	10.1	2.03	2.93	1.44	0.79	22	6
Sweden	9.1	1.84	2.67	1.45	0.72	20	5
Austria	8.3	1.68	2.53	1.51	0.68	19	5
Bulgaria	7.7	1.55	2.40	1.55	0.65	18	5
Denmark	5.4	1.10	1.73	1.58	0.47	13	3

Country	Population		Degressive Proportionality	Over- & Under-representation	Commission: Assessed Lots	European Parliament: Seats	
	inhabitants (in mil.)	share in EU-27 (in %)	vote share (in %)	1 = representation	1 = not assessed	1st chamber (elected)	2nd chamber (lottery)
Slovak Republic	5.4	1.09	1.73	1.59	0.47	13	3
Finland	5.3	1.07	1.73	1.63	0.47	13	3
Ireland	4.3	0.87	1.60	1.84	0.43	12	3
Lithuania	3.4	0.68	1.60	2.34	0.43	12	3
Latvia	2.3	0.46	1.20	2.60	0.32	9	2
Slovinia	2.0	0.41	1.07	2.63	0.29	8	2
Estonia	1.3	0.27	0.80	2.95	0.22	6	2
Cyprus	0.8	0.16	0.80	5.09	0.22	6	2
Luxemburg	0.5	0.10	0.80	8.32	0.22	6	2
Malta	0.4	0.08	0.80	9.71	0.22	6	2
EU-27	495.1	100.00	100.00	1.00	27	750	200

Table 1: *Degressive proportionality in the European Parliament and in the European Commission*

Deviations result from the fact that some of the numbers were rounded up, the number of inhabitants refer to figures from January 1, 2007.

Source: Eurostat (2008) *Total Population,*

www.epp.eurostat.ec.europa.eu/tgm/table.do?tab=table&init=1&plugin=1&language=en&pcode=tps00001>, 2008/11/17; European Parliament (2008); *Report on the Composition of the European Parliament,*

www.europarl.europa.eu/sides/getDoc.do?pubRef=-//EP//TEXT+REPORT+A6-2007-0351+0+DOC+XML+V0//EN>, 2008/11/14; own calculation.

8 Peter Stone

Lotteries and Probability Theory

A variety of decisions seem to require resort to a coin toss, die roll, or the drawing of straws — in other words, a fair lottery. This raises the question of what features distinguish fair lotteries from alternative procedures. The intuitive answer is that a fair lottery generates each of its possible outcomes with equal probability. But probability is a contentious term. There are a variety of conceptions of probability, and it may be the case that equiprobable lotteries are useful for decision making under some conceptions but not others. This paper considers four of the leading conceptions of probability — the frequentist, objective, subjective, and logical conceptions. It argues that unless the logical conception is adopted, it is impossible to make sense of the contribution that lotteries can make to decision making.

1 Introduction

Imagine a draft board charged with selecting one of two young men for military service at wartime. Both men are fit to serve; neither has any outstanding defects or extraordinary needs (e.g., no wife and seven children at home). How ought the draft board to decide between them? The intuitive answer is that it ought to toss a coin, draw straws, or otherwise employ a *lottery*.

This is far more than hypothetical speculation. Throughout history lotteries have been used to select military conscripts, and a great many other things as well. Anglo-American jurors, immigrants to the United States, admittees to desirable schools — all have been selected through lotteries, in accordance with the same intuition that underlies draft lotteries.[1] A growing literature, produced by philosophers, social scientists, and legal

---

1   Indeed, in the United States, efforts to curtail or modify conscription lotteries — by allowing draftees to buy their way out, or send a substitute — have been met with riots and other forms of strong protest.

scholars, has defended this intuition, exploring when lotteries are appropriate components of decision-making processes, and why.[2]

This paper contributes to this literature by investigating the question,
not of when or why, but of *what*. What makes a lottery a lottery? Specifically, what makes a lottery suitable for making a contribution to decision
making? Surely not just any coin toss would do when it comes to selecting
between potential military conscripts? Imagine using a coin known to
favour heads for this purpose. The obvious response is that the coin toss
should be *fair*, in the sense of selecting each outcome with equal probability. Fair lotteries—lotteries appropriate for decision making—are thus
equivalent to equiprobable ones. But this answer depends upon an adequate conception of probability. Probability, like many other founda-
tional concepts in political science and philosophy (justice, democracy,
freedom, etc.), is a hotly debated term. There are serious and persisting
disagreements over the right way to think about probability. An unchari-
table observer might even suggest that probability is an 'essentially con-
tested' term of political discourse—a term that is so intrinsically
contentious that disagreements over its meaning cannot be resolved by
rational discourse, but only by power relations.[3]

This paper addresses the problematic relationship between probability
and lotteries. It begins with the assumption that a fair (that is,
equiprobable) lottery is an appropriate method of making certain sorts of
decisions (like the military draft decision). It then examines four of the
leading conceptions of probability—the *frequentist, objective, subjective,*
and *logical* conceptions.[4] It asks whether probability, understood in terms
of each of these conceptions, would render this assumption plausible. If a
lottery were equiprobable in the frequentist (or objective, or subjective, or
logical) sense, would it make sense to make decisions using it? In answer-
ing this question for each conception, I shall use the toss of fair coin as an
illustration. If an equiprobable coin toss, defined using a given conception, were used to make a decision (like selecting a military conscript),
would this decision be defensible? After tackling each conception in turn,
the paper concludes that only the logical conception poses no serious

2   See in Bibliography: Aubert (1959); Greely (1977); Sher (1980); Broome (1984); Mulgan (1984);
     Kornhauser & Sager (1988); Elster (1989); Boyle (1998); Duxbury (1999); Goodwin (2005);
     Stone (2007); Dowlen (2008).

3   Connolly, William E., *The Terms of Political Discourse*, Lexington, KY, D.C. Heath, 1974.

4   I borrow this terminology from Karl Popper's *The Logic of Scientific Discovery* (New York: Basic
     Books, 1959), which distinguishes between competing conceptions of probability in a similar
     but not identical manner. Some modifications to Popper's categorization system are
     necessary, especially given Popper's own changing views regarding the nature of probability.
     (See Popper, 'The Propensity Interpretation of Probability', *British Journal for the Philosophy of
     Science*, 10, 1959, pp. 25-42.)

obstacles to the defense of decision making by lottery. The paper ends by considering this conclusion's implications.

Before proceeding, I should stress that not all lotteries are fair lotteries. Even a coin that yields heads eighty per cent of the time when tossed is still a lottery: it is simply not a lottery suitable for making the same decisions as a fair lottery. One can thus distinguish between fair (equiprobable) lotteries and *weighted lotteries* — lotteries that do not generate all of their outcomes with equal probability, and are thus 'weighted' towards some outcomes more than others. Some philosophers, most notably John Broome, have defended the use of weighted lotteries in decision making.[5] This paper does not address this issue; rather it presupposes that the decisions to be made are decisions for which equiprobable lotteries are appropriate. It also presupposes that the same understanding of probability suitable for defending equiprobable lotteries will also work for defending weighted lotteries, should such a defense be needed. In this way I maintain my focus on the process of identifying *which* conception of probability provides the best framework for understanding how equiprobable lotteries might prove desirable in decision-making processes.[6]

2 Four Conceptions of Probability

2.1 *The frequentist conception*

The frequentist conception of probability can quickly be dismissed. This conception, articulated most famously by Richard von Mises, defines probability as a property of a collection (possibly infinite) of events.[7] To say that the probability of a coin toss coming up heads is (say) .5, is to say that there is a class of events (tosses of the relevant coin) in which the relative frequency of heads is .5. But on this definition, as its detractors have often pointed out, there are no probabilities attached to single events, only

---

5   See Broome (1984), (1990).

6   One can speak of lotteries in terms of randomness as well as in terms of probability. Following Gregory Chaitin ('Randomness and Mathematical Proof', *Scientific American*, 232, 1975, pp. 47–52) I define a random sequence as one which cannot be fully characterized by any description less complex than itself. A random process is a process which generates sequences that can be so characterized. The outcomes in such a process are maximally unpredictable, in that no patterns exist in the outcomes that would allow for effective prediction in advance. And the outcomes of such a process must appear with equal frequency; if they did not, one could achieve some predictability by favoring the outcomes that appear more reliably. Intuitively, a lottery that constitutes a random process (so understood) should be equivalent to a fair/equiprobable lottery. The definition of probability I defend does have this implication, although I do not spell it out in the text.

7   Richard Von Mises, *Probability, Statistics and Truth.* 2nd revised English ed., Dover, New York, 1981.

collectives. This makes it impossible to speak of the probability that a given outcome will result from a process on a certain occasion. One can speak of the probability attached to a class of coin tosses — say, the class of all actual or potential tosses of a particular coin — but not of the probability that the next toss of a coin will come up heads. But this is precisely what is desired when speaking of a fair lottery as a means of effective decision making. For this reason, the frequentist conception is not suitable to the purpose at hand. (This is not to say, of course, that the observed frequencies generated by a process are irrelevant to the assignment of probabilities to it.)

2.2 The objective conception

The objective conception holds that probability is a property possessed by physical processes in the world, a property equivalent to a propensity to produce some result. This 'propensity' account of probability originated with Karl Popper, who came to regard probability as a *'property of the generating conditions'*[8] inherent in the process, making his view a *'new physical hypothesis* (or perhaps a metaphysical hypothesis) analogous to the hypothesis of Newtonian forces'.[9] Proponents of this theory agree that probability should be understood as a non-frequentist fact about the world (i.e., a fact about individual processes and not collections of outcomes). They further agree that a process possesses this property to the extent that it has a particular sort of propensity; they disagree, however, regarding the nature of the propensity.[10] A coin toss is thus objectively equiprobable if and only if its propensity to generate heads is equal to its propensity to generate tails.

The objective conception raises a number of philosophical problems. For example, it is questionable whether there are any objectively equiprobable physical processes at all, at least on the macro-level. (I set aside the difficulties posed by quantum physics here.) A coin toss, for example, is a determinate physical process, involving a moderately heavy object being launched into the air with a determinate initial velocity and spin (possibly with some additional effects, e.g., a bit of wobble). The results of such a toss could therefore be predicted with a high degree of accuracy, given sufficiently precise control over the act of tossing itself.

8   Popper originally embraced the frequentist conception of probability, and defended it in his *Logic of Scientific Discovery*. His subsequent revision of his views required him to revise his understanding of the space of alternative conceptions of probability (see note 4).

9   'The Propensity Interpretation of Probability', op. cit., 1959, pp. 34, 38. Also see Popper, *A World of Propensities*, Thoemmes Press, Bristol, 1997.

10   For a discussion of competing understandings of propensity, see Donald Gillies, 'Varieties of Propensity', *British Journal of the Philosophy of Science*, 51, 2000, pp. 807-35.

This is not a purely hypothetical scenario. Stage magicians have long developed the skill of tossing coins in a predictable manner. One statistician (not coincidentally, a former stage magician) has even constructed a coin-tossing machine that produces the same outcome each time with near-perfect reliability.[11] If one is to associate probabilities with a coin toss at all, one can only do so in terms of our lack of knowledge about the toss's initial conditions, not in terms of some physical property the toss possesses. It is unlikely that one could find any other archetypical 'lottery' (drawing straws, rolling dice, etc.) for which the probabilities amounted to objective physical propensities.

The objective conception also faces other, related, theoretical problems. As noted before, this conception requires probability to be a fact regarding physical processes, a fact independent of any agent's observation of those processes. This understanding is evident in Isaac Levi's description of the property of chance displayed by a coin toss.

> Coin *a* is able to land heads up on a toss. We may also say that it is possible for coin *a* to land heads up on a toss. The existence of actual or possible tosses of coin *a* is not implied by such claims. A property of the coin is being predicated, a property it has regardless of whether the experiment (tossing the coin) is ever conducted. Furthermore, *whether the coin has or lacks the property is independent of the attitudes of those who make the attribution.* In this sense, abilities or possibilities are real.[12]

This understanding of probability is implausible, for reasons first pointed out by A.J. Ayer.[13] The probability of an event occurring does not seem to be independent of the description of that event. And descriptions are always relative to an observer and what she knows about the process generating the event. Probability thus appears to have an ineradicable epistemic component, and this precludes a purely physicalistic understanding of probability, such as that put forward in the propensity theory.

This objection applies to any use to which the objective conception of probability might be put. There is also a strong objection, however, relating specifically to the use of the objective conception when talking about

---

11 See Esther Landhuis, 'Lifelong Debunker Takes on Arbiter of Neutral Choices', *Stanford Report*, 7 June 2004. * Also see David Lewis, 'A Subjectivist's Guide to Objective Chance' in *Philosophical Papers*, vol.II, Oxford University Press, 1987. Lewis argues at length that it would be impossible for an observer to determine the initial conditions of a coin toss with enough accuracy as to predict its outcome, at least in real-time. (There's not much point in 'predicting' the result of a toss after the coin has landed.) Lewis overlooks the possibility that the coin tosser could render the initial conditions predictable by exercising control over them.

12 My emphasis. Isaac Levi, *Hard Choices: Decision Making under Unresolved Conflict*, Cambridge University Press, Cambridge, 1986, p. 48.

13 A.J. Ayer, 'Two Notes on Probability' in *The Concept of a Person and Other Essays*, St. Martin's Press, New York, 1963.

lotteries and decision making. The goal, as indicated before, is to find a conception of probability according to which it is plausible to say that fair lotteries ought to play an important role in decision-making. But if probability is an objective property of physical processes, then objective equiprobability is neither a necessary nor a sufficient condition for a process to play such a role. Clearly, it is not sufficient. A process could generate outcomes with equal probability without this equality being perceived by an agent seeking to use the process to make a decision. If an agent falsely[14] believes that tossing a particular coin will almost invariably result in heads, if she then decides to use the coin toss in making a decision, few would say that she is using a fair lottery, even if the lottery is 'really' equiprobable. At a minimum, in order for a process to qualify as a fair lottery suitable for decision making the lottery must not only be really (objectively) fair, but it must also be *believed* to be fair.

However, if a process is believed to be fair, it is unclear why the lottery must itself be fair (in the sense of being objectively equiprobable). The perception of the lottery appears sufficient in its own right, at least if this perception is properly understood (see sections 2.3 and 2.4). Imagine, for example, that a draft board employs a lottery to select military conscripts. Everyone involved in the process perceives it to be fair, according to whatever criteria for fairness are deemed appropriate. At some point in the future, information comes to light suggesting that the lottery employed was not in fact fair according to those criteria. Does this fact imply retroactively that the draft board's selections were actually unfair? Intuitively, the answer is no.[15] But if that is the case, then objectively equal probabilities are not only insufficient for the lottery to be fair; they are unnecessary as well.

The objective conception of probability thus proves difficult to employ productively in decision-making processes. It is easy to understand why this should be the case. In order to prove useful in decision making, a conception of probability must make reference to beliefs—minimally, the beliefs of the agent(s) making decisions. The objective conception, which focuses purely on the physical world without any reference to agents' per-

14   But not necessarily wrongly. It could be the case that the agent has witnessed an unrepresentative sample of observations—perhaps an improbable run of heads generated by the coin toss—that has rationally led her to a false conclusion about the process.

15   The same answer was reached in federal court after the U.S. employed a draft lottery in 1970, the first since World War II. The lottery determined the order in which potential draftees would be called up according to their birthdays. An examination of the results of the lottery provided strong evidence that the lottery favored birthdays in some parts of the year over others. Nevertheless, the courts found no evidence that this fact was known at the time, or was intentional. They therefore let the results of the lottery stand. The 1971 lottery, fortunately, avoided making the same mistakes. See Fienberg (1971) and Elster (1989) pp. 42, 45-6.

ceptions of that world, lacks any such reference. A physical property of the world can do nothing for decision making if it is not perceived; moreover, at least some kinds of perception appear perfectly adequate for decision making *per se* and pose no problems in this respect, regardless of the actual nature of the physical world.

This is why a decision made by a fair lottery does not become unfair on the day that further information is discovered that might question the original perception of fairness. There is a gap between properties of the physical world and the world of decision making, a gap that can only be filled by reference to the beliefs of decision-makers. It therefore makes sense to turn to conceptions of probability that might potentially make up this gap.

2.3 *The subjective conception*

The subjective conception (sometimes known as the personalist conception) is the understanding of probability favored by most Bayesians.[16] It is in many ways the polar opposite of the objective conception. Whereas the latter regards probability as a physical property of the world, independent of any agent's beliefs, the former thinks of probability *exclusively* in terms of the beliefs of agents. In the subjective account, a statement concerning the probability of a coin toss coming up heads is a statement of the level of confidence an agent has that the coin will in fact come up heads. This statement is also a matter of fact, albeit a psychological and not a physical one. It is impossible for the individual to be wrong about his level of confidence, so long as she commits no logical inconsistencies (e.g., by affirming probability judgments about mutually exclusive events that add up to a total greater than one, or by refusing to update her beliefs properly in the face of new information).[17]

A fair lottery defined in terms of the subjective conception would indeed be relevant to decision making, because the facts determining the fairness of the lottery (the decision-maker's belief system) are certainly accessible to the decision-maker. The direct connection between belief and probability, however, generates different problems. As purely psychological phenomena, degrees of confidence are relative to the beliefs of a particular agent. Those beliefs are constrained by information, but not completely determined by it. Specifically, agents must update beliefs in light of new information in a certain way, on pain of logical inconsistency. Their initial beliefs (prior to receiving new information) are completely

---

16 Leonard Savage, *The Foundations of Statistics*, 2nd rev. ed., Dover, New York, 1972.

17 If the agent commits logical inconsistencies in formulating probability judgments, then she cannot coherently base her actions upon those judgments. These judgments therefore could not form the basis for her behavior (by deterring her from risky behavior, for example).

unconstrained, however. This implies that two agents possessing exactly the same information can reach different—possibly radically different—degrees of confidence in a given belief. This means different probability judgments are made on the basis of the same information; and since those degrees of confidence are purely subjective, it is not the case that one agent's probability judgments are more 'accurate' than those of any other. This is because, according to this conception, probability does not track anything common to both agents; it merely tracks the state of each agent's own internal belief system.

As a result, two agents might have different degrees of confidence in predicting the outcome of a coin toss, even if their information about the toss is identical. As a result, they will make different probability assignments to that toss. According to the subjective conception, there is no reason to expect such differences to be eliminable. Instead, it is simply the case that the probability of the toss coming up heads has one value for one agent, and another value for the other agent. This implies that this lottery might be fair to one agent but not fair to another—and there is no basis for talking of one or the other agent perceiving or failing to perceive the fairness of the lottery. The lottery simply is, or is not, fair depending upon the beliefs held by each agent. This fact poses a threat to any effort to use a lottery in circumstances in which multiple agents must judge the lottery as fair. Intuitively, people should be able to come to agreement as to whether a lottery is fair. The failure of the subjective conception to accommodate this intuition must be counted against it.

There is another, related, intuition that poses difficulties for the subjective conception. It ought to be possible for a decision-maker to be wrong about a fair lottery—for the decision-maker to believe that a lottery is fair when in fact it is not. This is particularly relevant when there are multiple parties to a decision, some of whom regard a lottery as equiprobable, others of whom do not. But the subjective conception leaves no room for this possibility. It is impossible, according to this conception, for a decision-maker to be mistaken about whether a process counts as a fair lottery.[18] If the agent is equally confident in predicting each of the outcomes of a coin toss, then by definition the agent must view that coin toss as fair. But surely people can mistakenly identify processes as fair lotteries, and

18 Self-deception, of course, is always a possibility. But this is not what one would ideally like to have in a probability conception. One would like to be able to say that an agent has reached an incorrect judgment about the probability that a given outcome will occur—much as one could say that an agent has reached an incorrect judgment regarding the answer to a mathematical problem. Self-deception would only make it possible to say that an agent is incorrect about the judgment she has in fact reached regarding the probability of a given outcome.

the subjective definition cannot make sense of this fact? (The objective conception, obviously, does not generate this problem.)[19]

Both of these objections stem from the fact that there is no critical distance between the beliefs of a decision-maker and the equiprobability of a lottery (or, more broadly, probability judgments in general). If the objective conception lacks the means to link decision-making to probability, then the subjective conception joins the two together too closely. It permits the decision-maker to use probability judgments, but not to use them *wrongly*. And any attempt to provide normative guidance to decision-makers presupposes that decision-makers are capable of doing the wrong thing. The project of defending lotteries rests on this presupposition; it assumes, for example, that it is possible for an agent to use a lottery when she should not, or to fail to use a lottery when she should, or to use an inferior (i.e., not fair) lottery when a superior (fair) alternative exists. The subjective conception, because of the overly close tie it creates between beliefs and probability judgments, renders those judgments inaccessible to normative analysis.[20]

2.4 The logical conception

The logical conception views probability as a measure of the degree of warrant that a body of evidence provides in support of a conclusion. This position is most famously associated with J.M. Keynes.[21] There are echoes of it, however, in theories that speak of probability in terms of the degree of *credence* that people may justifiably have in a proposition, given a body of evidence.[22] Two individuals with identical information must, accord-

---

19   The identification of probability with subjective belief in effect runs afoul of a variant of Ludwig Wittgenstein's argument against private languages (Ludwig Wittgenstein, *Philosophical Investigations*. 3rd ed., Prentice-Hall, Englewood Cliffs, NJ, 1973). If language were a purely private phenomenon, accessible only to a single agent, it would be impossible to describe a given utterance as a mistake in that language. Similarly, if probability is a purely private phenomenon, there is no way to regard an assertion of probability as mistaken.

20   Almost. As noted before, the Bayesian understanding of the subjective conception does render some limited normative judgments. An agent who fails to update her beliefs properly in the face of new information, for example, is clearly making a mistake. This understanding, however, leaves initial beliefs completely unrestrained. As a result, there is no set of probability judgments that a given agent at a given time cannot reach using a given quantity of information, given suitably defined prior beliefs.

21   John Maynard Keynes, *A Treatise on Probability*, Dover, New York, 2004.

22   See, e.g., Rudolf Carnap, 'The Two Concepts of Probability: The Problem of Probability', *Philosophy and Phenomenological Research*, 5, June 1945, pp. 513-32; and Lewis, op. cit., 1987. Both Carnap and Lewis distinguish between logical credence and objective *chance*, where the latter represents an objective conception of probability. Hacking (in *Logic of Statistical Inference*, Cambridge University Press, Cambridge, 1965) draws a similar distinction between 'support' and 'chance'. All three philosophers believe that a given level of observation of chance processes validates a given level of credence. This position is not necessary for the defense of the logical conception of probability, and so I do not assume it here.

ing to this conception, adopt the same probability assessment. If they differ, at least one of them has made a mistake. Put another way: according to the logical conception, justifiable disagreements over probability are ultimately reducible to differences in information.[23] A measure of probability indicates, not the level of belief a particular individual holds, but the level of belief any individual with access to a certain amount of information is rationally justified in holding.[24]

In the case of a lottery, the conclusions in question are predictions involving possible outcomes. A lottery is equiprobable, according to this conception, if the warrant for predicting that one outcome will occur when the lottery is employed is the same as the warrant for predicting that any other outcome will occur. This warrant will typically come, of course, from past observations of the lottery in action, but other information (e.g., scientific laws) might also be relevant.

The logical conception avoids the pitfalls of both the objective and the subjective conceptions. Unlike the objective conception, it establishes a clear relationship between probability and decision making. Unlike the subjective conception, it leaves room for mistakes. Agents are capable of acting upon probabilities, but they are capable of acting wrongly upon them. The probability that a coin will come up heads thus becomes a statement about what agents believe about the coin toss, but this statement says more than simply what particular agents happen to believe. This 'more' allows for the possibility that different agents will reach identical judgments regarding whether or not a given coin toss is fair, provided they can reveal all their available information to each other.

Whereas the objective conception defines probability in terms of what *is*, and the subjective conception defines it in terms of what people *believe*, the logical conception defines it in terms of what people *know*. This generates the correct level of critical distance between agents who must employ lotteries and the lotteries themselves. They are capable of recognizing and using fair lotteries, but they are also capable of making mistakes in doing so. This is not to say that there are no legitimate criticisms of the logical conception, merely that this conception best meets the needs of the project of defining a fair lottery. For this reason, criticisms of the logical conception are best addressed in the conclusion of this paper.

---

23   This is a form of what Robert Aumann calls the 'Harsanyi Doctrine' (Robert J. Aumann, 'Subjectivity and Correlation in Randomized Strategies', *Journal of Mathematical Economics*, 1, 1974, p. 92), although his focus is on disagreement *per se*, not justifiable or reasonable disagreement.

24   Of course, an individual might not be rationally justified in deriving the correct probability, any more than she would be rationally required to draw all warranted conclusions from the information she possesses. Making use of information requires effort, and depending upon what is at stake this effort might not be worthwhile.

3 Conclusion

To summarize, we can compare and contrast how a fair/equiprobable lottery should be understood in light of each of the three conceptions of probability discussed here. (I disregard the frequentist conception here, as its inapplicability to individual events renders it a non-starter in respect to our current framework of analysis.) Under the objective conception, a prediction of a lottery's outcome is impossible, and this impossibility is a physical fact about the world. Whether or not anyone in fact makes a prediction is irrelevant. Under the subjective conception, prediction of a lottery's outcome is not made. This is a fact about the decision-maker's psychology. According to the logical conception, prediction of a lottery's outcome is not possible, and this impossibility inheres in the relationship between the available evidence and a conclusion. The evidence simply does not warrant a prediction as to which outcome will in fact occur. More precisely, the evidence does not warrant predicting one outcome of the lottery any more than any other. Moreover, this relationship between evidence and prediction is known to the agent, and so, correctly, a prediction is not made.[25] This third conception is, I believe, the one most suitable for use in defining a fair lottery suitable for human decision making.

Acceptance of the logical conception has a number of implications for decision-makers interested in employing lotteries. It also poses a number of problems worthy of future research. I shall conclude this paper by briefly addressing each of these topics.

One implication of the logical conception of probability is that the status of a process as a fair lottery varies directly with the body of knowledge accumulated about it. It may be the case that at time t, the available evidence justifies regarding all of the outcomes of a process as equally probable; but that at time $t+1$, the (presumably increased) evidence favors predictions of some outcomes over predictions of others. Faced with such evidence, a decision-maker ought to treat the process as a fair lottery at time t and as a weighted (or non-equiprobable) lottery at time $t+1$. If at some point the evidence warrants a confident prediction of one and only one outcome, the agent might even be justified in viewing the process as not constituting a lottery at all. This seems to follow from the understanding of probability as purely a function of the relationship between evidence and warranted belief. This squares with the intuition that, should

---

25   The distinction between objective, subjective, and logical conceptions tracks, I believe, Karl Popper's division of reality into Worlds 1, 2, and 3, respectively (see Popper, *Objective Knowledge: An Evolutionary Approach*, Clarendon Press, Oxford, 1972). Popper himself does not make this connection, however, and space precludes me from pursuing it here.

people someday become capable of predicting the outcomes of an ordinary coin toss with mathematical precision, they would then be justified in refusing to use a coin toss in circumstances where a fair lottery was required. (This would not, however, retroactively render the past use of the lottery unfair. The lottery really was fair at time t, even if it is not fair at time $t+1$.)

The logical conception of probability has had many august defenders, most notably Keynes. But it is not currently in vogue due to the problem of defining the nature of the relationship between probability and evidence. Bayesians devoted to the subjective conception, for example, agree with Keynes that there is a definite method for updating given probabilities in the face of new evidence. But they also contend that there is no objective basis for assigning initial probability estimates prior to any updating. At the moment, then, probability estimates have an inextricably subjective component; efforts to eliminate this component simply shift it, 'just as attempts to iron out a wrinkle in a badly made suit of clothes will not remove it but simply send it elsewhere'.[26]

The problem posed by the Bayesian challenge is a real one. Efforts to define a rational basis for probability assignments in the absence of evidence have largely fallen short. The classic solution has always been the principle of insufficient reason, as formulated by Laplace, though not under that name.[27] The principle states that in the absence of evidence, one should regard all possible outcomes as equally likely. The difficulty with this principle lies in the fact, noted above, that probability judgments always exist under a description. Changing the description of a process thus changes the outcome set of that process. And if the principle of insufficient reason were true, then this would imply that a simple relabeling of the outcomes will change the probabilities associated with them. If the outcomes of a coin toss are described as 'heads, tails', then in the absence of evidence the principle of insufficient reason assigns a probability of ½ to each outcome. But if the outcomes are redescribed as 'heads, tails without bouncing first, tails after one or more bounces,' then the probability to be assigned to heads changes to $1/3$.[28]

Proponents of the subjective conception infer from this problem that the subjective element of probability is ineliminable (although they admit that, as the relevant body of evidence becomes large, the subjective com-

---

26   Colin Howson and Peter Urbach, *Scientific Reasoning: The Bayesian Approach*, Open Court, La Salle, IL, 1989, p. 54.

27   Marquis de Laplace, *A Philosophical Essay on Probabilities*, Dover, New York, 1951.

28   Keynes, op. cit., 2004, recognized the problem with the principle, which he called the 'principle of indifference.' He attempted to formulate a solution, but few today would regard it as satisfactory.

ponent becomes small almost to the point of vanishing—even though it never disappears entirely). But the difficulties posed by the principle of insufficient reason suggest an alternative possibility. Perhaps it is the case that, in the absence of evidence, numerical measurements of probability cannot be precisely formulated. Efforts to do so would then constitute a case of flouting Aristotle's memorable advice by imposing greater precision than the circumstances allow. Perhaps the more evidence that exists regarding a process, the more precise are the probability estimates that can be made from it. Probability is thus a measure of the warrant provided by evidence towards a proposition, but the precision of the measure varies with the quantity of evidence. As the evidential basis becomes better formulated so the task of formulating probabilities becomes less problematic—just as wrinkles are less of a problem the more carefully made a suit is.[29]

This approach has several advantages over the subjectivist solution. It is consistent, for example, with the intuition that probability judgments become more accurate, and hence more reliable for decision-making purposes, as the level of information supporting them increases. The standard Bayesian account renders this impossible. A Bayesian who observes ten coin tosses, and infers from them that the probability the coin will come up heads is ½, and a Bayesian who makes the same inference after observing 10,000 coin tosses, have reached an inference of exactly the same value. Both must regard the processes they have observed to be fair lotteries, and with the same degree of confidence. A probability judgment is a probability judgment, regardless of the level of evidence backing it up, at least for advocates of the subjective conception, and this result is highly counterintuitive.[30]

---

29   Isaac Levi, op. cit., 1986, pp. 118-19, distinguishes between *necessitarians*, who 'seek to identify principles of inductive rationality or "logic" so powerful that any agent is constrained by these principles and the information available to him to make numerically precise credal probability judgements of just one sort' and *personalists*, who 'doubt that principles of rationality so powerful as this can be obtained'. Levi wishes to defend a middle position between these two extremes, endorsing instead 'a point of view according to which one should refuse to restrict oneself to numerically definite probability judgements when the grounds for moving to such a position do not warrant favoring one way or making such judgements rather than another'. Levi appears here to endorse a logical conception of probability, but also affirms that precise probability assessments cannot be validly made under a variety of circumstances. Interpreted this way, Levi's position is quite close to my own.

30   Karl Popper calls this the 'paradox of ideal evidence.' See, e.g., Popper, *The Logic of Scientific Discovery*, op. cit., pp. 407-8. A Bayesian advocate of the subjective conception might respond that observed coin tosses make it possible to make estimates of the 'real' probability that the coin toss will come up heads. Additional observations facilitate more accurate estimates. But this response requires that people estimate the distribution of probabilities of a probability. The former are subjective, but the latter must be objective. There is no other way to make sense

If this approach is correct, then valid probability judgments are vague and fuzzy when evidence levels are low, and clean and precise when evidence levels are high. But this raises the question of how vague measurements get transformed into precise ones as evidence levels increase. There must be a continuum of measures ranging from no evidence to certain evidence. I do not know how to formulate such a continuum. All that matters here is that existence of this possible approach stands as an obstacle to the ready dismissal of the logical conception. The nature of the continuum and its impact on the feasibility of the logical conception would constitute an important avenue for future research.

One final question deserves comment here. I have spoken of the logical conception of probability as relating a given body of evidence to the level of warrant that this evidence provides for a prediction. But bodies of evidence do not exist in the abstract. They must be available in some sense, to an agent. But which agent is the relevant one? The question can be rephrased in terms of lotteries. If a fair lottery must be an equiprobable one, and if probability judgments are always relevant to a body of evidence, then who must possess the evidence in light of which lotteries are judged equiprobable? The subjectivist's concern returns here in a strong way. Different agents, with different bodies of evidence available to them, will, to the extent that they are rational, reach different probability assessments. This implies that one agent might judge a lottery fair, while a second might judge it weighted, and a third might judge it not to be a lottery at all. This is a problem if lotteries are supposed, for example, to ensure just outcomes.[31] If a fair lottery is necessary, say, in order to allocate a good justly, then a given allocative practice will be just or not depending upon the beliefs of the observer about the lottery being used. Doesn't this preclude any intersubjective agreement about the justice of allocative institutions?[32]

I do not believe this to be the case. Contemporary theories of justice do not presuppose that institutions are only just if every individual in them knows every fact about every institution, as well as the complete argument establishing that they are just. All that is required is that the facts and argument be readily available to any agent who seeks them out.[33] Similarly, if an allocative process involves a lottery, justice does not

---

of the 'real' chance that a coin toss will come up heads. And so this response must deal with all the problems raised by the objective conception.

31   See Stone (2007).

32   This concern is raised by Sher (1980) in the course of his own efforts to generate a satisfactory definition of a fair lottery. For my response to Sher, see Peter Stone, 'On Fair Lotteries', *Social Theory and Practice*, 34, no. 4, October 2008, pp. 573-90.

33   John Rawls, *Political Liberalism*, expanded ed. Columbia University Press, New York, 2005.

demand that every individual have all the evidence available for establishing whether that lottery is fair. All that is presumably required is that the evidence be readily available to any agent seeking to establish the justice of the allocative practice. This suggests that the proper answer to the question, 'which body of evidence is relevant when assessing whether a lottery is fair' is something like 'the total body of evidence available to the society employing the lottery.' This answer is consistent with the intuition that a collective body can be said to know something as long as the knowledge is in some sense available to that body. Beethoven's Ninth Symphony is known in twenty-first-century America even if most Americans could not reproduce the score at will.[34]

Once again, this answer is speculative and requires further work. In particular, it requires a theory of collective beliefs. Such a theory is hard to formulate, and I do not pretend to offer one here. All I hope to have established is that it is plausible to speak of evidence in an intersubjective manner suitable for assessing the appropriateness of putting lotteries to various social purposes. If lotteries appear to make valuable contributions to decision making, and if the logical conception of probability is the conception most appropriate for defining and defending these contributions, then there is good reason to investigate the idea of collective beliefs further.

34 Popper, op. cit., 1972, regarded musical compositions (as well as scientific theories, poems, etc.) as world three entities. This makes it all the more plausible that probability judgments should be similarly regarded.

Bibliography

This selected bibliography was compiled and annotated by a team consisting of the editors and Antoine Vergne.

Abert, James (1972), 'Since Grantsmanship Doesn't Work, Why Not Roulette?' *Saturday Review*, 55, no. 43.

Abramson, Jeffrey (2000), *We, the Jury: The Jury System and the Ideal of Democracy*, Harvard University Press, Cambridge Mass. [Evokes sortition amongst possible means of jury representation.]

Ackerman, Bruce A. & Fishkin, James S. (2004), *Deliberation Day*, Yale University Press, New Haven. [Deliberative democracy inspired by focus-grouping. In several procedures the groups are selected by sortition.]

Adeleye, Gabriel (1983), *Greek, Roman and Byzantine Studies*, 24, no. 4: 295-306. [Clarifies how the *dokimasia* as used and how it assumed greater political significance following the restoration of democracy in 403 BC.]

Amar, Akhil R. (1984), 'Choosing Representatives by Lottery Voting', *Yale Law Journal*, 93, no. 7.

Aristotle, *Politics*, books IV, 15; VI, 2. [Democracy described as the regime in which elections by lots outnumber elections by votes.]

Aristotle, *The Athenian Constitution*, trans. Moore in (1986), *Aristotle and Xenophon on Democracy and Oligarchy*, University of California Press, Berkeley.

Aubert, Vilhelm (1959), 'Chance in Social Affairs', *Inquiry*, 2, no. 1.

Barber, Benjamin R. (1974), *The Death of Communal Liberty*, Princeton University Press, Princeton NJ. [Identifies the use of lot as contributing to local democracy in the eastern Swiss Cantons.]

Barber, Benjamin R. (1984), *Strong Democracy: Participatory Politics for a New Age*, University of California Press, Berkeley. [Barber advocates sortition in the context of democratised local government.]

Barnett, Anthony & Carty, Peter (2008), *The Athenian Option: Radical Reform for the House of Lords* [1st ed. 1998], Imprint Academic, Exeter.

Becker, Theodore Lewis (1976), *Un-vote for a New America: A Guide to Constitutional Revolution*, Boston: Allyn and Bacon. [Proposes that half the House of Representatives to be elected by lot.]

Bennett, Deborah J. (1998), *Randomness*, Harvard University Press, Cambridge Mass.

Berg, Sven & Holler Manfred J. (1986), 'Randomized Decision Rules in Voting Games: A Model for Strict Proportional Power', *Quality and Quantity*, 20, no. 4. [Advocates sortition for selecting forms of vote.]

Bishop, David (1970), 'The Cleroterium', *The Journal of Hellenic Studies*, 90. [Includes comments about Dow, 1939.]

Bork, A.M. (1967), 'Randomness in the Twentieth Century', *Antioch Review*, 27, no. 1, Spring.

174 Sortition

Boyce, John R. (1994), 'Allocation of Goods by Lottery', *Economic Inquiry*, 32, no. 3.

Boyle, Conall (1998), 'Organizations Selecting People: How the Process Could Be Made Fairer by the Appropriate Use of Lotteries.' *The Statistician*, 47, no. 2.

Bromberger C. & Travis G. eds. (1987), 'Hasard et Sociétés', *Ethnologie Française*, février-mars.

Broome, John (1984), 'Selecting People Randomly', *Ethics,* 95, October.

Broome, John (1990), 'Fairness', *Proceedings of the Aristotelian Society*, Aristotelian Society.

Broome, John (1998), Review: Kamm on Fairness. *Philosophy and Phenomenological Research* 58, Nr. 4 (December): 955-961.

Buchstein, Hubertus (2009), *Demokratie und Lotterie: Das Los als politisches Entscheidungsinstrument seit der Antike: Das Los als politisches Entscheidungsinstrument von der Antike bis zur EU*, Campus Verlag, Frankfurt.

Bunting, William (2006), 'Election-by-lot as a Judicial Selection Mechanism', *New York University Journal of Law and Liberty*, 2, no.1. [Sortition for selecting judges.]

Burnheim, John (1985), *Is Democracy Possible? The Alternative to Electoral Politics*, Polity Press, London.

Burton, Abrams & and Settle, Russell F. (1976), 'A Modest Proposal for Election Reform', *Public Choice*, 28, Winter. [Cost saving sampling.]

Callenbach, Ernest & Phillips, Michael (1985), *A Citizen Legislature*, Banyan Tree Books, Berkeley. [2nd ed. 2008, Imprint Academic, Exeter.]

Carson, Lyn & Martin, Brian (1999), *Random Selection in Politics*, Praeger, Westport.

Carson Lyn & Martin, Brian (2002), 'Random Selection of Citizens for Technological Decision Making', *Science and Public Policy*, 29, no. 2.

Casti, J. & Karlquist, A. (1990), *Beyond Belief, Randomness, Prediction, Explanation in Science*, CRC Press, Boca Raton, Sweden.

Chaitin, Gregory J. (1988), 'Randomness in Arithmetic', *Scientific American,* July [Chaitin is probably the most interesting and exciting modern writer on randomness. He defines randomness in terms of algorithmic complexity.]

Chaitin, Gregory J. (2001), *Exploring Randomness*, Springer, London.

Condorcet, Marquis de (1793), *Plan de Constitution présenté à la Convention Nationale le 15 et 16 Février 1793*. Bibliothèque Nationale, Paris. [Paper from the Constitutional Committee in which lot is advocated to select a split legislature designed to facilitate debate.]

Condorcet, Marquis de (1994), *Foundations of Social Choice and Political Theory*, ed. McLean, I., Hewitt, F. & Edward E., Aldershot: Elgar. [Extracts from Condorcet's use of probability theory to explore elective schemes. Good introduction.]

Coote, Anna & Lenaghan, Jo (1997), *Citizens' Juries*, Institute of Public Policy Research, London.

Cordano F. & Grottanelli C. a cura di (2001), *Pubblicio sorteggio e cleromanzai: alcuni esempi*, Milano.

Crosby, Ned (2003), *Healthy Democracy*, Beaver's Pond Press, Edina MN.

Dahl, Robert A. (1970), *After the Revolution? Authority in a Good Society*, Yale University Press, New Haven. [Proposes sortition for selecting advisory councils to every elected official, from mayors, governors, members of the US House and Senate, and even the president.]

Dahl, Robert A. (1987), 'Sketches for a Democratic Utopia', *Scandinavian Political Studies*, 10, no. 3.

Delannoi, Gil (2003), 'Points de vue sur la démocratie, paradoxes de l'égalité, le tirage au sort' in Perrineau ed., *Le Désenchantement Démocratique*, Editions de l'Aube. [Explores sortition as a criterion for democracy and envisages different procedural options.]

Delannoi, Gil (2008), 'Selection by Lottery as an Antidote to Corruption', Ergopoliton, Athens/Centre de recherches politiques de Sciences-Po, Paris.

Dienel, Peter C. & Renn, Ortwinn (1995), 'Planning Cells: A Gate to "Fractal" Mediation' in Renn, Webler & Weidemann eds, *Fairness and Competence in Citizen Participation: Evaluating Models for Environmental Discourse*, Kluwer, Dordrecht.

Dienel, Peter C. (2002), *Die Planungszelle: der Bürger als Chance*, 5th ed. Westdeutsches Verlag, Wiesbaden. [1st ed. 1978]

Dow, Sterling (1939), 'Aristotle, the Kleroteria, and the Courts', *Harvard Studies in Classical Philology*, 50. [Dow successfully identifies the function of the Kleroterion.]

Dowlen, Oliver (2008), *The Political Potential of Sortition*, Imprint Academic, Exeter.

Duxbury, Neil (1999), *Random Justice: on Lotteries and Legal Decision-Making*, Clarendon Press, Oxford.

Eckhoff, Torstein (1989), 'Lotteries in Allocative Situations', *Social Science Information*, 28, no. 1, March.

Elster, Jon (1988), 'Custody by the Toss of a Coin?' *Social Science Information*, 27, no. 4 [Envisages sortition about the custody of children after divorce.]

Elster, Jon (1989), *Solomonic Judgements*, Cambridge University Press, Cambridge.

Elster, Jon (1992), *Local Justice: How Institutions Allocate Scarce Goods and Necessary Burdens*, Russell Sage Foundation, New York. [Mentions different uses of sortition.]

Engelstad, Fredrik (1989), 'The Assignment of Political Office by Lot', *Social Science Information*, 28, no. 1, March.

Ehrenberg, Victor (1927), ,Losung', in *Paulys Realencyclopädie der classischen Altertumwissenschaft*, Wissowa, Georg ed., vol. 13, Metzler, München.

Fienberg, Stephen E. (1971), 'Randomisation and Social Affairs: the 1970 Draft Lottery', *Science*, 171.

Fishburn, Peter C. & Gehrlein, William V. (1972), 'Towards a Theory of Elections with Probabilistic Preferences', *Econometrica*, 45, no. 8.

Fishburn, Peter C. (1977), 'Lotteries and social choices', *Journal of Economic Theory*, 5, no. 2.

Fishburn, Peter C. (1978), 'Acceptable Social Choice Lotteries' in *Decision Theory and Social Ethics: Issues in Social Choice*, ed. Göttinger, Hans & Leinfeller, Weiner, Reidel, Dordrecht.

Fisher, R.A. (1949), *The Design of Experiments*, Oliver and Boyd, Edinburgh. [A very useful work for understanding exactly what random selection brings to experimental design.]

Fishkin, James S. (1995), *The Voice of the People: Public Opinion and Democracy*, Yale University Press, New Haven.

Fox, J.A & Tracy, P.E. (1986), 'Randomised Response: a Method for Social Surveys', *Quantitive Applications in the Social Sciences*, Sage.

Frey, Bruno S. & Stutzer, Alois (2005), 'Ein Vorschlag zu mehr Demokratie in Internationalen Organisationen', *Zeitschrift für Staats – und Europawissenschaft*, 3, no. 3. [Recommends sortition for the selection of officials in international oragnisations.]

Gangale, Thomas (2004), 'The California Plan: A 21st Century Method for Nominating Presidential Candidates', *PS: Political Science and Politics*, 37, no. 1. [Suggests sortition for the ordering of US primaries.]

Gastil, John (2000), *By Popular Demand: Revitalizing Representative Democracy Through Deliberative Elections*, University of California Press, Berkeley.

Gataker, Thomas (2008) [1st ed. 1627], *The Nature and Uses of Lotteries: A Historical and Theological Treatise*, reprint Imprint Academic, Exeter. [The bible for all serious students of sortition. Gataker distinguishes between valuable uses of sortition and its use for gaming and superstitious practices.]

Gilbert, Felix (1965), *Machiavelli and Guicciardini*, Princeton University Press, Princeton N.J. [Excellent historical introduction to context and debate of institutions in the Florentine Republic.]

Glotz, Gustave (1907), 'Sortitio' in *Dictionnaire des antiquités grecques et romaines d'après les textes et les monuments*, ed. Daremberg, Charles & Saglio, Edmondo, Hachette, Paris.

Gobert, J. (1997), *Justice, Democracy and the Jury*, Aldershot, Ashgate. [A valuable work that approaches sortition from the working practice of the jury system and assesses its democratic potential from this perspective.]

Godwin, W. (1971), *An Enquiry Concerning Political Justice*, Clarendon, Oxford. [Godwin is very critical about the use of sortition. For him it represents a dereliction of responsibility.]

Goodwin, Barbara (1984), 'Justice and the Lottery', *Political Studies*, 32, no. 2.

Goodwin, Barbara (2005), *Justice by Lottery*, [1st ed. 1992], Imprint Academic, Exeter. [A classic on the use of sortition to distribute the goods of society.]

Goudappel, Flora (1999), 'The Dutch System of Lottery for Studies', *European Journal for Educational Law and Policy*, 3.

Greely, Hank (1977), 'The Equality of Allocation by Lot', *Harvard Civil Rights – Civil Liberties Review*, 12.

Gretton, Richard (1912), 'Historical Notes on Lot-Meadow Customs at Yarnton, Oxon', *Economic Journal*, 22, no. 85, March.

Green, T.A. (1985), *Verdict According to Conscience*, University of Chicago Press. [An excellent account of the rise of the jury system in England and Britain.]

Grote, G. (1888), *A History of Greece from the Earliest Period to the Close of the Generation Contemporary with Alexander the Great 1846-56*, J. Murray, London. [Grote explores sortition, but mainly in respect to the selection of the *archon*.]

Grötzinger, Gerd (1998), Weltbürgerschaft und Nationalitätslotterie' in *Demokratischer Experimentalismus*, ed. Brunkhorst, Hauke, Suhrkamp, Frankfurt am Main. [Suggests the creation of a 'second nationality' which would be allocated by lot to every human being.]

Guicciardini, Francesco, 'Del modo di eleggere gli uffici nel Consigli Grande' in *Dialogo e discorsi del Reggimento di Firenze* (1932), a cura di R. Palmarocchi, Laterza, Bari, pp. 218-259. [Paired speeches for and against the use of lot, probably the only surviving dialogue of its type on the subject. Another vital work.]

Guicciardini, Francesco, *History of Florence* (1964), trans. Grayson, abridged, intro. by Hale, J.N., Sadler and Brown, London. [Contains a brief discussion on the use of lot in the Second Republic.]

Guicciardini, Francesco, *The History of Italy* (1984), trans. and ed. Alexander, Princeton University Press, Princeton NJ. [Guicciardini sets up another, briefer historical dialogue on sortition based on the events of 1494. Less convincing and thorough than *Del modo*.]

Hacking, Ian (1988), 'Telepathy: Origins of Randomness in experimental design', *Isis*, 79. [A little-known, but very revealing paper.]

Hacking, Ian (1990), *The Taming of Chance*, Cambridge University Press, Cambridge.

Hansen, Mogens H. (1990), 'Political Powers of the People's Courts' in *The Greek City from Homer to Alexander*, ed. Murray, O. & Price, S., Oxford University Press, Oxford.

Hansen, Mogens H. (1991), *The Athenian Democracy in the Age of Demosthenes*, Blackwell, Oxford. [The most thorough modern account of the Athenian system.]

Harrington, James, *The Political Works of James Harrington*, (1977)[1st ed. 1661], ed. Pocock, Cambridge University Press. [Useful as a cross reference to *Oceana*, and to determine Harrington's attitude to Athenian democracy and the use of lot in that context.]

Harrington, James, *Harrington: The Commonwealth of Oceana and A System of Politcs* (1992)[1st ed. 1661], ed. Pocock, Cambridge University Press, Cambridge. [Harrington advocates lot for nominators in the Venetian style and for a number of other important uses in his model republic. He does little, however, to explain exactly why it was to be used.]

Harris, John (1975), 'The Survival Lottery', *Philosophy*, 50, no. 191.

Harris, John (1978), 'Hanink on the Survival Lottery', *Philosophy*, 53. [In response to Hanink's who commented the 1975 article.]

Haspel, Abraham E. (1985), 'Drilling for Dollars: The Federal Oil-Lease Lottery Program'? *American Enterprise Institute Journal on Government and Society*, 9.

Headlam, James Wycliffe (1933), *Election by Lot at Athens* [1st ed; 1891], Cambridge University Press, Cambridge. [A classic in the re-discovery and re-evaluation of sortition.]

Herodotus, *The Histories*, book III, § 80-84. [In this simple but most ancient typology for political regimes sortition is connected to democracy.]

Hirose, I. (2007) 'Weighted Lotteries in Life and Death Cases', *Ratio – Oxford*, 20, no. 1.

Hofstee, Willem K.B. (1983), 'The Case for Compromise Models in Education Selection and Grading' in *On Educational Testing*, ed. Anderson, S. & Helmick, J., Jossey-Bass, San Francisco.

Hofstee, Willem K.B. (1990), 'Allocation by Lot: A Conceptual and Empirical Analysis', *Social Science Information*, 29, no. 4.

Isocrates, *Areopagiticus*, § 20-29. [Critical remarks about the Athenian democracy, comparing elections by lot with elections by vote, with a preference for the latter.]

Jackson, S. & Brashers, D.E. (1986), 'Random Factors in ANOVA (Analysis of Variance)', *Qualitative Applications in Social Sciences*, 98, Sage.

Katz, Al (1973), 'Process Design for Selection of Hemodialysis and Organ Transplant Recipients', *Buffalo Law Review*, 22, no. 2.

Kishlansky, Mark A. (1986), *Parliamentary Selection: Social and Political Choice in Early Modern England*, Cambridge University Press, Cambridge. [Kishlansky gives details of some uses of sortition in the development of Parliamentary selection procedures.]

Knag, Sigmund (1998), 'Let's Toss for It: A Surprising Curb on Political Greed', *The Independent Review*, 3 no. 2.

Kornhauser, Lewis A. & Sager, Lawrence G. (1988), 'Just Lotteries', *Social Science Information*, 27, no. 4.

Kroll, J.H. (1972), *Athenian Bronze Allotment Plates*, Harvard University Press, Cambridge Mass.

Lanthenas, Fr. (1792), *Des Elections et du mode d'élire par listes épuratoires*, Bibliothèque Nationale, Paris, FR.BNF 11911005 [A paper in which Lanthenas suggests that lotteries could be useful in certain circumstances to select Primary Assemblies.]

Ledyard, John O. & Palfrey, Thomas R. (1994), 'Voting and Lottery Drafts as Efficient Public Goods Mechanisms', *The Review of Economic Studies*, 61, no. 2.

Leiman, Sid Z. (1978), 'The Ethics of Lottery', *Kennedy Institute Quarterly Report*, 4.

Lesueur, Théodore, *A French Draft Constitution of 1792. Modelled on James Harrington's Oceana*, (1932), ed. Liljergen, S. B. & Lund, C.W. [A comprehensive constitutional plan that involves the use of sortition at the citizen's point of entry to the political process.]

Lewis, David (1989), 'The Punishment that Leaves Something to Chance', *Philosophy and Public Affairs*, 18, no. 1. [Sortition used to allocate forms of punishment.]

Lichtman, Douglas (1996), 'The Deliberative Lottery: A Thought Experiment in Jury Reform', *American Criminal Law Review*, 34.

Lockard, Alan A. (2003a), 'Decision by Sortition: A Means to Reduce Rent-Seeking', *Public Choice*, 116, no. 3.

Lockard, Alan A. (2003b), 'Sortition', in *Encyclopedia of Public Choice*, Kluwer Academic Publishers, Norwell MA/Dordrecht.

Manin, Bernard (1997), *The Principles of Representative Government*, Cambridge University Press, Cambridge. [One of the best modern starting points for the exploration of sortition and its relationship to modern democratic practice.]

Mavrodes, George I. (1984), 'Choice and Chance in the Allocation of Medical Resources: a Response to Kilner', *The Journal of Religious Ethics*, 12, no. 1. [Against Kilner's argument about the natural fairness of sortition.]

McCormick, John P. (2006), 'Contain the Wealthy and Patrol the Magistrates: Restoring Elite Accountability to Popular Government', *American Political Science Review*, 100, no. 2.

Meier, Christian (1956),'Praerogativa Centuria' in *Paulys Realencyclopädie der classischen Altertumswissenschaft*, München.

Montesquieu, *The Spirit of the Laws*, book II, 2. [1st ed. 1748] [In this important passage Montesquieu is the last of the great political thinkers to equate democracy with the frequent and habitual use of sortition.]

Morris, Robert (1770), *A Letter to Sir Richard Aston*, 2nd ed., printed for Geo Peach, London. [Pamphlet in favour of the randomly selected jury.]

Mueller, Dennis C., Tollinson, Robert D. & Willet, Thomas D. (1972), 'Representative Democracy via Random Selection', *Public Choice*, 12, Spring.

Mulgan, Richard G. (1984), 'Lot as a Democratic Device of Selection', *The Review of Politics*, 46, no. 4.

Najemy, John M. (1982), *Corporatism and Consensus in Florentine Electoral Politics, 1280-1400*, University of North Carolina Press, Chapel Hill. [The most comprehensive work on the use of sortition in Florentine politics up to the end of the First Republic.]

Noland (1701), *The Free State of Noland*, printed for D. Brown, London. [An anonymous pamphlet that advocates the use of lot as part of a comprehensive republican electoral system for England.]

O'Leary, Kevin (2006), *Saving Democracy: A Plan for Real Representation in America*, Stanford University Press, Stanford.

Ostrom, Elinor (1990), *Governing the Commons*, Cambridge University Press, Cambridge. [Olstrom brings to light a number of key uses of lotteries in the distribution and organisation of shared resources, but does not develop an analysis of sortition itself.]

Paine, Thomas, *Complete Works*, (1945), ed. Foner, Citadel Press, NewYork. [Paine makes a number of suggestions for the use of lot.]

Plato, *Protagoras*. [Argument between Protagoras and Socrates about the principle of competence in the Athenian democracy.]

Plato, *The Laws*. [Suggests some uses of sortition in the near-perfect society envisaged in this dialogue.]

Pope, Maurice (1989), 'Upon the Country. Juries and the Principle of Random Selection', *Social Science Information*, 28, no. 2, June. [A small pamphlet on the value of the randomly-selected jury as a representative body.]

Repp, T. G. (1832), *A Historical Thesis in Trial by Jury, Wager of Law, and other Co-ordinate Forensic Institutions in Scandinavia and Iceland*, Thomas Clark, Edinburgh. [An old but invaluable contribution to the development of the jury from its Scandinavian origins.]

Rhodes, P.J. (1985), *The Athenian Boule*, Oxford University Press, Oxford.

Rinnuccini, Alamanno, 'De Liberate' in Watkins (1978), *Humanism and Liberty*, University of South Carolina Press, Columbia. [Includes a brief defence of the use of lot to counter the power of patronage in Florentine electoral politics.]

Röcke, Anja (2005), *Losverfahren und Demokratie*, LIT, Münster.

Rous, George (1771), *A letter to the Jurors of Great Britain. Occasioned by the Opinion of Lord Mansfiel*, Geo Peach, London. [A defence of the randomly-selected jury.]

Rousseau, *On the Social Contract* [1st ed. 1762], in *Rousseau's Political Writing* (1988), ed. Ritter & Bondarella, Norton, New-York. [Rousseau comments on the use of sortition early in *On the Social Contract*.]

Saunders, Ben (2008), 'The Equality of Lotteries', *Philosophy*, 83, no. 3.

Scheirer, James C. & Fienberg, Stephen E. (1971), 'Draft Lottery: Validity of Randomness', *Science*, 172.

Sher, George (1980), 'What Makes a Lottery Fair?' *Nous*, 14, no. 2.

Singer, Peter (1977), 'Utility and the Survival Lottery', *Philosophy*, 52, no. 200.

Sintomer, Yves (2007), *Le Pouvoir au peuple: jurys citoyens, tirage au sort et démocratie participative*, La Découverte, Paris.

Snider, John (2007), 'From Dahl to O'Leary: Thirty-six years of the Yale School of Democratic Reform', *Journal of Public Deliberation*, 3, no. 1.

Stewart, J.H. (1951), *A Documentary Survey of the French Revolution*, Macmillan, New York. [Good for finding details of the use of lot in the post-Terror period.]

Stone, Peter (2007), 'Why Lotteries Are Just', *Journal of Political Philosophy*, 15, no. 3.

Stone, Peter (2008), 'Voting, Lotteries, and Justice', *Polity*, no. 2, 40.

Stone, Peter (2009), 'The Logic of Random Selection', *Political Theory*, 37, no. 3, June.

Streater, John (1659), *Government described. Viz what monarchie, aristocracie, oligarchie and demoracie is. Plus a model of the commonwealth or free state of Ragaus*, London. [A contemporary of Harrington discovers the use of sortition in Ragusa (Dubrovnik).]

Sutherland, Keith (2004), *The Party's Over*, Imprint Academic, Exeter.

Sutherland, Keith (2008), *A People's Parliament*, Imprint Academic, Exeter.

Szaniawski, Klemens (1991), 'On fair Distribution of Indivisible Goods' in *Logic and Ethics*, ed. Geach, Peter, Kluwer. [Mentions sortition as means for fair distribution but considers its implementation impossible.]

Thiele, Carmen (2008), *Regeln und Verfahren der Entscheidungsfindung innerhalb von Staaten und Staatenverbindungen*, Springer, Berlin.

Todhunter, I. (1865), *A History of the Mathematical Theory of Probability from the time of Pascal to that of Laplace*, Macmillan, Cambridge. [Vital for understanding the value (and the problems) of using probability law to investigate the function and potential of sortition.]

Tolbert, Caroline J., Redlawsk, David P. & Brown, Daniel C. (2009), 'Reforming Presidential Nominations: Rotating State Primaries or a National Primary?' *PS: Political Science & Politics*, 42, no. 1, January.

Traill, J.S. (1975), *The Political Organisation of Attica*, Hisperia Supplement XIV, Princeton, New Jersey. [One of the best short works on the structure of the Athenian *polis*.]

Vergne, Antoine (2009), '*Kleros* et *Demos*: Le tirage au sort est-il l'avenir de la démocratie?' in *Die Zukunft der Demokratie*, ed. Bedorf, Thomas, Heidenreich, Felix & Obrecht, Marcus, Lit Verlag, Berlin.

Waring, Duff (2005), *Medical Benefit and the Human Lottery: An Egalitarian Approach to Patient Selection*, Springer, Dordrecht.

Warren, Mark & Pearse, Hilary eds (2008), *Designing Deliberative Democracy: The British Columbia Citizens' Assembly*, Cambridge University Press, Cambridge.

Wasserman, David (1996), 'Let Them Eat Chances: Probability and Distributive Justice', *Economics and Philosophy*, 12, no. 1.

Weller, Thomas (2009), Repräsentation per Losentscheid? Wahl und Auswahlverfahren der Procuradores de Cortes in den kastilischen Städten der frühen Neuzeit' in Weller, Dartmann & Wassilowski, *Technik und Symbolik vormoderner Wahlverfahren*, München.

Wolfle, Dael (1970), 'Chance, or Human Judgment?' *Science*, 167, February.

Wolfson, Arthur M. (1899), 'The Ballot and other Forms of Voting in the Italian Communes', *American Historical Review*, 5, no. 1, October. [An early short paper that gives details of the uses of sortition in the communal period of development of the Italian city-state.]

Xenophon, *Memorabilia*, book I, 2. [Contains critical remarks about sortition attributed to Socrates.]

Zeckhauser, Richard (1969), 'Majority Rule with Lotteries on Alternatives', *Quarterly Journal of Economics*, 83, no. 4.

Online articles

Boyle, Conall, 2006, 'Who gets the Prize: The Case for Random Distribution in Non-market Allocation', see: www.conallboyle.com

Brown, Marc, 2004, 'Citizen Panels and the Concept of Representation', see: www.allacademic.com

Lerner, Michael, 2000, 'Corporations Reimagined, see: www.findarticles.com/p/articles/.

Litvak-Poulin, David, 'Citizens' Democracy. Setting the Paste for a Democratic Revolution through the use of Random Selection of Citizens in Political Institutions', see: www.citizensparliament.org.au

Rehfeld, Andrew 2005, *The concept of constituency: political representation, democratic legitimacy, and institutional design*, Cambridge University Press. see: www.loc.gov/catdir/enhancements

Stasz, Cathleen & Christian von Stolk, 'The Use of Lottery Systems in School Admissions', RAND Europe working paper series (WR460), see: www.rand.org/pubs